INDIA AND SAARC

INDIA AND SAARC

Suman Sharma

GYAN PUBLISHING HOUSE
New Delhi-110 002

1. Jacket Front Page : SAARC Emblem
2. Jacket Back Page : SAARC Secretariat Complex in Kathmandu

(Courtesy : 'SAARC in Brief' — SAARC Secretariat Kathmandu, Nepal)

INDIA AND SAARC
(Reference)

ISBN : 81-212-0771-1

Published in 2001 in India by
Gyan Publishing House
5, Ansari Road,
New Delhi-110 002
Phone : 3282060, 3261060 Fax : 3285914
E-mail : gyanbook@del2.vsnl.del.in

Laser Typesetting at : Com Biz Online, Daryaganj, New Delhi-2
Printed at : Mehra Offset Printers, Delhi-110 002

To my Daughter
Sakshi

Contents

Preface

The paradigm shift from 'geo-politics' to 'geo-economics' in international relations after the end of the cold war and India's own policy shift in the '90s to accept the liberal pro-market reforms agenda has put India in a new perspective. India's relative economic stability in the aftermath of the East Asian financial crisis of 1997 and her overt nuclearisation in 1998 further enhanced India's importance and evoked a great deal of interest in India's regional policy.

In the post-cold war global context the extra-regional powers have been facilitating the process of regionalism in South Asia. A universal trend towards regionalism has further provided a sense of urgency to the process of regionalism in South Asia. In this context the Indo-centrality of South Asia has quite obviously sharpened focus on India's policy in the region. This study aims to evaluate India's policies and objectives with reference to SAARC within the broader frame work of its approach to regional cooperation in Asia. The focus of interest in this study is on how post-cold war developments have shaped, influenced and facilitated Indian policy objectives in the region with reference to SAARC.

India's approach to regionalism was to soften the intra-South Asian political and strategic divergence through greater economic and cultural cooperation. Post-cold war imperatives of economic liberalisation and globalization, as well as absence of the spill over of great power rivalry on South Asia gave India a greater opportunity to give desired shape to the process of regionalism in South Asia.

This study traces the roots of regionalism in Indian policy dating back to the years of struggle for independence. India's initiative and role in holding Asian Relations Conference, Conference on Indonesia, the Bandung Conference and such other initial efforts towards regionalism have been studied.

The emergence and evolution of SAARC have been examined in detail keeping in focus India's early responses and subsequent approaches and priorities - economic, cultural, political/strategic. This covers the period between 1980-85. Secondly, the early years of SAARC, its institutionalisation and slow and gradual progress during 1985-90 period have been examined.

An attempt has been made to analyse how post-cold war developments have affected India's approach to regional cooperation process in Asia in general and SAARC in particular. India's initiatives and interest in both sub-regional and wider Asian groupings like ASEAN and Indian Ocean Rim Association have been taken into account to examine how it would affect SAARC.

I owe a deep sense of gratitude to Professor S.D. Muni whose guidance and keen interest in my work were a source of inspiration. His words of encouragement and frank criticism motivated me to improve the quality of my work. I am also thankful to Prof. Kalim Bahadur and Professor C.P. Bhambri who were extremely supportive in my endeavour.

I am extremely thankful to Sh. I.K. Gujral, former Prime Minister of India, Sh. Bhabani Sengupta, veteran journalist, Sh. M.K. Rasgotra and Ambassador Ram, former Foreign Secretaries of India and Dr. V.R. Panchmukhi, Director General of Research and Information System for the Non-Aligned and other Developing Countries (RIS), New Delhi for granting me interviews which provided authenticity to my research findings.

My thanks and gratitude are also due to Ambassador K.K. Bhargava, former Secretary General of SAARC, and Sh. Muchkund Dubey, former Foreign Secretary of India. They have been extremely helpful with their advice for improving the quality of my work.

It would have been extremely difficult to complete the work in time without the assistance and help from the personnel of different libraries which I frequented during last three years. I must mention Nehru Memorial Museum and Library, Teen Murti, New Delhi; Research and Information System for the Non-Aligned and other Developing Countries, New Delhi; Institute of Defence Studies and Analyses Library, New Delhi; ICWA Library, Sapru House, New Delhi; Central Secretariat Library, Shastri Bhawan, New Delhi and Moti Lal Nehru College Library, University of Delhi.

I am extremely thankful to the Indian Council of Social Science Research (ICSSR), New Delhi for providing me financial grant which enabled me to visit Bangladesh, Sri Lanka and Nepal for collection of source material and data for my work. My thanks are also due to Gargs of Gyan Publishing House who not only promptly agreed to publish this study but also put it on priority in their otherwise very tight publishing schedule.

July, 2001 **Suman Sharma**

1

Introduction

The process of decolonisation after the end of the second world war created a large number of state-actors in world politics necessitating a re-definition of international relations. No sooner the war was over, the leading powers sought to divide the world into competing spheres of influence. The grand objectives of the United Nations Organisation notwithstanding, the international politics witnessed an ideological divide between two camps - one led by the United States of America and the other by the Soviet Union. Both camps scouted for allies among the newly independent states of Asia, Africa and Latin America and indulged in a fierce cold war. Some of the newly independent nations, with India in a leading role, tried to provide an alternative world-view independent of the two power-blocs.

The cold war, however, continued unabated and acquired new dimensions with the advancement in technology and weapons of mass destruction. Simultaneously, increasing economic interaction and growing interdependence among nation-states gave rise to problems which could not be resolved within the territorial limits of sovereign states. Mutual interest in co-existence to resolve these problems necessitated cooperation among states. Some theorists believe that the institutions, which are evolved to deal with these problems and issues get accepted by the citizens.[1] The institutionalisation of such regionalism has an obvious implication in dilution of the centrality of the nation-state. It is assumed that this phenomenon initially applies to issues of 'low politics', i.e., trade and commerce and later with increasing sophistication to the issues of 'high politics' involving shift of loyalties from the nation-state to the supranational institutions. This model of regionalism conforms to the evolving West European experience on regionalism.

The regional integration of Western Europe has been achieved through a painstaking, long effort since early 1950s in the aftermath of European devastation in the Second War. Europe was forced to rethink the doctrine of nationalism, political sovereignty and economic autarchy in favour of some kind of political union or federation. The economic regeneration of Western Europe was actively supported by the US which also ensured its security vis-á-vis Eastern bloc. There was a universal yearning for a peaceful and harmonious future devoid of war. It was in this context that Western Europe evolved and created an impressive supranational institutional arrangement and achieved a significant level of economic integration. European Union (EU) thus has a European Council comprising of all national Heads of government, the elected Presidents of France and Finland and the President of the European Commission; a Council of Ministers which shares legislative functions with the elected European Parliament; a civil bureaucracy in the form of European Commission with significant executive powers delegated by the Council; and a European Court of Justice which decides how community law should be applied to specific cases or whether it is being applied uniformly across the Union.

The treaty of Maastricht, which established EU, entered into force in November 1993. Earlier, a single European Market came into being in January 1993. EU is a symbolic construct comprising of three pillars :

* the first pillar represents European Communities (the former European Economic Community no longer mere economic was renamed European Community);
* the second pillar represents the idea of a Common Foreign and Security Policy (CFSP); and
* the third signifies Home Affairs and Justice.

The present President of the European Commission, Mr. Romano Prodi, sometime ago termed EU as a 'hard but successful venture'. Mr. Prodi while recounting the difficulties in integrating Europe suggested that there was lack of an overall vision of the future of Europe, its shape and strategic role, which in other words, he described as absence of a political design. While conceding the need for a new political dimension in Europe, Romano

Prodi asserts that the present community construction, largely based on economic cooperation, is an important political element in the whole construction and that the economic and monetary union and political union are two sides of the same coin.[2]

The evolution of West European regionalism has witnessed two contending viewpoints—one arguing for gradual linking of economies with joint control and creation of a federal structure; and the other wanting to confine European integration to intra-governmental cooperation. There is a strong segment of Euro-skeptics who doubt whether the EU will be durable. The British Foreign Secretary, Robin Cook some time ago maintained that the "high tide of European integration has passed".[3] Likewise Danish Prime Minister Pol Nyrup Rasmusseu in 1998 observed that there existed "no big decisive new issues in the EU requiring new treaties...There will always be elderly gentlemen who dream of great projects, but do not necessarily have the support of the people."[4] The skeptics maintain that EU lacks democratic legitimacy and perhaps European Monetary Union (EMU) would be the last great project of European integration. The functionalist argument for regional integration into supranational federal institutions and a shift of political allegiance away from the nation-state may not, therefore, be very valid.

The European experience cannot be postulated as the model to be copied by other regions, more so, in South Asia where "the very issues of 'low politics' that proved to be positive forces for integration and regionalism (in Europe) are highly charged ones and directly related to nation and state building."[5] There are strong civilisational and cultural bonds in South Asia. Yet this remarkable unity gets distorted by divisive and contentious politics in the region. In the era of globalization South Asia might be compelled to rethink and transcend the limits of divisive politics for the sake of a common prosperous future.

While the European effort at integration started only after the devastation caused by the Second World War, India has been aspiring for a larger identity of Asia and even beyond on the strength of ancient cultural influence and a glorious anti-colonial movement in the first half of twentieth century.

India and Regionalism in Asia

A relatively unknown facet of the ancient history of South and

South-East Asia is the spread of Indian culture and thought in these areas. Objective observers in this regard concede that the ethnocentric historians of Europe have not done justice to India's position in the world. There is evidence in literature based on Indian sources, accounts of Arab travellers and Chinese historical accounts to establish Indian influence (Hindu and Buddhist), covering a period of about thirteen hundred years from the beginnings of the first or second century AD to the end of the fifteenth century. Further, there are many old inscriptions, copper plates and magnificent ruins of ancient monuments like Angkor and Borobudur (Indonesia) to speak of India's pre-eminence in a widespread area in South-East Asia. India's geographical location at the confluence of South East, West and Central Asia also makes it geostrategically central to Asia.

Pre-independence Initiatives Towards Regionalism

The idea of transnational/regional/Asian identity in search for a meaningful role in international affairs has been an important ingredient of Indian mindset during struggle for independence from the British Empire. In fact, the Indian National Congress kept its focus on India's possible role in Asia during freedom struggle. It was as early as in 1920 that Gandhiji wrote of the growing solidarity of the Asian countries. In 1922, C.R.Das, President of Indian National Congress urged India's participation in an Asian Federation which he regarded as inevitable.[6] A resolution to this effect was adopted by the Congress in 1928. In 1945 Pt. Jawaharlal Nehru declared that the small states of the world would have no future and that they were sure to be reduced to the status of satellite states, and, therefore, he advocated creation of South Asian Federation of India, Iran, Iraq, Afghanistan and Burma.[7]

Even before India's formal independence from the British rule, the leaders of the Indian National Movement convened an Asian Relations Conference in New Delhi in March 1947. In this conference there was a general agreement on the issues of freedom for the colonial areas, the need for uplifting the status of women in Asia, the importance of inter-Asian communication and the urgency of supplementing political freedom by economic process. However, there was a lurking distrust among the small Asian countries towards their powerful neighbours despite this general agreement.[8] An attempt was made to create an Asian Relations Organisation which continued as a non-official organisation for about a decade before being wound-up in 1957.

Post-independence Initiatives Towards Regionalism

After independence India took initiative and convened a Conference on Indonesia in New Delhi in January 1949. The objective of the Conference was to discuss the Indonesian struggle for freedom. This Conference unlike earlier ones, was official in character and political in nature. Jawaharlal Nehru the then Prime Minister of India while strongly criticising the Dutch action against Indonesia, also made a fervent appeal for greater interaction among Asian countries.

It was during this phase that an Afro-Asian group emerged. India's attitude to the question of regional cooperation took a distinct shape after 1951, when the President of the Philippines announced his intention of convening an international conference to consider formation of anti-communist association of South-East Asia on the pattern of North Atlantic Treaty. This marked the beginning of differences in approach and perceptions of regional cooperation among Asian states. India was not in favour of such politically oriented groupings and felt that an anti-communist bloc was no answer to Asia's problems.

India's approach to regional cooperation took a different turn when the United States agreed to give military aid to Pakistan in 1954, thus upsetting the entire balance of power in the region, and brought the superpower rivalry at the doorsteps of South Asia. Nehru strongly criticised the formation of military pacts like SEATO and Baghdad Pact.

However, the attempts for regional cooperation continued at various levels. The Bandung Conference, which is regarded as the highest point of Afro-Asian attempt in this direction, struck a common approach to the problems facing Asia. In this Conference differences emerged between Nehru and other Asian leaders regarding the general tone of the Conference. In fact, this Conference demonstrated that the varying patterns of conflicts between the great powers had more to do with mutual relations of Asian nations than any geographical contiguity or mutuality of interests. In this Conference Indian attempts failed both to prevent ideological cleavages simmering at the plenary sessions and also in discussion on specific bilateral issues. As a consequence, the Indian approach to regional cooperation took a different shape and the kind of regionalism that India looked forward to in Asia received a further setback in the wake of armed conflict between India and China, the two Asian giants, in 1962.

Emergence of Regional Groupings

The erosion of cold war and universal realisation among the third world countries for self-help and collective help in pursuing the goals of economic progress and development, impelled the countries of South Asia to forge a regional grouping despite their earlier misgivings and apprehensions. India with her experience of initial efforts to organise the Asian community and recent history of conflicts in the region cautiously welcomed the initiative of Bangladesh in 1980 for an association of South Asian nations, namely, India, Pakistan, Sri Lanka, Bangladesh, Nepal, Bhutan and Maldives. Five years later, after a painstaking, gradual step-by-step progress, the seven South Asian nations launched South Asian Association for Regional Cooperation (SAARC) in 1985. India's objective in SAARC was to promote economic cooperation despite political differences among the member countries. India believed that such cooperation would lead to peace, harmony and greater stability in South Asia.

The initial years of SAARC were marked by significant political developments in the world culminating in the demise of the cold war and dismemberment of the Soviet Union. The end of the cold war brought about a fundamental change, a paradigm shift in international relations. The predominant strain was of the primacy of economics in a market driven international politics. There have also been significant attempts by the world's rich to consolidate 'regionally' in order to prepare for the global future. Almost every country in the rich club of the Organisation of Economic Cooperation and Development (OECD) is a member of some sort of regional cooperative arrangement.

As already noted, Western Europe achieved an advanced state of economic integration and much more after the creation of European Union (EU) in 1993. The emergence of a free trade area of North American Continent (NAFTA) has further fuelled the phenomenon of regional cooperative arrangements. In fact, nearly all countries of Latin America, Caribbean and continental Africa are also involved in some or the other form of regional cooperation. The countries of South-East Asia had already come together to form the Association of South-East Asian Nations (ASEAN). The

Gulf countries came together in a cooperative arrangement called Gulf-Cooperation Council (GCC). There is a Southern Cone Market (MERCOSUR) in Latin America, a South African Customs Union (SACU) and an upcoming powerful bloc of Asia-Pacific region Asia Pacific Economic Cooperation (APEC). In fact, with APEC and the newly emerging Indian Ocean Rim-Association for Regional Cooperation (IOR-ARC) an entirely new dimension of 'open-regionalism' has been added to the concept of regionalism. Open-regionalism seeks to promote the objectives of free-global trade without attempting to form a trade-bloc as such. We thus find that the urge to merge into some form of cooperative arrangement seems to have become almost universal.

India and SAARC

In this fast-changing international context, this study aims at evaluating India's policies and objectives with reference to SAARC within the broader framework of its approach to regional cooperation in Asia.

This study traces the roots of regionalism in Indian policy dating back to the years of struggle for independence. India's initiative and role in holding Asian Relations Conference, Conference on Indonesia, the Bandung Conference and such other initial efforts towards regionalism have been studied.

The emergence and evolution of SAARC have been examined in detail keeping in focus India's initial response and subsequent approaches and priorities—economic, cultural, political/strategic. This covers the period between 1980-85. Secondly, the early years of SAARC, its institutionalisation, slow and gradual progress during 1985-90 period have been examined.

An attempt has been made to analyse how post-cold war developments have affected India's approach to regional cooperation process in Asia in general and SAARC in particular. India's initiatives and interest in both sub-regional and wider Asian groupings like ASEAN and Indian Ocean Rim Association have been taken into account to examine how it would affect SAARC.

During its freedom struggle against the British, Indian National Congress aimed at evolving an Eastern Federation comprising of Asian countries. The unifying bond at this point of time was opposition to imperialism. The ideas of freedom struggle spilled over to the initial years of independence and India's foreign policy was inspired by the ideology of non-alignment in pursuit of world peace and security. However, India's dream for Asian unity was frustrated by the cold-war, a hostile neighbourhood and failure of initial efforts which commenced even before India became independent. These initiatives for regional unity lacked economic content. There was also lack of clarity on the specific region sought to be evolved into an organised entity.

India's policy was that of extreme caution to the moves for organising South Asia in late 70s and early 80s. The cautious approach could be attributed to the past failures, superpower rivalry in Afghanistan, interference of extra-regional powers in the region and extremely hostile neighbourhood. The options for Indian policy, however, were limited. India could not afford to stay out of a regional grouping. India decided to take the plunge for the regional association of SAARC on the condition that contentious, bilateral issues would be excluded from the agenda.

India's policy as a member of SAARC was to seek regional peace and harmony by emphasising on sociocultural factors and cooperation in economic areas. India believed that by pushing socioeconomic cooperation and invoking commonality of culture and heritage, the nations of South Asia can overcome the problems created by the political and strategic divergence in the region.

After the end of the cold-war South Asia witnessed a reduced scale of extra-regional interference, a sense of urgency to catch-up with the globalizing economic order, and most significantly from India's point of view, lessening of tensions with her neighbours with the exception of Pakistan. These developments facilitated Indian policy objectives in the region and India could nudge SAARC into the core areas of economic cooperation.

India's central position in South Asia, asymmetry in its size, power potential and economic strength vis-á-vis other members of SAARC and unabating Indo-Pak hostility can be mentioned as some important factors, among others, which influence Indian policy in the region.

Indian regional policy venture in SAARC can, at best, be seen as partially successful. The organisation evolved an institutional framework within a short span of time. It has also embarked on an ambitious programme of economic cooperation and has generated considerable dynamism at the social, NGO/Civil Society levels.

There is a basic conflict between India's efforts to keep anti-India bilateral political issues out of SAARC agenda and a strife torn political environment of the region.

India while seeking to promote regional peace through its policy of 'bilateralism' and socio-economic cooperation in the 'non-political' forum of SAARC, has also been looking for sub-regional and extra-regional linkages to realise her perceived potential for a larger role in world affairs.

REFERENCES

1. David Mitranny, *A Working Peace System*, Chicago, 1966, p.11; Also see E. Haas, *Beyond the Nation State: Functionalism and International Organisation*, Stanford, 1964. David Mitranny initiated the idea of functionalism to project the potential of the United Nations and this was further pursued by Ernest Haas to explain the institutionalisation of European integration in the Common Market. The functionalist argument maintains that function should determine institution and the problem its own solution. The institution and solution attract allegiance and loyalty once they are seen working.
2. Prime Minister Romano Prodi "The European Union : A hard but successful venture" (Speech at European University Institute, San Domenico Di Fiesole, June 20, 1996). Mr. Prodi was Prime Minister of Italy in 1996.
3. *The Economist,* London, 3 January 1998.
4. *The Financial Times*, 29 May 1998.
5. Dr. Paikiasothy Saravanamuttu, "Globalisation and Economic Regionalism in South Asia: An Unfriendly Context for an Arduous Task?" in Victor Gunewardena (ed.) *Regional Cooperation and Integration: Perspectives from Europe and South Asia,* Colombo,1998, p. 37.
6. For details see, The Presidential Address of C.R. Das in the Indian National Congress Plenary Session in 1922 in A.M. Zaidi and S.G. Zaidi (ed.). *The Encyclopaedia of the Indian National Congress*, Vol. VIII, 1921-1924, New Delhi, 1981, pp. 117-18.
7. J.S. Bright (ed.), *Before and After Independence*, (Collection of Nehru's Speeches 1922-50), New Delhi,1950, p. 279.
8. "Asian Relations", *Report of the Proceedings and Documentation of the First Asian Relations Conference*, New Delhi, March 1947.

2

India and Regionalism in Asia

Here we attempt to explore the genesis of the idea of regionalism in Asia and trace the roots of regionalism in Indian policy dating back to the years of struggle for independence. India by virtue of its pivotal position in Asia and a unique, spectacular mass movement for freedom acquired leadership of the colonised nations, particularly in Asia and Africa and bequeathed to the world an alternative vision of international relations different from the cold-war politics. The failure of Indian initiatives to bring together the nations of Asia and Africa in the wake of decolonisation has been examined in the light of the regional and global foreign policy objectives of the Indian National Congress and the non-aligned free India.

Regional Spread of Ancient India

The idea of 'India and regionalism' evokes the image of an ancient Indian past when her influence spread far and wide—in East, South East, North and West Asia. This influence was due to the old universalistic conceptions "based on the transcendence of the immediate, the local and the temporal through the cultivation of the mind and a search for comprehension and meaning in an admittedly mysterious and complex reality, and led to a moderation and containment of selfish and expansionist drives in human personality".[1] The modern conception of universalism which unfolded during the last two centuries in the European continent, on the other hand, "was based on the expansion of a local civilization and on dominance over the rest of the world, legitimized by a belief in the manifest destiny that was peculiar to Judeo-Christian religiosity in the post-medieval age."[2] It was probably this basic contradiction between the visions of the East and the West which during twentieth century catapulted India to the leadership role against imperialism of the West in Asia and Africa. While the image of ancient 'Greater India' created apprehensions among the countries of Asia, India was looked upon as a guide and leader during its glorious freedom struggle against British imperialism. The imperial policy of the British envisaged a strategic position for India in their international strategy. George N. Curzon thus said:

> The Indian Empire is in the strategic centre of the third most important portion of the globe.... But her central and commanding position is nowhere better seen than in the political influence which she exercises over the destinies of her neighbours near and far, and the extent to which the fortunes revolve upon an Indian Axis.[3]

Indian Freedom Movement and Ideas on Regionalism

However, even before the Indian National Congress (INC) in the vanguard of India's struggle for independence, could conceive of complete freedom from British empire, they tried to articulate India's regional position in world affairs.[4] Bal Gangadhar Tilak, the Indian statesman, was nominated by the INC to attend the Peace Conference held at Versailles after the First World War. He wrote to the President of the Peace Conference after he was denied permission to attend the Conference. Outlining India's position he said:

> India is self-contained, harbours no design upon the integrity of other States and has no ambition outside. With her vast area, enormous resource, and prodigious population, she may well aspire to be a leading power in Asia. She could, therefore, be a powerful steward of the League of Nations in the East for maintaining the peace of the world.....[5]

Tilak, despite his militant image, could not envisage India working against the imperial interest of Britain in world affairs. This situation however, drastically changed in 1920, when Gandhi acquired leadership of the Congress. INC adopted Gandhi's plan of non-cooperation against the British in 1920 and called upon Indian people not to offer themselves as recruits for service in Mesopotamia.[6] In 1921, Gandhi declared that if there were a war between Britain and Afghanistan, he would certainly assist the Amir of Afghanistan if he waged war against the British Government. He said:

> I would openly tell my countrymen that it would be a crime to help a Government which had lost the confidence of the nation to remain in powel.[7]

In a similar vein the Congress Working Committee (CWC) in its meeting held in June 1921 in Bombay advised Indian soldiers not to cooperate with British Government against the Turkish Nationalist Government.[8]

Foreign Policy Perspective in Pre-independence India

The All India Congress Committee (AICC) in its Bombay session held in July 1921 took note of a resolution passed by the citizens of Bombay in April 1921 urging AICC 'to promote feelings of amity and concord with neighbouring States with a view to establish goodwill and sympathy to formulate a clear and definite foreign policy for India'.[9] Realising that Britain was using India's position and resources to promote its imperialistic designs in India's neighbourhood, the AICC in a historic declaration in Delhi on November 4-5, 1921, affirmed for the neighbouring and other non-Indian States that:

(i) the present Government of India in no way represent Indian opinion and that their policy has been traditionally guided by considerations more of holding India in subjection than of protecting her borders;

(ii) India as self-governing country can have nothing to fear from the neighbouring states or any state as her people have no designs upon any of them, and hence no intention of establishing any trade relation hostile to or not desired by the people of such states; and

(iii) the people of India regard most treaties entered into with the Imperial Government by neighbouring states as mainly designed by the latter to perpetuate the exploitation of India by the Imperial power, and would therefore urge the states having no ill-will against the people of India and having no desire to injure her interest, to refrain from entering into any treaty with the Imperial power.[10]

Asiatic Federation

Anti-imperialism became the cornerstone of the foreign policy of Congress and provided an opportunity for the states of Asia to come together. Gandhi observed that the common lot no less than territorial homogeneity and cultural affinity was bringing the Asiatic races wonderfully together and they seemed determined to take their fullest share in the world politics.[11] The INC saw the emergence of a great Asiatic Federation as inevitable and participation of India in the union of the oppressed nationalities of Asia as the precursor to the freedom of every nationality to bring about world peace. The Congress world-view maintained that no nation on earth can really be free when other nations are held in bondage.[12]

Pursuing the idea of an Eastern-Federation Congress discussed political ideas that scaled the ramparts of the Himalayas and most of the surrounding seas to recognise that the freedom of Asiatic nations would contemplate the organisation of an Eastern-Federation.[13]

Policy on Neighbouring States

The Indian National Congress under the leadership of Gandhi was extremely careful and sensitive towards the Indian neighbours oppressed by the imperialists.[14] The AICC sent a congratulatory message in 1921 to the Burmese people on their struggle for freedom from the British Indian administration. Gandhi made it clear that free India would recognise Burmese independence and would not try to absorb it into India. Accordingly, he asserted in 1922 that he had never been able to take pride in the fact that Burma had been made part of British India. He maintained that the Burmese had a civilisation of their own.[15] The AICC in 1924 expressing sympathy with the Burmese people asked the Indian settlers in Burma not to seek any separate rights for themselves at the cost of the indigenous population. Similarly, Gandhi, on a visit to Ceylon in 1927, advised the Indian settlers to throw their lot entirely with the Ceylonese people.

It was, however, China which received a very special attention of the Congress. The AICC in 1925 conveying its sympathy to the Chinese people in their struggle for national unity, protested against the use of Indian troops in China. Earlier, the same year Gandhi described the use of Indian soldiers for shooting Chinese people as humiliating and degrading spectacle.[16]

India's pivotal role in the fight against imperialist repression was aptly described by Dr. M.A. Ansari in his presidential address to the forty second session of INC held in 1927 in Madras. He said:

> India holds in her hands the remedy for this universal misfortune, for, she is the key-stone of the arch of Imperialism. Once India is free the whole edifice will collapse. The best guarantee for the freedom of Asia and the peace of the world, is a free and self-governing India.[17]

Further, continuing with the Congress vision of an Eastern Federation, Dr. Ansari maintained:

> In the conflict between Europe and Asia, Asia has been worsted because Europe could take concerted action against her piecemeal and defeat her in detail. The only hope of success in our efforts to check the forces of European Imperialism and Capitalism lies in Eastern nations coming closer and taking a more intimate interest in the problems facing them.[18]

The INC in 1928 taking its ideas on Asian regional unity further, directed the CWC to correspond with the leaders and representatives of other Asiatic nations and to take further steps to summon the first session of a Pan-Asiatic Federation in 1930 in India. The domestic and international dimensions of anti-imperialism of the INC provided the basic foundation of the Indian Foreign Policy. This policy of the Indian Congress was sharply pronounced in the inaugural session of the League Against Imperialism held at Brussels in February 1927. Pandit Jawaharlal Nehru representing the Congress at the League affirmed India's alignment with all other anti-imperialist forces of the world.[19]

A significant, positive fall out of this conference at Brussels was direct contact between Asian giants—India and China—leading to a formal declaration by the two stressing the need for a joint policy and recognising that Indo-Chinese cooperation was the key to Asiatic liberation.[20] The declaration thus read as follows:

> ... For more than three thousand years the people of India and China were united by the most intimate cultural ties. From the days of Buddha to the end of Mogul period and the beginning of British domination in India, the friendly intercourse continued uninterrupted.
>
> Since the infamous opium war of 1840-44 Indian mercenary troops have been sent again and again to China in

support of British capitalist brigandage in that country. For 87 years Indians have been permanently stationed as policemen in Hong Kong and Shanghai. Time and again they have been used to shoot down Chinese workers and have thus created ill-will in China against the people of India.

... We must now resume the recent personal, cultural and political relations between the two peoples. British imperialism which kept us apart and done us so much injury is now the very force that is uniting us in a common endeavour to overthrow it.[21]

The INC in its plenary session in Madras in 1927 passed a resolution assuring the Chinese people of its fullest sympathy in their struggle for freedom and condemned the action of the Government of India in dispatching the Indian troops to China, demanding their immediate withdrawal. The very next year the Congress, in a unanimous resolution, sent its warmest greetings and congratulations to the people of China on their having attained full and complete freedom and nationhood ending the era of foreign domination in their country. In the same resolution the Congress sent greetings to the people of Egypt, Syria, Palestine and Iraq assuring their full sympathy in their struggle for emancipation from the grip of Western imperialism which in the opinion of the Congress was a great menace to India's struggle for freedom.[22] In the historic Lahore session in 1929, Congress declared full Independence from British imperial rule as their ultimate objective. There was thus unity of outlook in Congress policy on internal and external problems facing the oppressed people of Asia and the world.

Regional Agenda Against Imperialism

The persistent strain of anti-imperialism in the policy of INC was accompanied by the Gandhian doctrine of Non-violence which inspired its opposition to war particularly during the period between two world wars.[23] The Indian leadership realized better than the European statesmen that imperialism and war were related phenomena and therefore must be opposed by the freedom loving people of the colonized nations. Amidst gathering war clouds between the growing Fascist Powers in Europe and Far East and the imperialist powers of Western Europe, Nehru articulated Congress-ideology in his Presidential address to the Lucknow session of the INC in 1936 in the following words:

> Capitalism in its difficulties took to fascism with all its brutal suppression of what western civilization had apparently stood for; it became, even in some of its homelands, what its counterpart had long been in the subject colonial countries. Fascism and Imperialism thus stood out as the two faces of the now decaying Capitalism.... They represented the same forces of reaction and supported each other, and at the same time came into conflict with each other, for such conflict was inherent in their very nature.... Nationalism in the East, it must be remembered, was essentially different from the new and terribly narrow nationalism of Fascist countries; the former was the historical urge to freedom, the latter the last refuge of reaction.[24]

Expressing this historical urge to freedom, Congress served the final 'Quit India' notice on British imperialists in August 1942. Even while doing so the AICC kept its regional Asiatic agenda in place when in this historical resolution it was observed that "the freedom of India must be the symbol of and prelude to the freedom of all other Asiatic nations under foreign domination. Burma, Malaya, Indo-China, the Dutch-Indies, Iran, Iraq must also attain their complete freedom."[25] The regional policy of the pre-independence Congress was further elaborated in the AICC resolution passed in a meeting held in September 1945 at Bombay. This resolution expressed anxiety at the attempts that were being made to maintain the political and economic subjugation of Burma, Malaya, Indo-China and Indonesia and declared:

> To continue imperialist domination over these countries, under whatever name or guise, would be a denial and repudiation of the professions made by the United Nations during war time and would sow the seeds of future wars. India, desiring the freedom of all Asiatic, as well as other countries would deeply resent the continuation of an imperialist policy in South-East Asia. In particular the AICC would take strong objection to the use of Indian troops in maintaining imperialist domination over any of these countries of South East or Western Asia.[26]

Pledge on Free India's Regional Policy

In a further significant statement for the future policy of free India the AICC resolution of September 1945 mentioned that "a free India will inevitably seek the close and friendly associations with her neighbouring countries and would especially seek to develop common policies for defence, trade and economic and cultural development with China, Burma, Malaya, Indonesia and Ceylon as well as the countries of the Middle East."[27]

The INC nursed a sense of grievance that despite India's importance and leadership against colonialism, India could not secure its rightful due place as a member of the Security Council of the United Nations on account of its colonized status. The CWC in July 1945 adopted a resolution expressing strong resentment against the position allotted to the smaller nations in the United Nations Organisation. The Committee observed that the Great-Powers not only dominated and completely controlled the new organization but were placed above and beyond the law they had themselves helped in framing. In accordance with its perception of India's role in national and international fields, the CWC felt that India must attain the status of an independent and sovereign state, having a place in the highest councils of nations, and in a position to contribute to the maintenance of peace, security and freedom.[28]

It was in keeping with this grandiose image of India that the INC considered India to be the central actor in Asia. Thus Jawaharlal Nehru, who more than anyone else represented Congress views on Foreign Policy matters, observed:

> "whether one talked of the Middle East or South East Asia or China, all impinged on India and all depended on India economically, politically and strategically. They could not help looking at India and India could not help looking at them. In the modern world it was inevitable for India to be the centre of things in Asia."[29]

Nehru also maintained that the small States of the future world had no future in store and they were certain to be reduced to the status of the satellite States. He advocated the creation of a South Asian Federation of India, Iraq, Iran, Afghanistan and Burma.[30]

Follow up of Indian Pre-independence Ideas on Regionalism: Afro-Asian Movement

Asian Relations Conference (1947)

The CWC could not follow up on the directive of the Congress (1928) to take steps to summon the first session of the Pan-Asiatic

Federation in 1930 in India due to its preoccupation with mass Civil Disobedience Movement against the Empire. However, on the eve of Indian independence inspired by Nehru, the Indian Council of World Affairs (ICWA) picked up these threads and convened an Asian Relations Conference (ARC) in New Delhi in March 1947.[31] The Conference was attended by 28 countries including the then Soviet-Asian Republics and Egypt. There were observers from the UNO, Arab League and several institutions from Sydney, London, Moscow and New York. Eight different subjects by five groups were discussed in the Conference. These were as follows:

(i) National Movements for Freedom;
(ii) Racial Problems and Inter-Asian Migrations;
(iii) Transition from Colonial to National Economy; Agricultural Reconstruction and Industrial Development; Labour Problems and Social Services;
(iv) Cultural Problems;
(v) Status of Women and Women's Movements.[32]

The steering committee of the Conference took two important decisions — one, that the Conference would not adopt resolutions but would merely accept a report embodying the consensus of opinions expressed in various discussion forums; and two, that a sub-committee of fifteen persons be set up to consider the advisability of establishing a permanent institute.[33]

The political importance of the Conference was underlined by the presence of eminent representatives of several countries although they attended the Conference on behalf of non-political organisations. These included Dr. Sutan Shariar, Prime Minister of Indonesia; S.W.R.D Bandarnaike, Minister for Local Administration in the Government of Ceylon and later its Prime Minister; General Aung San, the Burmese nationalist leader who later became the Prime Minister of free Burma and Jawaharlal Nehru himself. The Chinese protested at the invitation to Tibet and French did so in respect of Vietnam. The Indian Muslim League boycotted the Conference alleging that the show was an attempt by the Indian Hindu Congress to spread its influence abroad. The ICWA issued a communique that the Conference would deal mainly with cultural, economic and like subjects. The Conference, nevertheless, because of its historical importance and eminent attendance acquired a political and a sort of 'official' status.

In his inaugural address, Nehru set the tone when he said:

> There was a widespread urge and awareness that the time had come for us, peoples of Asia, to meet together, to hold together and to advance together.[34]

Nehru further observed:

> For too long, we of Asia have been petitioners in Western courts and chancelleries. That story must now belong to the past. We propose to stand on our own feet and to cooperate with all others who are prepared to cooperate with us. We do not intend to be the playthings of others.[35]

In an eloquent and balanced manner Nehru provided an appropriate introduction to this historic Conference. Sisir Gupta has noted four major elements in Nehru's speech: the proclamation of Asia's arrival on world scene; the stress on the need for Asian unity; the need to avoid the expression of the anti-Western sentiments; and the need for greater cooperation.[36] It was Nehru's contention that Asia should work for larger ideal of 'one world' and not for any grouping which comes in the way of this larger world group. However, in order to attain this one world, Nehru thought the countries of Asia should cooperate among themselves.

There was tremendous enthusiasm among delegations attending the Conference. The speakers referred to awakening and new birth of Asia, cultural unity of Asia, a continent of peace which is fearful of the prospect of the new world war; realistic outlook and hard work the need of the hour in Asia, etc.

Nehru, in his inaugural address said:

> The freedom we envisage is not to be confined to this nation or that or to a particular people but must spread out over the whole human race. That universal freedom also cannot be based on the supremacy of any particular class. It must be the freedom of the common man everywhere....[37]

A delegate from Ceylon expressed the fear of small countries that they might be faced with aggression, not necessarily political but economic and demographic by big brothers like India and China. The general consensus of the Conference on issues discussed in this group were the following:

(i) that it was against any continuation of foreign domination in any part of Asia;

(ii) that the Asian countries will avoid any assistance for the continuation of such domination;

(iii) that assistance should be given to national movements wherever possible; and

(iv) that people belonging to one country and living in another should identify themselves with the latter.[38]

The outcome of the Conference lacked clarity due to its decision that there should be no resolutions. The Conference, nevertheless, decided to establish an Asian Relations Organisation (ARO) in New Delhi with following objectives:

(a) to promote the study and understanding of Asian problems and relations in their Asian and world aspects;

(b) to foster friendly relations and cooperation among the peoples of Asia and between them and the rest of the world; and

(c) to further the progress and well being of the peoples of Asia.[39]

A Provisional General Council of the ARO representing all participating nations was constituted. This Council elected Jawaharlal Nehru as its President. The ARO was to be composed of the national units of each affiliated Asian countries. These units were to be non-governmental in character. The council was directed to frame the Provisional Constitution of the Organisation and it was decided to hold the next general Conference in China in 1949.

Given the objectives it was expected that the Asian Relations Organisation would develop into the political and economic aspects of an Asian federation. However, the provisional council did not meet a second time and even provisional constitution could not be framed. The Organisation was quietly wound up in 1957 without even a second opportunity of meeting. The second meeting was scheduled to be held in 1949. Analysing the reasons for the failure of ARO an Asia watcher observed:

> If circumstances had been ideal, the Asian Relations Organisation might have grown into something very large and important. In the event it was no more than a nut crushed between the jaws of a steel press closing under the weight of immense events — the rivalry between India and China, the Communist revolutionary take over in China, the suspicion of

India in South and South-East Asian countries, and the rending apart of British India into India and Pakistan.[40]

The distrust, suspicion and rivalry of Asian nations must have come as a rude shock to the intellectual idealism and honesty of purpose of Jawaharlal Nehru. "Faced with the hostility of China, the suspicion of South-East Asia and the indifference of Arabs, India had no bricks with which to build any kind of Asian structure".[41]

The reactions of Western and Russian media to the holding of Asian Relations Conference makes an interesting reading. *The New Chronicle of London* discovered a certain nervousness apparent in European capitals lest some conspiracy for an anti-Western bloc was being hatched. The *New York Times* warned that the Western world would do well to watch carefully what was happening in Delhi since it might have large potentialities. The *Times of London* declared that the world had a new force to reckon with the awakened spirit of Asia. *The Russian Izvestia* noted that the decision to have a permanent organisation produced a negative reaction from the countries in the American sphere of influence.[42] The alarming reaction of the media of ex-colonial powers which brutally kept the Asian nations apart into different imperial systems was indeed very amusing. The very thought of Asians coming together unnerved them. Unfortunately the Asians riven by dissension and apprehensions of their own creation did not disappoint the Western imperialists who were on the verge of a vicious cold war with the Soviet-bloc and would soon be scouting for allies.

Jawaharlal Nehru's approach in ARC was that the Conference was not directed against any race or region, that it ought not to deal with bilateral internal disputes and that there were no leader and no followers among the participants. This approach was to continue in future in all Afro-Asian conferences held during the decade and a half after Indian independence, viz., the New Delhi Conference on Indonesia, January 1949; the Baguio (Philippines) Conference, May 1950; the Colombo Powers Conference, April 1954; the Bogor Conference, December 1954; the Afro-Asian Conference, April 1955, Bandung (Indonesia); the Simla (India) Conference, May 1955; the Brioni Conference, July 1956; the New Delhi Conference, 1961; and the Belgrade Conference, 1961.[43]

Conference on Indonesia (1949)

The New Delhi Conference on Indonesia was convened by

India in 1949 in the aftermath of Dutch police action in Indonesia in December 1948. This effort by a small European country to re-enter an Asian country after the exit of British imperialists from the mainland South-Asia was taken as an affront by the resurgent Asia. Asia was not hopeful of any firm action against Holland by the UN Security Council dominated by the Western powers who were in the process of institutionalising West European Union in the form of North Atlantic Treaty Organisation (NATO). The Conference attended by India, Afghanistan, Australia, Burma, Ceylon, Egypt, Ethiopia, Iran, Iraq, Lebanon, Pakistan, the Philippines, Saudi Arabia and Yemen, and observers from Kumintang China, Nepal, New Zealand and Thailand condemned the Dutch aggression and called for the release of the arrested members of the Government of the Indonesian Republic, withdrawal of Dutch troops from the capital Jogjakarta and from Indonesia at large with a view to transfer power by January 1, 1950 to the United States of Indonesia.[44]

The Conference was ostensibly called to discuss only Dutch aggression in Indonesia. However, the indication of failure of the Asian Relations Organisation prompted Nehru to suggest the formation of a permanent Asian Organisation and to make an open appeal for regional integration. He said:

> We see creative and cooperative impulses seeking a new integration and new unity. New problems arise from day to day which, in their implications, concern all of us or many of us. The Americans have already recognized a certain community of interests and have created machinery for the protection and promotion of common interests. A similar movement is in progress in Europe. Is it not natural that the free countries of Asia should begin to think of some more permanent arrangement than this Conference for effective mutual consultation and concerted effort in the pursuit of common aims-not in a spirit of selfishness or hostility to any other nation or group of nations, but in order to strengthen and bring nearer fulfilment the aims and ideals of the Charter of the United Nations ?.[45]

The Conference termed as 'the first Asian Political Conference' by the Syrian representative and described by Phillipino General Romulo as "the first inter-governmental Conference on the political level to be held in Asia", was sharply divided on the issue of a permanent Asian organisation. While some countries endorsed the idea, others objected to its being out of agenda and hence not feasible for consideration. There were differences too on the exact shape of this organisation among the supporters of the idea. Arabs wanted to create an anti-Isareli bloc and General Romulo wanted an Asian front against Communism. The final resolution on the issue was an insipid expression of the opinion that "participating governments should consult among themselves in order to explore ways and means of establishing suitable machinery, having regard to the areas concerned, for promoting consultation and cooperation within the framework of the United Nations."[46]

The New York Times had reported deep concern of the United States and the European colonial powers over the possible development through this Conference of the atmosphere for the growth of regionalism and racialism. Nehru, however, made it clear that his intention was to act within the UN agencies and that no 'Asian bloc' or 'brown bloc' would come from this conference".[47] It must have been with a tremendous sense of relief that the New York newspaper carried an assessment of this conference to say:

> ...Asia is feeling its muscles. However, the record indicates that statesmen like Pandit Nehru and General Romulo can be counted upon to shy away from fostering racial or geographical antagonisms. India particularly is anxious to avoid the ideological cleavage that now separates the democracies from the Soviet sphere....[48]

Interestingly, Soviet newspaper *Pravada* also attacked Nehru for being anti-Soviet and interpreted the Asian Conference on Indonesia as an attempt to establish an anti-Soviet bloc.[49]

Post-Second War International Situation and Asian Regionalism

The victory of Communist movement in China in 1949 changed the political context of Asia. The cold war ambience with its impact on all regions of the world was taking a firm shape. India had declared its firm commitment to stay clear of East-West antagonism. The Korean war in mid-1950 further complicated the Asian scene. Sisir Gupta notes two consequences out of this situation: an erosion of Indian urgency for regional integration and an immense difficulty in conceiving any association in Asia which would be consistent with the need of avoiding alignment and invoking the potential sympathy of the two blocs in the solution of the Asian problems.[50]

An Afro-Asian group was formed in the United Nations in December 1950 to hold consultations and coordinate their actions in the UN on matters of war and peace in the wake of Korean-war. The non-aligned India, Burma and Indonesia came together within the Afro-Asian group.

Nehru's belief in India's responsibility to bring Asian countries together was firmly entrenched in India's foreign policy approach.[51] Nehru felt convinced that there was a keen desire on the part of Asian countries to work together, to confer together and generally to look to one another. Nehru also deprecated the talk of India's leadership in this regard when in Baguio Conference held in 1950 he said:

> Some people talk rather loosely, and if I may say so, rather foolishly, of India becoming the leader of this or the leader of that or the leader of Asia. Now, I do not like this at all. It is a bad approach, this business of leadership. But it is true that because of various factors... a certain special responsibility is cast on India. India realizes it and other countries realize it also. The responsibility is not necessarily for leadership, but for taking the initiative sometimes and helping others to cooperate.[52]

In the emerging post-second war international situation and in view of the Korean war, India in early fifties was interested in an Asia free from cold war and military alignments. India wanted Asia to become an area of peace. The cold war was considered immoral as against non-alignment with a moral basis. On June 12, 1952 Nehru thus said in Indian Parliament:

> I should like an ever increasing number of countries in the world to decide that they will not have another war, whatever happens. I should like the countries in Asia—I speak about our neighbours—and other countries also to make it clear to those warring factions and those great countries that are explosively bitter against each other that they themselves will remain cool and not enter the arena of warfare whatever happens and that they will try at least to restrict the area of conflict....[53]

The Colombo Conference[54] convened in 1954 to consider inter-alia the Indo-China situation could not contribute in any significant manner to regionalism in Asia except that it proved to be the starting point for the historic Afro-Asian Conference at Bandung. The cold war realities had started impinging on India's neighbourhood in South and South-East Asia by now. Pakistan and some South-East Asian countries joined U.S. sponsored alliances of SEATO and Baghdad Pact. Likewise U.S. decision to provide military aid to Pakistan in 1954 fundamentally changed the regional situation in Asia. Nehru voiced his concern on U.S. decision in following words:

> This is a matter on which constitutionally or otherwise it is none of our concern what Pakistan and the U.S.A. are doing. But practically it is a matter of most intense concern to us and something which will have very far-reaching consequences on the whole structure of things in South Asia and especially in India and Pakistan.[55]

These developments were destabilising for Asia and a negation of Nehru's ideas on non-aligned peace area for Asia. A U.S. analyst commented that U.S.-Pakistan alliance was " not for its purported defense value against Soviet aggression but for the very reason Pakistan has sought aid—as a counterforce to the confirmed neutralism of Jawaharlal Nehru's India."[56]

The Panchsheel

Nehru was not to be cowed down by the cold war rhetoric. He put forth his five principles of peaceful coexistence as an alternative vision to the 'immorality' of cold war. The five principles later known as 'Panchsheel', officially admitted by the Indian Government as a restatement in more specific terms of the principles embodied in the United Nations Charter were as follows:

(i) Mutual respect for each other's territorial integrity and sovereignty.

(ii) Mutual non-aggression.

(iii) Mutual non-interference in each other's affairs.

(iv) Equality and mutual benefit.

(v) Peaceful coexistence.[57]

Nehru maintained that the idea of peaceful coexistence was not new and was rooted in ancient Indian thought and culture. He said:

> These principles form the basis of our relations with other nations. We are convinced that on this basis the relationship

between the countries will be healthy, peaceful and cooperative, because it rests on equality and mutual respect and peaceful coexistence, and rules out aggression and internal interference. Trouble arises when one country dominates over another or interferes in another's internal affairs. If 'Panchsheel' is fully and sincerely adopted by all countries, peace would be assured everywhere, and cooperation would follow.[58]

Although not backed by the economic power of the state, the concept of Panchsheel was a serious threat to the ideology of the cold warriors, particularly in the newly liberated zone of Asia. Only a few months later at the time of Afro-Asian Bandung Conference, Panchsheel was accepted as a regulating basis of relations between India and China, North Vietnam, Yugoslavia and Cambodia and between Burma and China and Yugoslavia.[59] Nehru considered Panchsheel as a challenge of Asia to the rest of the world. He hoped that this question would be posed at the Afro-Asian Conference in all its straightness and that each country would be asked to say whether it stood for non-aggression and non-interference or not.[60]

Bandung Conference (1955)

The Bandung Conference, considered to be the high point of Afro-Asian attempt to develop common policies and approach to their problems, was convened by the five Colombo Conference participants, i.e., Burma, Ceylon, India, Indonesia and Pakistan in April 1955. The Conference attended by 29 Asian and African nations included almost all nations which had gained freedom from colonial rule. The communique issued at the end of preparatory Bogor Conference outlined the objectives of the Bandung Conference:

(a) to promote goodwill and cooperation between the nations of Asia and Africa to explore and advance their mutual as well as common interests and to establish and further friendliness and neighbourly relations; and

(b) to view the position of Asia and Africa and their peoples in the world of today and the contribution they can make to the promotion of world peace and cooperation.[61]

The final Bandung Communique stressed the desire for economic cooperation among participating countries and recommended early establishment of a Special United Nations Fund for economic development. It asked for the allocation of a greater part of its resources by the World Bank to Asian-African countries and the early establishment of an International Finance Corporation to promote equity investment.[62]

The Bandung Conference declared that colonialism in all its manifestations is an evil and should speedily be brought to an end, and called upon the powers concerned to grant independence to dependent people. To promote world peace and cooperation it was considered essential to make the United Nations universal. It called on the Security Council to support the admission of those States which were qualified for admission in terms of the Charter; and to increase the representation of Asian-African States in the Security Council. It also called for disarmament and the prohibition of the use of nuclear weapons. The declaration on the promotion of world peace and cooperation specifically exhorted nations to be free from mistrust and fear and with confidence and goodwill towards each other practise tolerance and live together in peace with one another as good neighbours and develop friendly cooperation. The principles to be observed for this purpose were in essence based on the concept of Panchsheel. Indonesia's Sukarno had underlined the most important purpose of the Bandung Conference in the following words:

> We Asian and African leaders understand that Asia and Africa can prosper only when they are united and that even the safety of the world at large cannot be safeguarded without a united Asia-Africa.[63]

The result of the Conference and subsequent period of Asian-African history could not fulfil this primary purpose of the Conference. In fact the Western media was gleefully satisfied at the outcome of the conference. Thus the *Times*, London observed:

> Thus at Bandung it was not Mr. Chou who felt the force of continual sniping, and sometimes heavy shelling from Turkey, Iraq, the Philippines, Siam, Pakistan and Ceylon... it was Mr. Nehru and his friends whose hopes were dashed and whose plans were wrecked by this anti-Communist assault, and the two of the attackers were among the five sponsors...The corollary of this move directed against Mr. Nehru and his friends that he was hardly called upon to act as a mediator between China and the rest. At times one almost felt that it was Mr.

> Chou who was playing such a part on behalf of Mr. Nehru...yet ...if Asia as a concept and political entity is to survive Mr. Nehru is its embodiment....[64]

And the *New York Times* observed :

> One of the most surprising developments at Bandung, it was agreed, was Premier Nehru's inability to keep the conference on the course he had chartered for it. He was described by reporters as increasingly irritable and snappish as he was frustrated in his effort to prevent ideological conflict at the open sessions, and second, to prevent discussion of specific issues such as Palestine.[65]

G.H. Jansen has noted a remarkably accurate forecast of Bandung Conference by a secret committee set up in the U.S. State Department. The report of the committee predicted that China would be moderate, in order to raise her prestige and show herself diplomatically acceptable; because of the diversity of the membership, the conference resolutions were likely to stick to general principles; for the same reasons the conference was not expected to result in any kind of regional alliance, but it was expected to make plans for further meetings to advance the principles it adopted; Chou En-lai would be cautious and reasonable, and there would be a struggle for leadership between him and Mr. Nehru, who was expected to give the meeting a non-racial lead. The conference would endorse the Five Principles of Panchsheel.[66]

Some of the participants in the conference — the Philippines, Japan, South Vietnam, Laos, Thailand, Turkey, Pakistan, Ethiopia, and Libya were considered 'friends' of the U.S. in this report. These friends were expected to display a positive and constructive attitude at the conference but resist any anti-American proposals. The Bandung Conference thus became a hot bed of cold war politics and a story of rivalry between India and China. It failed to promote the cause of Afro-Asian regionalism.

The Bandung economic proposals were sought to be revived by the Prime Minister Bandarnaike of Ceylon in 1959. He sent a memorandum to 29 Bandung participants and to Malaya and Singapore suggesting a discussion on the ways and means to carry out the economic resolutions of the Bandung Conference. The memorandum included issues such as establishment of a free trade area or a common market, establishment of a regional development bank, coordinated planning in food production, cooperation in industrial development, a unified policy on foreign investment, establishment of joint atomic research centres and collective action to safeguard shipping interests to ensure fair and stable export prices for primary products. The response to the memorandum was very poor. The Prime Minister of Ceylon was later assassinated.[67]

Failure of Afro-Asian Movement

The ideas and ideology of the Indian National Congress on regional solidarity of colonized nations of Asia and Africa evolved in the final stages of the Indian struggle for independence. India by its geographical and historical importance and grand presence of Gandhi and Nehru acquired the leadership of anti-colonial movements in Asia and Africa. The Indian National Congress generated a historic mass movement and ideology to bring together countries of Asia on a common anti-imperialistic plank.

The unifying spirit of anti-imperialism, however, dissipated during early initiatives for consolidating the gains of freedom. This was primarily due to lack of a focussed effort to create a specific regional identity and a supporting institutional framework, a very vicious post-second war division of the world into warring ideological camps, rivalry between India and China and apprehensions of their smaller neighbours that their identity would be submerged and they would be swamped by the 'big two'.

The failure of Indian initiatives on regionalism was also partly attributable to the high goals set for the Indian policy by Nehru. A well meaning statesman and intellectual giant in Nehru wanted to realize the vision of world-peace through a conflict-free Asia and Africa by means of Panchsheel. In the process, however, he ignored the harsh realities of power-play and underestimated the 'skills' of the Western powers in ensuring the division of the third world to perpetuate their influence and power. The prediction of the secret committee of the U.S. State Department proved to be prophetic, not merely in respect of Bandung Conference but also in respect of Indian policy to promote regionalism in Asia, i.e., a mere endorsement of general principles without any substantive, specific achievement.

India's initial efforts at Asian regionalism were marked by confusion about the region which it should promote for cooperation and collective identity.[68] India had strong geographical, historical and cultural linkages with the West and South-East Asia. She could also not remain untouched by the events and problems in the Far East. However, the wider Asia comprised of nations with geographical, cultural, political and economic diversity. A common anti-colonial sentiment was not enough to sustain these countries into a common regional bond. Nehru's statement in Indian Parliament on March 8,1949 after the Conference on Indonesia reflected the lack of clarity in Indian outlook. Nehru said:

> Recently there was the Conference on Indonesia held at India's insistence in New Delhi and many countries from Asia attended it, besides Egypt, Ethiopia, Australia and New Zealand. That conference forcibly brought several matters before the world's eye and at the conference one of the resolutions passed was that we should explore methods of closer cooperation ....possibly we might have another conference to consider the possible lines of cooperation .... We have not yet decided what the region of cooperation might be, because,... India is interested in several regions in Asia. Whether all should be grouped together or separately. I do not know. That is for us to consider together and to decide what is more feasible....[69]

The Indian confusion on regionalism was further confounded since Nehru, the most important architect of Indian foreign policy after independence had set his focus on a larger goal. In the same speech as above before Indian Parliament in March 1949, Nehru outlined his ideas when he said:

> ...I would beg the House to look upon the matter from the wider point of view that I have placed before it, that is the emergence of India and Asia in the modern trend of human affairs, the inevitability of India playing an important part by virtue of her tremendous potential, by virtue of the fact that she is the biggest political unit in terms of population today and is likely to be in terms of resources also. She is going to play that part. If we have to play that part we have to look upon this question from this bigger point of view and not from the small difficulties and problems that face us and that part must essentially be one of promoting peace and freedom in the world, of removing racial inequalities.[70]

Sisir Gupta reflecting on the problems and prospects of regional integration in Asia found that in developing countries like India, foreign policy was not the function of mass opinion but rather of modernized elite groups often represented by one man or a group of men who represented the urges and aspirations of the elite. The foreign policy of India was thus largely seen as creation of Jawaharlal Nehru. The lack of communication among the elites of different Asian countries and the tendency of the Indian elite to identify with European values and problems was seen as a serious difficulty in the process of regional integration in Asia.[71] Nehru's attempt at imitating Western experience in regionalism was, therefore, considered unrealistic because he did not distinguish between the Western and Asian situations in this regard. S.D. Muni and Anuradha Muni observe:

> ...In the third world, the external and strategic factors play an extremely important role. There exists strategic schism and discord in the third world as against harmony and consensus in this respect behind European regionalism.... No attempt to study regionalism in the third world can therefore be meaningful without proper reference to the factors of the primacy of politics, including strategic/security factors and the role of the external powers and forces.[72]

The external powers and forces were not favourably disposed towards Asian regionalism. The Western ex-colonial powers were particularly apprehensive of Asia coming together on an anti-colonial plank. The cold war rivalry of superpowers resulted in their efforts to wean away newly independent states of Asia into military pacts and ideological alliances. This was not in consonance with the Indian articulation of third world solidarity in accordance with the principles of non-alignment. The emergence of mainland China as a communist country and Sino-Indian rivalry in Asia further aggravated the political and strategic divergence in Asia. This virtually sealed the prospects of an institutional structure emerging from the deliberations of Afro-Asian conferences.

The economic aspects of cooperation were neglected during initial moves towards regionalism in Asia. The Asian economies ravaged by colonial exploitation were in dire need of regeneration. A regional effort at that stage for economic reconstruction would have provided an excellent catalyst for evolving an Asian established in 1947 had provided the initial basic ideas for evolving a regional economic cooperative framework in Asia. Some initiatives were taken in the areas of trade promotion and coordinated planning in the region. The Bandung Conference document referred to the issues of mutual technical assistance, stability of raw material prices, holding of Asian or sub-regional trade fairs etc.[73] However, no significant progress or achievement could be made in respect of regional economic cooperation.

The Colombo Plan

A Colombo Plan for economic and technical cooperation was earlier launched in 1951 by Burma, Cambodia, Ceylon, Indonesia, Japan, Laos, Nepal, Pakistan, the Phillippines, Thailand, Vietnam (South), Malaya, Singapore and British Borneo. However, later India convened a conference at Simla in May 1955 inviting all Colombo Plan members. The agenda for this conference was utilisation of special allocations for development of intra-regional trade, setting up of a machinery to provide credit for Asian nations that were in short-term balance-of-payment difficulties and for the creation of a permanent secretariat for the Colombo Plan. The response to Indian invitation was lukewarm — a very low level representation by most countries with Burma declining the invitation and Sri Lanka objecting to any multilateral arrangement. The Colombo Plan on account of political and economic divergence in Asian countries and lack of outside support, could not become a vehicle for economic regeneration of Asia.[74] The U.S. supported Marshal Plan for its ideological allies in Western Europe, on the contrary, achieved a remarkable reconstruction of Western Europe.

India's Policy Objectives

The apprehensions about India's long-term objectives among her South Asian neighbours was also a serious impediment in the emergence of regionalism in Asia. The deliberations of different groups constituted during the Asian Relations Conference provide a useful insight into the mindset of the smaller Asian nations. In the round table discussion on the group on 'National Movements for Freedom', a Burmese delegate referred to India being a tool in the hands of the British imperialism for subjugating countries around India and mentioned Burma, Ceylon, Malaya and Indonesia feeling the pressure either of Indian troops or of Indian economy. This delegate hoped that India after getting freedom would not use its the hands of the British imperialism for subjugating countries around India and mentioned Burma, Ceylon, Malaya and Indonesia feeling the pressure either of Indian troops or of Indian economy. This delegate hoped that India after getting freedom would not use its army for suppressing the freedom movement of any country and also feared that the European capitalism and exploitation might be replaced by 'brown exploitation' in the course of Burma getting assistance to rebuild its ruined economy.[75]

In yet another group discussion on 'Racial Problems and Inter Asian Migration' these fears found expression in the words of the Burmese delegate:

> Burma was between two great powers. It was terrible to be ruled by a Western power, but it was even more so to be ruled by an Asian power. Burma was naturally frightened by the possibility that the British imperialism may be substituted by an Indian or Chinese imperialism.[76]

S.D. Muni quite appropriately captures the Indian dilemma in promoting Asian regionalism during early 50s when he observes:

> The attitude of small neighbours constrained India from taking initiatives for regionalism after 1949. India almost reluctantly participated in the Baguio Conference (1950) and subsequently let Sri Lanka and Indonesia take initiatives. India's opposition to military pacts sponsored by the Western Powers, right since the Baguio Conference and specially after the U.S. military aid to Pakistan in 1954, turned it lukewarm towards the ideas of Asian regionalism, which in the then existing context could not avoid cold war orientation. This appeared to be a complete negation of the principles of non-alignment and peaceful co-existence to which India stood fully committed.[77]

Indian policy orientation towards regional cooperation in Asia got a new lease of life in the larger context of non-aligned movement and North-South polarisation of the world during 1960s and 1970s. The United Nations also continued its supportive efforts to promote regionalism in Asia under the concept of ECAFE. The ECAFE Ministerial Conference at Bangkok in 1968 produced hopes of a modest action programme for greater economic cooperation in Asia. In the wake of the oil-crisis of 1973 and sharpening of North-South divide, we witnessed articulation of South's efforts towards acceptance of the objectives of an equitable New International

Economic Order (NIEO) by the United Nations General Assembly in 1974 and promotion of the idea of South-South cooperation.

Conclusion

To sum up, India, inspired by the anti-colonial sentiment and resurgence of Asianism, wanted to forge the unity of newly independent nations of Asia and Africa for reconstruction of the nations ravaged by Western imperialism. Inherent in Indian policy pronouncements and efforts was a strong desire to play a larger political role for world peace and a secure international order. The grand political vision of independent India's initial policy was confronted by the hostility of the cold war and political aspirations of her newly created neighbour Pakistan and rivalry of her ancient neighbour China.

India's initial efforts failed to unify Asia and she suffered the rude shocks of wars with China (1962) and Pakistan (1965). These initial efforts to promote regionalism also lacked economic content and were inspired primarily by the grand world-view of Jawaharlal Nehru who wanted to pursue the higher ideals of world peace through the ideology of non-alignment.

However, despite the fact that the economies of the region were competitive rather than complementary, India was willing to collaborate with the countries of the region in economic sphere. A beginning was also made in the form of Colombo Plan as a result of the initiative taken earlier by the Commonwealth Foreign Ministers. The Plan envisaged survey of the needs of the area, an assessment of the available resources and manpower and providing an international framework for a regional cooperative effort. However, the Colombo Plan idea on economic cooperation did not make much headway in the absence of a central organisation, a headquarter or a permanent secretariat. The efforts of the United Nations later to promote economic cooperation in the region through the mechanism of ECAFE were again more in the realm of possibility rather than reality. Indian policy during this period developed linkages with non-aligned movement and consequent pursuit of regional economic interests through the struggle for a New International Economic Order.

REFERENCES

1. Rajni Kothari, *Towards a Just World,* Working Paper No. 11, World Order Model Project, Institute for World Order, New York, 1980, pp. 2-3.
2. *Ibid*., p. 3.
3. George N. Curzon, *Problems of the Far East*, London, 1896, pp. 8-9.
4. For details see Jawaharlal Nehru, *Autobiography*, London, 1940; N.V. Rajkumar, *The Background of India's Foreign Policy*, AICC, New Delhi, 1953; Bimla Prasad, *Origins of India's Foreign Policy*, Galcutta, 1960; Sisir Gupta, *India and Regional Integration in Asia*, Bombay, 1964; Satyavrata Ramdas Patel, *Foreign Policy of India: An Inquiry and Criticism*, Bombay, 1960, Norman D. Palmer, "Foreign Policy of Indian National Congress before Independence", in K.P. Misra (ed.), *Foreign Policy of India*, New Delhi , 1977.
5. C.F. Andrews and Girija Mukherji, *The Rise and Growth of Congress in India*, London, 1938, pp. 270-71.
6. Mesopotamia (Iraq) was used as a base for operations against Turkey during the First World War. However, in 1920 there were strong protests against British domination which turned into a mass rebellion in Iraq. The rebellion was ultimately crushed with the help of troops from India; For details please see Jawahar Lal Nehru's *Glimpses of World History*, New Delhi, 1982, pp. 773-76.
7. M.K. Gandhi, "The Afghan Bogey", *Young India*, May 4, 1921, Ahmedabad Published by Navjeevan Trust, 1981, Vol. III, p. 139.
8. A.M. Zaidi, *INC, The Glorious Tradition*, Vol. II, (192-1927) Texts of Resolutions passed by the INC, the AICC and CWC, New Delhi, 1987, pp. 59-60.
9. *Ibid*., p. 34.
10. *Ibid*., p. 38, Also see, Bimla Prasad, *Origins of Indian Foreign Policy*, Calcutta, 1960.
11. M.K. Gandhi, "The Spirit of the East", *Young India*, Ahmedabad, April 14, 1920, Navjeevan Trust, 1981, Vol. II.
12. For details refer to the Presidential Address of C.R. Das in the INC of 1922, in A.M. Zaidi and S.G. Zaidi (ed.), *The Encyclopaedia of the Indian National Congress, India at the Cross Roads*, Volume Eight,1921-1924, New Delhi, 1981, pp. 117-18.
13. Mohmed Ali presiding over INC, 1923, n. 12, p. 287.
14. *Far Eastern Economic Review*, September 21, 1961, Hong Kong, contains a 48 page special survey of India's economic and political relations with her neighbours.

15. M.K.Gandhi, *Young India*, Ahmedabad, January 26, 1922,Navjeevan Trust, 1981,Vol. 4.
16. *Ibid.* July 30, 1925, (Vol. 7).
17. *The Encyclopaedia of the INC*, Volume Nine, 1925-1929, n.12 , p. 234.
18. *Ibid.*, pp. 254-55.
19. For details see, Jawaharlal Nehru, *Autobiography*, London, 1940.
20. Before having contacts with China it was Japan which impressed the leaders of the Indian National Congress. The Victory of Japan over Russia in 1905 demonstrated the fact that there was nothing inherently superior about Britain. They were also deeply impressed by the Japanese slogan of 'Asia for the Asians'. However, few years later the leaders were disappointed with Japan's international conduct, military adventure against Burma, Korea and China; For details see, Werner Levi, *Free India in Asia*, Minneapolis, University of Minnesota,1952, p. 23; Sisir Gupta, *India and Regional Integration in Asia*, Bombay, 1964.
21. Text of the Report submitted by Jawaharlal Nehru to the All India Congress Committee in the International Congress Against Imperialism held at Brussels in February 1927, Bimal Prasad, n. 4, Appendix 1, pp. 295-96.
22. *The Encyclopedia of INC*, Vol. IX, n. 12, pp.306-07 and p. 538; Also see Bimla Prasad, *Origins of Indian Foreign Policy,* Calcutta, 1960.
23. For details see J.C Kundra, *India's Foreign Policy (1947-54) —A Study of Relations with the Western Block*, Netherlands, 1955; K.P. Karunakaran, *India in World Affairs (1947-50),* London, 1952.
24. *The Encyclopedia of the INC* Vol. XI, 1936-1938, n.12, pp. 86-87.
25. Quit India Resolution by AICC, Bombay, August 7-8, 1942 in A.M. Zaidi, *INC: The Glorious Tradition* Vol. IV : 1939-1950, n. 8, pp. 161-65.
26. *Ibid.*, p. 197.
27. *Ibid.*, p. 197.
28. Please see CWC resolution passed in its meeting July 3-15, 1945 at Shimla. A.M. Zaidi, *INC. The Glorious Tradition*, n. 8, Vol. IV, pp. 207-08.
29. Jawaharlal Nehru, "Inter-Asian Relations" *India Quarterly*, October 1946.
30. Please see J.S. Bright (ed.) *Before and After Independence*, New Delhi,1950, p. 379. These views were expressed by Nehru in August 1945.

31. The first Pan-Asian Conference was held in Baku in 1920 under the leadership of USSR. Nearly 1800 delegates from all parts of Asia including China attended the Conference ; For details see G.N. Acharya, "A Review of India's Foreign Policy 1948-61", *Far Eastern Economic Review*, Hong Kong, September 21,1961, p. 557.

32. "Asian Relations" - *Report of the Proceedings and Documentation of the First Asian Relations Conference*, New Delhi, March-April ,1947, Asian Relations Organisations, New Delhi, 1948, p. 3; Also see Jawaharlal Nehru, *India's Foreign Policy-Selected Speeches* (1946- April 1961) New Delhi, 1961, H. Venkatsubbiah, "Forty years of Asian Relations Conference 1947", in Eric Gonsalves (ed) *Asian Relations*, New Delhi, pp. 71-75.

33. For details on Afro-Asian Movement see G.H. Jansen, *Afro-Asian and Non-Alignment*, London,1966; S.L. Poplai, *Asia and Africa in the Modern World*, Bombay, 1955; K.M. Panikkar, *The Afro-Asian States and their Problems*, London, 1959; K.P. Karunakaran, *India in World Affairs (1947-1950) and also (1950-53)*, London, 1952; Lalita Prasad Singh, *The Politics of Economic Cooperation in Asia-A Study of Asian International Organisations*, Columbia, 1966.

34. *Asian Relations*, n. 32, p. 22.

35. *Ibid*., p. 22.

36. Sisir Gupta, *India and Regional Integration in Asia*, Bombay,1964, p. 34; Also see Werner Levi, *Free India in Asia*, Minneapolis, University of Minnesota, 1952.

37. *Asian Relations*, n. 32, p. 74.

38. *Ibid*., p. 74

39. *Ibid*., Also see Bimal Prasad,"Trends in Asian Relations, 1947-87 : An Overview" in Eric Gonsalves (ed.) *Asian Relations*, pp. 66-69.

40. G.H. Jansen, *Afro-Asia and Non Alignment,* London, 1966, p. 72. Also see Asia and Africa in the Modern World, S.L. Poplai, Bombay, 1955.

41. *Ibid*., p. 73.

42. *The Hindu*, 26 March, 1947.

43. For details see G.S.Pohekar, *India's Relations with Asia and Africa*, Harold.Laski Institute of Political Science, Ahmedabad, 1964; T. Yu George, *Intra-Asian International Relations,* USA, 1977; Satyavrata Ramdas Patel, *Foreign Policy of India :* An *Inquiry and Criticism*, Bombay, 1960.

44. Jansen, n. 33, pp. 91-92. Also see K.M. Panikkar, *The Afro-Asian States and their Problems*, London, 1959; J.C. Kundra, Indian Foreign

46. Jansen, n. 33, p. 74.
47. For details on this conference also see Yuri Nasenko, *Jawaharlal Nehru and India's Foreign Policy*, New Delhi, 1977
48. Jansen, n. 33, p. 95.
49. *Ibid.*
50. Sisir Gupta, n. 36, p. 45.
51. For details see Jawaharlal Nehru, n.45; Also see K.P. Karunakaran, *India in World Affairs*, Vol. II: February1950-December1953, Bombay, 1958.
52. Nehru, n. 45.
53. Nehru, n. 45, p. 58.
54. This Conference attended by Burma, Ceylon, India, Indonesia and Pakistan also discussed the issues of H-Bomb, the question of Tunisia and Morocco and that of Communism. India wanted to single out the issue of H-Bomb and Indo-China but other countries were interested in emphasising different issues—Kashmir for Pakistan, communist danger for Ceylon, economic cooperation for Burma and Afro-Asian Conference for Indonesia were priority issues.
55. *The Times of India*, November 16, 1953.
56. Selig.S. Harrison, *Case History of a Mistake*, New Republic, August 10, 1959 as quoted by Sisir Gupta, n. 36, p. 56.
57. For details see M.S. Rajan, *India in World Affairs* 1954-56, ICWA, New Delhi, 1964, pp. 52-57.
58. Nehru, n. 45.
59. Jansen, n.33, pp.128-29; For details also see S.L. Poplai, *Asia and Africa in the Modern World,* Bombay, 1955.
60. *Ibid.*, p.192.
61. For final communique see George McTurnan Kahin, *The Asian-African Conference*, Bandung, Indonesia, April 1955, New York, 1956.
62. *Ibid.*, pp. 76-85.
63. Speech by President Sukarno at the opening of the Asian-African Conference, April 18, 1955 in n. 61, p. 40.
64. *The Times* (London), 26 April 1955.
65. *The New York Times*, 24 April 1955.
66. Jansen , n. 33, pp.185-86.
67. Kahin, n. 61, p. 84-85.
68. S.D.Muni, Anuradha Muni, *Regional Cooperation in South Asia*, New Delhi, 1984, p.12.

69. S.L. Poplai (ed.), *Selected Documents on Asian Affairs: India 1947-50 (Vol. 2) External Affairs*, Bombay, 1959, pp. 35-36
70. *Ibid*., pp. 38-39.
71. Sisir Gupta, n. 36, pp. 85-113.
72. Muni and Muni, n. 68, p. 5.
73. Kahin, n. 61, pp. 77-78.
74. S.D. Muni, *Post-Cold War Regionalism in Asia: with special reference to the SAARC Sub-Region*, Institute of Developing Economies, Singapore, No. 258, February 1996, p. 21.
75. Asian Relations, n. 32, p. 72
76. *Ibid*., p. 73
77. Muni and Muni, n. 68, p. 15.

3

Genesis of SAARC (1980-85)

The failure of the Afro-Asian movement notwithstanding, India emerged as the leader of the non-aligned movement (NAM) in the post-colonial world. Nehru's pursuit of economic development through industrialisation and his mission for world peace sought to be achieved by the ideology of non-alignment gave India's foreign policy an international status.[1] The Indian policy of non-alignment in respect of South Asia was intended to limit the penetration of cold war politics into the region.[2]

India's political position in the world and Asia, in particular, suffered a serious setback in 1960s on account of deterioration in relations with China resulting in the humiliating war of 1962. Further, three years of drought and agricultural failure during third five year plan (1961-66) brought India on the brink of an economic collapse. India had to import food to prevent starvation and the World Bank in 1966 enforced devaluation of Indian currency.[3] There was a widespread impression in the West that India would not survive long as a united country, and would not be able to feed itself and develop as a viable state.[4] Nehru's death in 1964 also signalled a break from the policies of freedom struggle. But, later events, particularly India's decisive victory against Pakistan in 1971 resulting in creation of Bangladesh, achievement of self-sufficiency in food production and nuclear test explosion at Pokhran (1974), restored India's credibility and image in international power politics. The year 1971 was thus a turning point for South Asia and for India's role in the region.[5] Emergence of India as a regional power in South Asia and failure of the U.S. and China to help Pakistan in 1971 war with India enhanced the fear and mistrust of India's neighbours about her behaviour in the region.[6] Earlier, the Indo-Soviet Treaty of Friendship signed in 1971 had to some extent undermined India's non-aligned status in the post-Nehru period. The Soviet invasion of Afghanistan in December 1979 and Western response to this brought the cold war on the door-steps of India.

Proposal for Regional Cooperation by Bangladesh

It was against this background that the idea of a South Asian Regional Cooperation (SARC)[7] was mooted by President Zia-ur-Rahman of Bangladesh in 1980. President Zia-ur-Rahman of Bangladesh discussed the possibility to organise regional cooperation for the common good of the people of South Asia during his visits to Nepal, India, Pakistan and Sri Lanka in late 70s and in 1980.[8] Encouraged by the positive response from South Asian capitals, the Ministry of Foreign Affairs of the Government of Bangladesh formulated a proposal for regional cooperation in South Asia and circulated the proposal among the countries of the region in November 1980. The proposal, taking note of the fact that the countries of the region had been cooperating with one another under different fora like United Nation's Economic and Social Commission for Asia and Pacific (ESCAP), the non-aligned movement (NAM) and the Commonwealth, asserted that the full potential of regional cooperation had not been fully exploited in South Asia. The proposal argued for an arrangement of regional cooperation in the spirit of mutual trust, understanding and sympathetic appreciation of the political aspirations existing among the countries of the region, as well as based on respect for the principles of sovereign equality, territorial integrity, non-interference in internal affairs of other nations and mutual benefit.[9]

Rationale for Regional Cooperation

Explaining the motivation behind President Zia-ur-Rahman's initiative the proposal gave a strong rationale for regional cooperation in South Asia:

(i) While other regions had evolved institutional arrangements for consultations on matters of mutual interest and cooperation in the economic, social and cultural fields on a regional basis, and had consequently benefited immensely from such cooperation, South Asia comprising one-fifth of the world population was the only region which did not have any such arrangements for regional cooperation. West Europe despite highly competitive economies had introduced a wide-ranging and well developed system of cooperation. The West-Europe thus emerged as one of the strongest economic forces in the world.

(ii) Despite differences in perceptions among the countries of South Asia about certain specific events or political situation in the world, the beginning of cooperation on a regional basis might be a positive force which could generate a climate of harmony leading to a better perception of commonalities among the countries of the region which share common values rooted in their social, ethnic, cultural and historical traditions.

(iii) All developing countries had accepted the economic and technical cooperation on regional basis as a strategy within the framework of economic cooperation among developing countries (ECDC) and technical cooperation among developing countries (TCDC).

ECDC was an integral part of New International Economic Order (NIEO) which was accepted by the world community in the United Nations General Assembly (UNGA) in 1974 as an objective to be pursued for an equitable international order.

(iv) A regional cohesion could give an effective voice to South Asia in international forums. The people of South Asia could play a role commensurate with their intrinsic global importance by establishing an institutional arrangement for consultation and cooperation.

(v) South Asian economic cooperation through joint ventures could create a wider market for commodities requiring large-scale production providing a scope of utilisation of hitherto unexploited resources.[10]

Politico-Strategic Context of South Asia and Regional Cooperation

The proposal for regional cooperation in South Asia was made in the wake of significant political developments in the context of the second cold war.[11] The West, particularly the United States was making efforts to establish a regional security arrangement in the South and South-West Asia in the wake of Soviet invasion of Afghanistan.[12] At the same time due to Iran-Iraq conflict, a move to establish a Gulf-Cooperation Council (GCC) with the blessings of the US was made to respond to the security situation in the Gulf.[13] As already noted, South-East Asia had earlier initiated moves to set up a pro-west ASEAN.[14] Given the history of the failure of Indian moves to bring together Asian nations after decolonisation, it was also significant that the present initiative was taken by a smaller Indian neighbour. The assessment and reaction of Pakistan, of which Bangladesh was an eastern-wing till 1971, was of crucial significance in the context of Indo-Pak hostility.[15] A Pakistani scholar considering the Bangladesh proposal for regional cooperation as an unprecedented initiative made by a President desirous of playing a key role on the regional front, expressed Pakistani assessment in the following words:

> President Zia-ur-Rahman might have perceived that such a regional forum would help neutralize India's position of advantage in relation to the smaller nations of South Asia. Informal discussions with Bangladesh officials revealed their view that the only way to restrain India's overbearing attitude was through the discipline inherent in the membership of a regional organization.[16]

The initial Pakistani reaction was thus summed up in the light of the above assessment in the following manner:

(i) In political terms, Pakistan was apprehensive that, because of its overwhelming strength, India might overshadow Pakistan in the region. As India was the biggest country among the South Asian states, it was possible that SAARC could become an instrument of Indian hegemonistic designs.

(ii) In economic terms, Pakistan had also specific fears of Indian domination of future trade and commercial links with that country, especially if these were advanced in the industrial infrastructure and the regional trade market. At the same time, Pakistan sensed, that, in case of non-participation, it would be excluded from enjoying beneficial trade relations with the other members of SAARC.

(iii) It was also thought that, in such a regional organisation, the interests of the smaller nations would converge which could compel India to behave in a more responsible and reasonable manner.[17]

The Indo-centric nature of South Asia overwhelmingly gets reflected in the policies of the smaller South Asian States.[18] It is alleged that the spirit of 'five Principles' or 'Panchsheel' is not always reflected in the Indian attitude towards her neighbours. India's South Asian diplomacy is characterized by bilateralism which excludes third party mediation including that of the United Nations in her disputes with neighbours. This is suspected by her neighbours to be the Indian version of Monroe Doctrine.[19]

The asymmetry of size, population, power potential between India and her neighbours is touted by South Asian states to justify their search for extra-regional support to countervail 'big India'. A Bangladeshi observer thus maintains that most of the ruling elite of South Asia have been consciously pursuing the tactics suggested by the ancient Indian thinker Kautilya in his dictum in 'Arthshastra' that "do not trust your neighbour who is your natural enemy, but rather look for support from the states beyond who are your natural allies, or, as a supplementary principle, if you have to be surrounded by two or more larger states, play them off against each other."[20] The ruling class of Pakistan is considered to have reaped the maximum benefits out of the South Asian tension:

> Pakistan ruling class, instead of removing the basis of such suspicion and distrust, made these elements central to their foreign policy.[21]

The politico-strategic context of South Asia immediately preceding the formulation of the Bangladesh proposal was, however, considered favourable to the idea of regional cooperation. S.D. Muni notes:

> This milieu was due to the emergence of what may be called like-minded regimes in the sub-continent in the first half of 1977 following changes in India from Mrs.Gandhi to the Janata, in Pakistan from Bhutto to Zia-ul-Haq, in Sri Lanka from Mrs. Bandarnaike to Jayawardene, and in Bangladesh from an atmosphere of uncertainty to the consolidation of General Zia-ur-Rahman. These new regimes not only shared the hatred of their respective predecessors, but also tended to

look at the East-West strategic issues in a manner that was generally sympathetic to the West. At the regional level they sought to lay greater emphasis on mutual understanding and harmony in approaching bilateral and multilateral issues. The new Indian leaders even termed their South Asia policy one of " beneficial bilateralism"....[22]

However, Indira Gandhi's return to power in India in early 1980 disturbed this seemingly pro-Western inclination of the regional cooperation move. Mrs. Gandhi's regime was not in favour of Soviet presence in Afghanistan. Her policy was to promote the prospects of a negotiated political settlement of Afghan problem respecting the non-aligned status of that country. India, under Mrs. Gandhi, nevertheless did not want to associate with any regional move which could be interpreted as anti-Soviet.

The U.S. administration wanted a cooperative regional security framework in South and South-West Asia in reaction to Soviet aggression in Afghanistan. Prior to regional cooperation proposal from Bangladesh, President Zia-ur-Rahman, as if echoing the U.S. move, suggested holding of a six-nation South Asian summit (excluding Maldives) for creation of a climate of regional harmony through establishment of a framework for regional cooperation. India, however, made it clear that for her to associate with the proposal, the strategic and security aspects would have to be excluded from the regional cooperation move.[23] Analysing India's dilemma and policy predicament S.D. Muni observed:

> ... India could not reject the proposal either because the idea of regional cooperation in itself was a positive one and could play a useful role in India's own regional policy. An outright rejection of the proposal by India could also give legitimacy to the neighbouring states going ahead with it on their own. This in effect would have made the forum an instrument of neighbours "ganging-up" against India. It would also have aggravated India's isolation in the region, which was already becoming pronounced on issues such as the Indian Ocean, Kampuchea and Afghanistan. India, therefore, had to be careful in its response to the proposal. It activated its diplomacy to see that the proposal was moderated and redefined so as to become compatible with essential aspects of its perceived interests in the region.[24]

India's Response and the Scope of the Proposal

In the context of prevailing political and security environment in South Asia and the mindset of its neighbours, India apprehended that the initiative for South Asian Regional Cooperation might be an attempt to build a disguised anti-Soviet and pro-US strategic front.[25] As already noted India wanted withdrawal of Soviet troops from Afghanistan, but at the same time was against any U.S. move which might have brought fierce superpower rivalry in the region. Reflecting informal consultations, the proposal from Bangladesh categorically maintained:

> ...such cooperation is not, however, intended to take the form of any new block or alliance. The institutional arrangements set up for such cooperation would strictly conform to the principles of non-alignment to which all the countries in the region are firmly committed.[26]

There were genuine apprehensions in India, given the history of bilateral disputes in the region, that the proposed regional forum, might be used by her neighbours to 'gang up' against her[27] and try to settle such disputes to her disadvantage.[28] The proposal, however, to counter such apprehensions, asserted that the experience of regional cooperation in other parts of the world indicated the possibility of such cooperation despite bilateral problems among the countries of the region. Rather, it was maintained that as regional cooperation would grow, it would generate a climate of mutual understanding reducing the scope for such disputes.[29]

The proposal also listed several possible areas of cooperation in the fields of agriculture, science and technology, transport, market, promotion, education and culture. A draft declaration proposed to be adopted by the countries to launch the regional forum appended with this proposal mentioned promotion of peace and stability in the region through adherence to the principles of United Nations Charter and non-alignment as one of the objectives of regional cooperation in South Asia. It also expressed determination to uphold respect for the principles of sovereignty, national independence, territorial integrity, non-interference in one another's internal affairs, non-use of force and peaceful settlement of disputes.[30]

The proposal from Bangladesh was rather ambitious and even

suggested an institutional structure with Heads of Government of member states at the apex to meet once annually or as often as necessary to give directions, provide guidelines and review the activities of the organisation. It suggested a council of Foreign Ministers of Member States as the principal functional organ responsible for finalizing the recommendations for consideration of the summit leaders and implementation of the decisions of the summit meetings and also suggested setting up of a Secretariat to be headed by a Secretary General as the principal executive of the organisation.[31] Not to leave anything to chance, this proposal even outlined the steps required for preparation of the Summit Meeting. It was suggested that the proposal be considered as a working paper on which ideas/response of other Governments would be obtained to crystallize and finalise concrete programmes for consideration of the first preparatory meeting of Foreign Secretaries. Later, the Foreign Ministers of the member states were to finalise recommendations for the Summit on the following issues:

(a) Feasibility of regional cooperation and policy recommendation on the general approach to such cooperation.

(b) Possible areas of cooperation.

(c) The framework for regional cooperation/draft declaration.

(d) Agenda for the Summit Meeting.

(e) Finalisation of the date and venue of the Summit Meeting.[32]

Follow-up of Bangladesh Proposal: 1981-83

In pursuance of this proposal, the Foreign Secretaries of seven South Asian countries, namely, Bangladesh, Bhutan, India, Maldives, Nepal, Pakistan and Sri Lanka gathered in Colombo in April, 1981 to consider the possibility of regional cooperation. India's reaction to the Bangladesh proposal was that of extreme caution.[33] In this very first meeting Indian Foreign Secretary at the outset restrained the enthusiasm of Bangladesh and other smaller states when commenting on Bangladesh paper he said:

> ... We fully subscribe to the view expressed therein that in the foreseeable future, regional cooperation in South Asia has to be confined to economic, technical, scientific, social and cultural fields. It is inevitable that there will be some differences of emphasis if not perception in regard to a preliminary document of this nature. We feel that till detailed examination

has taken place it would be premature to consider the institutionalisation of regional cooperation through the establishment of a Secretariat, etc.[34]

Pre-Conditions by India

Further in a very forthright and pragmatic manner the Indian Foreign Secretary R.D. Sathe put forth two important pre-conditions for regional cooperation in South Asia. He said:

> At this stage it would also be useful to stress that we reach unequivocal agreement on what I would call the "ground rules" which should govern regional cooperation exercise and which in fact appear in the Bangladesh paper itself. Here I would submit that the principle of avoiding discussions in regional framework of all bilateral and contentious issues and of unanimity as the principle on the basis of which decisions in regard to regional cooperation are taken should be followed scrupulously.[35]

Step-by-Step Approach

This meeting agreed for the need of regional cooperation as a complement of already existing bilateral and multilateral cooperation among the countries of South Asia and decided to proceed step-by-step on the basis of careful and adequate preparation for early realization of such cooperation.[36] As a first step, the Foreign Secretaries agreed to set up Five Study Groups, one each on Agriculture, Rural Development, Telecommunications, Meteorology and Health and Population Activities. It was also agreed to set up a Committee of the Whole comprising senior officials of the seven countries to identify and report on other areas of possible cooperation. The Indian Foreign Secretary R.D. Sathe gave a firm and clear indication of India's policy of gradual movement towards regionalism in South Asia. In his concluding speech in the first meeting he said:

> We have an obligation to lay a solid and secure foundation on which regional cooperation can be built. If there are delays one should not become pessimistic, Rome was not built in a day. Neither were other regional groupings established without several meetings and thorough discussions. In fact, I would submit that while we should no doubt profit from the experience of other regions in the world,we should not replicate or copy those patterns. A pattern of regional cooperation

> in South Asia should evolve itself. We do not have to jump steps ahead and create an organisational superstructure without first agreeing upon arrangements, modalities and programmes of regional cooperation.[37]

Interestingly, Pakistan and Nepal[38] also favoured step-by-step approach like India, while Sri Lanka,[39] Maldives,[40] and Bhutan[41] were unequivocal in their support to the idea of regional cooperation in South Asia. In a note to the Committee of the Whole set up to identify additional areas of cooperation, India suggested widening the scope of the study on telecommunication to include cooperation in the sector of postal services, merger of the study groups on agriculture and rural development and new study groups in the areas of culture covering sports, education, films, theatres, production of text-books, organisation of seminars and exhibitions, regional film festivals etc.; infrastructure to cover transport, shipping, tourism and market promotion; and scientific and technological cooperation.[42]

A significant suggestion by India was for South Asia to adopt a common stand as a group at the North-South Dialogue, ECDC, in the UNCTAD, and ESCAP sessions and in the World Bank and other UN fora connected with aid to developing countries and other aspects of development cooperation. It also suggested a common strategy directed towards the achievement of NIEO involving reforms in the international monetary system, stabilisation of prices of commodities of common interest for their joint marketing and measures for facing competition from synthetics in the world market.[43]

The Committee of the Whole met in Colombo during August 31- September 2, 1981 and after detailed deliberations identified 13 areas for possible cooperation to be considered by the Foreign Secretaries.[44] The second meeting of Foreign Secretaries was held at Kathmandu, Nepal during 2-4 November, 1981.The Secretaries agreed to endorse the recommendations of the five study groups and convert these into working groups.[45] It was also decided to initiate cooperation in the areas covered by these groups through immediate and long-term implementation programmes. The report of the Committee of the Whole was considered and it was decided to form three study groups on the following three additional areas of cooperation:

Study Group	*Co-ordinator Country*
(i) Transport	Maldives
(ii) Postal Services	Bhutan
(iii) Scientific and Technological Cooperation	Pakistan

India's Cautious Approach

The Kathmandu meeting also deliberated on the issue of convening a meeting of Foreign Ministers in 1982 as agreed in the first meeting of the Secretaries. While Bangladesh, Sri Lanka, Maldives and Bhutan wanted a firm commitment to hold a meeting at the ministers' level, India and Pakistan advocated lower level meetings. The Indian Foreign Secretary R.D. Sathe maintained:

> ...When we have worked out a substantial programme of cooperation, we should move in the direction of recommending to our Foreign Ministers to convene a meeting at their level in order to launch such a programme and to provide guidance for further progress.[46]

The third meeting of the Foreign Secretaries which was held in Islamabad, Pakistan during 7-9 August, 1982 considered the reports of the study groups on three new areas (Transport, Postal Service and Scientific and Technological Cooperation) constituted in the second meeting, and their recommendations unanimously accepted. These Groups were converted into Working Groups. The recommendations of the Working Groups on earlier agreed areas of cooperation were endorsed for their expeditious implementation. A meeting of the representatives of the various official national planning organisations of the seven countries was recommended to be convened in New Delhi before the next meeting of the Foreign Secretaries. A Study Group on Sports, Arts and Culture was formed and the Committee of the Whole was made responsible for nominating the coordinator country.

It was agreed in this meeting to hold the first meeting of the Foreign Ministers in 1983. This was to be preceded by the meetings of the Foreign Secretaries and of another Committee of the Whole. This Committee was set up to prepare an Integrated Programme of Action in the agreed areas of cooperation. The Committee was to recommend modalities and mechanism for implementation, co-ordination and monitoring of the mutually agreed Programme of

Action. It was also required to provide indications of the financial implications of the short-term component of the Integrated Programme of Action, and to recommend funding modalities and arrangements for its long-term component.[47]

India, in the third meeting, was keen to incorporate Tourism and Trade as the areas of cooperation in the agenda. The Indian Foreign Secretary M. Rasgotra mentioned 'trade' as a field of great importance for regional cooperation. He said:

> ...In fact, in many other regions of the world, cooperation in trade was established at a relatively early stage starting with certain specific sections. As developing countries we all have understandable difficulties in liberalising trade flows which might necessitate drastic changes in our trade regimes. But it should be possible to consider limited cooperation based on a regional system of trade preferences, cooperation among state trading agencies and trade related institutions and cooperation in the marketing and processing of commodities of interest to countries of the region....[48]

The Indian Foreign Secretary in consonance with his country's cautious and step-by-step approach mentioned about the meeting to be convened at the level of Foreign Ministers. He cautioned:

> ...At our level we have made some important progress. A lot more remains to be done; we have yet to complete our task of presenting to the ministers a concrete and comprehensive action-oriented programme including specific measures for its co-ordination and implementation. For this a few more meetings at our level would seem necessary, though this need not mean an unduly, extended time frame for the meeting at the level of Foreign Ministers.[49]

The Committee of the Whole met at Colombo, Sri Lanka during 10-13 January 1983 and identified activities for short-term and long-term cooperation. The short-term activities were as follows:

(i) Exchange of Data.

(ii) Exchange of Expert Service.

(iii) Training and Research.

(iv) Holding of seminars/workshops.[50]

Similarly, long-term activities were identified by the Committee as given below:

(i) Establishment of regional institutions for training and research;

(ii) Creation/strengthening of linkages among existing national institutions in the seven South Asian Countries in the agreed areas of cooperation;

(iii) Strengthening of infrastructural support in such areas as postal services, telecommunication, railways, highways, shipping, meteorology, etc. which would require capital investment by participating countries.[51]

The Committee also discussed the modalities and mechanisms for implementation, coordination and monitoring of the action programmes and the financial implications and arrangements for financing. It also recommended that the Foreign Secretaries might decide regarding the utilisation of the EEC ($ 1,50,000); and the International Telecom Union, ITU ($ 2,20,000) offers of assistance. The Indian delegation suggested that the Committee of the Whole should recommend the establishment of a Ministerial Council as the apex body to meet periodically to provide political guidance for cooperation programmes. It was, however, agreed to leave this for a higher level decision.

The fourth meeting of Foreign Secretaries was held in Dhaka, Bangladesh during 28-30 March 1983. This meeting endorsed the recommendations of the Sectoral Working Groups and of the Committee of the Whole. It approved an Integrated Programme of Action suggested by the Committee of the Whole. A committee designated as the Standing Committee was proposed at the level of Secretaries for the implementation of the Integrated Programme of Action.

The meeting welcomed the offers of assistance from the EEC and the ITU for activities connected with regional cooperation in South Asia. The Secretaries noted with satisfaction the report of the meeting of the representatives held in New Delhi on 24-25 January 1983 and agreed to hold such meetings periodically.

Affirming that necessary preparatory work for a Ministerial level meeting had been successfully completed and that stage for launching implementation of regional cooperative activities had been reached, the Secretaries agreed that the meeting of Foreign Ministers be held at New Delhi.[52]

The Indian Foreign Secretary, M. Rasgotra, again wanted tourism and trade and industry to be included in the items for cooperation. He said:

> The Standing Committee...should meet as often as necessary and at least once a year. It could attend to the task among others, of identifying new areas of cooperation. In this respect our work is far from complete and my delegation would strongly recommend that studies should be commissioned straightaway in two important areas, namely tourism in its various aspects and cooperation in trade and industry.[53]

However, Indian suggestion was not acceptable to Pakistan, Bangladesh and Nepal. In addition to the argument against venturing into too many fields, too soon, an underlying streak of apprehension of India's domination in these fields, particularly in the field of trade and industry, might also possibly be the factor behind this stance.[54]

Political Push for South Asian Regionalism (1983-85)

The process for regional cooperation in South Asia moved a significant step further when the Foreign Secretaries decided to raise the level of interaction to the political plane.[55] In August 1983 the Foreign Ministers of the seven South Asian countries met in New Delhi to adopt a declaration on South Asian Regional Cooperation. This important Ministerial Meeting took following important decisions:

(i) The Integrated Programme of Action for cooperation in the fields of Agriculture, Meteorology, Health and Population Activities, Postal Services, Rural Development, Science and Technology, Telecommunications, Transport and Sports, Arts and Culture be implemented;

(ii) It was decided that the Foreign Ministers would meet once a year to review the progress of regional cooperation;

(iii) A summit meeting of the Heads of State/Government be recommended to be held—the dates be finalized in the next meeting of the Foreign Ministers in the Maldives;

(iv) The Foreign Ministers signed the declaration on South Asian Regional Cooperation setting out the objectives; and

(v) Approved principles of such cooperation incorporating provisions regarding institutional and financial arrangements.[56]

Declaration of South Asian Regional Cooperation (SARC)

The objectives of SARC as set out in the declaration were inter-alia, promotion of the welfare of the peoples of South Asia and improvement in the quality of their life, promotion and strengthening of collective self reliance among the countries of South Asia; and acceleration of economic growth, social progress and cultural development in the region. The principles of sovereign equality, territorial integrity, political independence, non-interference in internal affairs of other states and cooperation for mutual benefit were reiterated in the declaration. It was envisaged that the cooperation would be complementary to, rather than a substitute for, the existing bilateral cooperation.[57]

The institutional arrangements finalised in the declaration provided for a Technical Committee for each area of cooperation; an Action Committee for implementation of the projects in case more than two countries but not all countries of the region are involved; and a Standing Committee at the level of Foreign Secretaries for the coordination and monitoring of the Programme. The Technical Committees were required to submit periodic reports to the Standing Committee. Likewise Action Committees could be constituted only with the approval of the Standing Committee. The Standing Committee was to function with following terms of reference:

(i) Approval of projects and programmes, and the modalities of their financing;

(ii) Determination of inter-sectoral priorities and overall coordination of Programmes of Action.

(iii) Mobilisation of regional and external resources;

(iv) Identification of new areas of cooperation based on appropriate studies.[58]

Two important conditions reflecting Indian position were incorporated as General Provisions under the institutional arrangements, viz., decisions at all levels would be taken on the basis of unanimity, and bilateral and contentious issues would be excluded from the deliberations.[59]

The financial arrangements in the declaration provided for voluntary participation of each country. It was also stipulated that subject to the approval of the Standing Committee, resources may be availed from external agencies in case of projects and programmes for which sufficient financial resources could not be mobilised within the region.[60]

India's Approach to SARC

The Indian position towards regional cooperation was well articulated by Prime Minister Indira Gandhi in her inaugural address to the meeting of the Foreign Ministers. Mrs. Gandhi while underlining the commonalities of geography, experiences, aspirations, challenges and the civilisation, also talked of each country's 'individual personality, distinctive perception and a different political system'. She further affirmed[61]:

> Our policy is not to interfere in the affairs of others. But ours is a troubled region, most of our countries are multi-racial and multi-religious. It would be idle to pretend that we are not affected by what happens elsewhere. Even as we meet, there are disturbing and tragic developments in our neighbourhood.[62]

Mrs. Indira Gandhi asserted India's policy of non-alignment to 'seek peace with development among ourselves and in the world as a whole'. She was quite categorical when she outlined the Indian ideology and policy in following words:

> The regional grouping that brings us together is not aimed against anyone else. Nor are we moved by any ideological or military considerations. Our cooperation in no way limits each country's freedom of judgement....
>
> ...We are all equals. We are against exploitation and domination. We want to be friends with all on a footing of equality. We should be ever vigilant against the attempts of external powers to influence our functioning.[63]

Some South Asian scholars consider these remarks of the Indian Prime Minister indicative of India's long-term objectives of the SARC as being 'much broader than the achievement of collective self-reliance in economic matters'.[64] At the same time India's extreme caution towards regional cooperation was reflected in her opposition to the Bangladesh-proposal which suggested that SARC declaration could include a specific name for the regional endeavour, establishment of a Council of Ministers, designation of a 'South Asia Day' and recommendation for holding a Summit Meeting in 1984.[65]

The launching of SARC aroused world-wide interest. This was reflected in the messages received from the UN Secretary General, Executive Secretary of ESCAP, ASEAN, President of Indonesia and the Prime Minister of Thailand. There was extensive coverage in the foreign media as well.

Global Economic Issues in SARC

The second meeting of the Foreign Ministers was held at Male, Maldives on July 10-11, 1984.[66] This meeting laid strong emphasis on a collective regional approach to global economic issues. The Indian Foreign Minister P.V. Narasimha Rao in his speech in the meeting dwelt at length on the grim international security and economic environment.[67] He thus said:

> ...We have witnessed an intensification of conflict in many parts of the globe. The arms race continues unabated and threatens world peace and security. All this has had an inevitable fall-out in our own region. Meeting as we do in the middle of the Indian Ocean, we cannot but recall with regret that our long hard struggle to rid the Indian Ocean of tension and conflict has yet to bear fruit....[68]

Continuing in the same vein the Minister mentioned about the international economic situation and the plight of developing countries particularly in South Asia. He said:

> The situation is equally grim on the economic front, some developed countries are now beginning to emerge from the recession. But the recovery is by no means strong and its promised impact on the developing countries is nowhere in evidence. Meanwhile the stalemate in the North-South dialogue continues. The debt burden of many developing countries has reached crushing proportions and threatens not only the prosperity and stability of these countries but also the commercial banking system in the industrialised world. The flow of resources to developing countries, instead of increasing, has actually diminished. The level of resources agreed upon for IDA VII is lower even in nominal terms than that of IDA VI. This is a matter of particular concern to the countries of this region who are major recipients of IDA resources.[69]

The Foreign Ministers reviewed the world economic situation and expressed concern over deteriorating economic and social conditions in developing countries and their disappointment at the lack of progress in adopting international support measures in this respect as well as the continued stalemate in negotiations in international economic cooperation. They also regretted that despite pleas from developing countries, resources available to IDA VII had not been augmented and further urged donor countries to provide increase in the flow of resources in real terms over the level of IDA VI so that the requirements of the existing as well as the new borrowers could be met.[70] It was also decided in the meeting that the Foreign Minister of Maldives, in his capacity as the Chairman should formally convey the concern of South Asian countries to the leaders of the industrialised countries, in particular, to the Prime Minister of Japan.[71]

The Foreign Ministers also agreed that increasing emphasis should be placed on operational activities and the formulation of specific regional projects—for this purpose consideration was thought necessary at the level of Ministers in some of the vital agreed areas of cooperation. The Ministers expressed satisfaction at the progress made in implementing the Integrated Programme of Action in a relatively short time and stressed the urgent need for improved telecommunication and air transport links, especially between the capitals of the South Asian countries.

The Foreign Ministers urged member countries of SARC to actively pursue proposals put forward by the Seventh Non-aligned Summit[72] and the Group of '77 at various forums. They also reaffirmed their resolve to co-operate closely in all relevant fora in seeking appropriate solution to the problems affecting developing countries.[73]

On the crucial issue of summit meeting of SARC countries, the Indian Minister observed:

> ...Obviously such a meeting will require thorough preparation so that we are in a position to put something concrete before our leaders. Before we initiate the preparatory process, we would need to have a clear perception of what we should aim to achieve at the summit.[74]

India, obviously was not in a hurry to hold the summit meeting. It was agreed to recommend to the respective Heads of State or Government that the First Summit of South Asian countries be held in Dhaka in the last quarter of 1985 to be preceded by a meeting of the Foreign Ministers in Bhutan in May, 1985 to serve as the preparatory meeting for the Summit.[75]

The Third Meeting of the Foreign Ministers was convened at Thimpu, Bhutan during 13 -14 May, 1985 against the backdrop of heightened tension between India and Sri Lanka over 'Tamil problem'. Sri Lanka initially did not want to participate in protest against a statement made by the then Indian Minister of State for External Affairs in the Upper House of Indian Parliament about the Sri Lanka Government's alleged involvement in fomenting divisions amongst the Tamils. A special envoy of Sri Lanka, however, later joined the deliberations at Thimpu.[76] The envoy fully endorsed the decisions taken by the representatives of the other six countries.[77] On the most important issue of Summit meeting, the Indian Minister of State for External Affairs clarified his Government's position as under:

> As the scope of SARC activities grows, we must ensure that we have an adequate framework to provide the necessary institutional support. This will be an important issue before the first SARC summit to be held this year...
>
> ...It is a matter of satisfaction that a consensus has been reached at the Standing Committee that a South Asian Association for Regional Cooperation will be created. My delegation is in favour of a Council of Ministers and the establishment of a Secretariat at the appropriate time.[78]

India's Note of Caution

While extending full support to the evolving process of South Asian Regionalism the Indian Minister sounded a note of caution:

> I would like to conclude by affirming once again our full support for the further evolution of SARC—both conceptually and institutionally. We extend our hand in solidarity, knowing fully that what we are seeking to achieve cannot be done with ease. The present international scene continues to be dictated by noble platitudes and harsh realities. History has shown that even when benefits of working together are positive and self-evident, vested and narrow interests tend to entangle the gains that could accrue from such cooperation... We must increase our self-reliance and reduce our susceptibilities to pressures both within and outside our control. Divided we are vulnerable,

> united we will move forward to a bright future in pursuit of freedom and peace, so essential for it.[79]

The Ministers decided that the first summit meeting would be held at Dhaka, Bangladesh on 7-8 December 1985 to formally launch the South Asian Association for Regional Cooperation (SAARC)[80]. They also exchanged views on the basic documentation for the summit meeting.

In their fourth meeting at Dhaka on December 5, 1985 the Foreign Ministers of SARC countries discussed the overall preparations for the first SARC Summit and reviewed the activities under the Integrated Programme of Action. The Ministers recommended a Draft Charter, Declaration and Emblem of the South Asian Association for Regional Cooperation (SAARC) for adoption by the Summit. Three days later, on December 8, 1985, the Heads of State/Government of Seven South Asian Countries launched the SAARC.

Conclusion

India's regional policy objectives after independence were circumscribed by Nehru's prescriptions of non-alignment and peaceful co-existence with neighbours. India, therefore, considered suspicion of her neighbours that she might harbour hegemonistic ambitions and misuse SARC to further her objectives, as unjustified. India was extremely sensitive to the intrusion of great powers in the South Asian region and wanted to keep their influences at bay to preserve its ideology of non-alignment. This policy orientation was appropriately explained by Madhav Rao Scindia, an important figure in Indian ruling establishment in 1984 in following words:

> ... a country may be larger in size but in the global context, other countries, though smaller, do have their own geostrategic importance. In other words, size and military strength are not the only relevant factors. In any case, hegemonistic ambitions in a developing country could ultimately gravitate against its own national interest. However strong economically or militarily a country may be in terms of a particular region, we have to merely cast a glance at developments in regional crisis areas after World War II to realize that regional dissension or aggression has quickly led to the deep involvement of the great powers.[81]

India's distaste for extra-regional influences in South Asia was also borne out of her assessment that the intrusion of outside powers was a major factor for destabilization which made SARC difficult to launch. India wanted to resist the intrusion of both the Super Powers into the region. Scindia thus maintained:

> The presence of one superpower has always sooner or later been followed by the entry of the other, and it would not serve the interests of any of us to convert South Asia and the region in to a cockpit of superpower rivalry which it is fast becoming. The Soviet presence in Afghanistan, the American profile in Pakistan and Sri Lanka, and the presence of Israeli and British commando instructors in Colombo can have sinister long-term ramifications.[82]

Closely inter-linked to India's efforts to keep off extra-regional influences in South Asia, was her desire to promote cordial, tension-free relations with neighbours. While the proposal for regional cooperation was modified on India's insistence to exclude contentious bilateral issues from the agenda, this could not be interpreted to mean that the cooperation was to be confined to the economic and non-political issues only.

India considered friendly relations with the neighbours, particularly with Pakistan, as the key to the success or failure of regional cooperation. The ruling establishment in India considered it pointless to venture into unexpected areas of SARC without addressing the fundamental question of bilateral relations and particularly Indo-Pak relations. On Indo-Pak equation Madhav Rao Scindia observed:

> ...However, it can as well be argued that SARC would lead to cementing friendship between the two nations. Though it has rightly been laid down that no bilateral issue would be raised in the SARC forum, can it be denied that in matters concerning the region as a whole, a general atmosphere of cooperation through the aegis of SARC would undoubtedly have a salutary effect on bilateral relations too?[83]

India's policy was to facilitate evolution of a regional forum unhindered by the contentious bilateral, political issues and at the same time to create an enabling environment through this regional effort to resolve bilateral disputes and disharmonies without extra-regional interference.

India considered the issue of trade to be an important element in regional cooperation. Its exclusion in SARC declaration was attributed to the fear of India's neighbours that a liberal trade regime would work to the advantage of 'big' India. India's approach in this regard, however, had been to suggest a carefully balanced interdependence and a division of labour based on local factors that can provide strength to the region's economic base and infrastructure.[84] However, considering the politico-strategic divergence in the policy perceptions of India and her neighbours, India deliberately followed the policy of hastening slowly the process of regional cooperation in South Asia.

The broad set of objectives of SARC on promoting 'collective self-reliance' and contributing to mutual trust and understanding and appreciation of one another's problems, etc., were interpreted as not confined to economic cooperation only but could possibly extend to political and strategic areas later.

S.D. Muni thus reads a subtle Indian policy objective in respect of her approach to SARC in 'evolving a comprehensive regional consensus' to political realm.[85] It was indeed significant that despite the absence of essential ingredients of common ideological/ political perception and common foreign policy orientations, the move for evolving a regional cooperation forum could reach the launching stage in South Asia. These were probably the compulsions of the international, political and economic situation that South Asian nations were left with no option but to come together to seek collectively regional peace and progress.

REFERENCES

1. For details on basic features of India's foreign policy see J. Bandhyopadhyay, *The Making of India's Foreign Policy*, Bombay, 1970; Bimal Prasad (ed), *India's Foreign Policy-Studies : Continuity and Change*, New Delhi, 1979; K.P. Misra (ed.) *Foreign Policy of India-A Book of Readings*, New Delhi, 1977; V.P. Dutt, *India's Foreign Policy*, New Delhi 1984; Ashok Kapur, and A. Jayaratnam Wilson, *The Foreign Policy of India and Her Neighbours*, New York, 1996; A. Appadorai and M.S. Rajan, *India's Foreign Policy and Relations*, New Delhi,1985.
2. For details see S.D. Muni, "India's Political Preference in South Asia", *India Quarterly*, New Delhi, January 1975, pp. 23-26.
3. The devaluation was forced upon India by the Aid India Consortium which made resumption of aid flows contingent upon devaluation. The

devaluation and liberalisation package was clearly in conformity with the ideological position held by international and multilateral aid agencies. The devaluation was 36.5 per cent if computed as the decrease in the dollar value of the rupee. For further details see P. Sen, *Imported Inputs and the Theory of Currency Devaluations*, Unpublished Ph.D. Dissertation, John Hopkins University, Ballimore,1982; also by the same author "1966 Devaluation in India: A Reappraisal", *Economic and Political Weekly,* Vol. XXI, No 30, January 26,1986, pp. 1322-1329; I.J. Ahluwalia, Industrial Growth in India: Stagnation since the Mid Sixties, Oxford University Press, Delhi,1985; J.N. Bhagwati and T.N. Srinivasan, *Foreign Trade Regimes and Economic Development in India*, National Bureau of Economic Research, New York,1975.

4. K.Subrahmanyam, "Strategic Aspects of SARC", *Mainstream, SAARC Summit Special,* New Delhi, December, 1985, p.36.
5. Robert W. Bradnock, *India's Foreign Policy Since, 1971,* London, 1990, p. 1.
6. For a detailed analysis of apprehensions of India's neighbours regarding its hegemonic role see, Leo Rose and S. Kumar, "South Asia", in W.J. Field and G. Boyd (ed.), *Comparative Regional Systems,* New York, 1980; B. Buzan in Buzan and Rizvi, *South Asian Insecurity and Great Powers*, London, 1986; Mohammed Ayoob, "India in South Asia: The Quest for Regional Predominance", *World Policy Journal*, 1990, pp.107-35.
7. The Acronym 'SARC' is used for referring to the regional grouping in the formative years prior to the official designation of an Association in December, 1985.
8. President Zia-ur-Rahman discussed the issue of a South Asian regional approach in respect of Afghanistan situation with Indian Prime Minister Indira Gandhi in New Delhi in January 1980. (This was followed by the visit of a senior Indian official for further talks in Dhaka.) President Rahman also discussed the question with King Birendra of Nepal in Dhaka in March 1980 and sent his envoys to other South Asian countries to explore the possibilities of a regional arrangement. His call for a six nation summit (Maldives did not figure in this call) in May 1980 was the product of these exploratory talks. For details see S.D. Muni, "SARC: Building Regionalism from Below", *Asian Survey*, Vol. XXX, No. 4, April 1985, pp. 391-405.
9. A Paper on the Proposal for Regional Cooperation in South Asia- prepared by the Ministry of Foreign Affairs, Government of Bangladesh, From SARC to SAARC : *Milestones in the Evolution of Regional Cooperation in South Asia (1980-1988)* Vol. I, SAARC Secretariat, Kathmandu, 1988, p.1.

10. *Ibid.*, pp. 2-3. The arguments were given in the Bangladesh paper.
11. For details see Strategic Analysis (Special issue on the second cold war), IDSA, New Delhi, Vol. 8, No. 2-3, May-June 1983.
12. For a detailed analysis of political and strategic implications of the Bangladesh proposal see S.D. Muni, Anuradha Muni, *Regional Cooperation in South Asia,* New Delhi, 1984, pp. 30-43, S.D. Muni, SARC: Building Regionalism From Below, *Asian Survey*, April, 1985, pp. 391-405.
13. Gulf Cooperation Council (GCC) was established in Riyadh in February 1981 comprising United Arab Emirates, Bahrain, Kuwait, Qatar, Oman and Saudi Arabia. For details see, Percy S. Mistry, *Regional Integration and Development: Panacea or Pitfalls*, RIS Occasional Paper, New Delhi, 1995, pp. 2-10.
14. The countries of South-East Asia (Indonesia, Malaysia, Thailand, the Philippines and Singapore) perceiving a common threat from communism to their security decided to forge ASEAN in 1967. For the role of the West and the U.S. in setting up ASEAN see Chintamani Mahapatra, *American Role in the Origin and Growth of ASEAN*, New Delhi.1990.
15. For a detailed Pakistani point of view see Ross Masood Hussain, *SAARC-Evolution and Prospects: a view from Pakistan*, FES, Islamabad, 1991; *South Asian Regional Cooperation*, Institute of Regional Studies, Islamabad, June, 1983; Daniel F. Waterman, *SAARC : A New Framework for Regional Cooperation*, East West Center, April, 1986, pp. 24-27; Mubashir Hasan "Alternative to Dependence" in Pran Chopra (ed.) *Future of South Asia*, Delhi, 1986; Imtiaz H Bokhari, "South Asian Regional Cooperation : Progress, Problems, Potential and Prospects", *Asian Survey,* April, 1985, pp. 371-91.
16. Hussain, n.15, p. 2.
17. *Ibid*, p. 2.
18. According to Sir Ivor Jennings India was looked upon by its neighbours as a mountain that might, at any time, send down destructive avalanches. For details see his *The Commonwealth in Asia*, London,1953, p. 113; Also see Leo Rose and S. Kumar, "South Asia", in W.J. Field and G.Boyd (eds.), *Regional Systems*, New York,1968, pp. 264-68.
19. Monroe Doctrine, enunciated by the U.S. President Monroe in 1823 and still important in rationalizing US foreign policy, maintains that the US can countenance no intervention in the American continent by a foreign power and would not itself intervene in disputes in Europe. For details see R.B. Rais 'South Asian Regional Cooperation Problems and Prospects', a paper presented at the second conference on Indian

Ocean Studies, Perth, Western Australia, 5-12, December, 1984, p.1; Also See J.C. Saigal, "Economic Cooperation and Integration in Latin America: A Review of Historical Experience", a paper presented at the International Conference on South Asian Regional Economic Cooperation, organised by Bangladesh Economic Association, Dhaka, January 21-23, 1985, p. 4.

20. Atiur Rahman, *Political Economy of SARC*, Dhaka, 1985, p. 15. For Bangladeshi perspective also see Syedur Rahman, "Issues and Agenda for South Asian Regional Cooperation. A Bangladeshi Perspective", *Asian Survey,* April, 1985, pp. 405-26; Rehman Sobhan, *Political Dimensions of South Asian Cooperation*, Kanesalingam (ed.) Marga Institute, Colombo, 1990 pp. 27-67; Shamsul Haq, "Problems and Promises", in Pran Chopra (ed.), *Future of South Asia*, Delhi, 1986, pp. 56-87.
21. *Ibid*, p.16.
22. Muni, "SARC: Building Regionalism from Below", n. 12, p. 393.
23. For details *Ibid.*, pp. 393-96.
24. *Ibid.*, p. 396.
25. Following Soviet military intervention in Afghanistan in the last week of December, 1979, the U.S. for obvious strategic reasons sought to highlight the security implications of this development and prompted a co-ordinated regional response. The U.S. President in his State of Union Address on January 23, 1980 stressed that U.S. objective in the prevailing situation was to encourage the establishment of a 'cooperative regional security framework' in South and South-West Asia. President Carter even sent high level emissaries to India and Pakistan to explain this framework and persuaded the antagonistic neighbours to 'evolve a regional approach' in the changed situation; For details see S.D. Muni ,"SARC: Building Regionalism from Below", n. 12, pp. 394-95.
26. A paper on the Proposal for Regional Cooperation, n. 9, p. 2.
27. Author's interview with Sh. M. Rasgotra, a former Indian Foreign Secretary on May 16, 2000. Sh. Rasgotra was informed by some highly placed sources in Bhutan that there might be an attempt by India's neighbours to "gang-up" against her.
28. For instance attempt by Bangladesh to bring in Nepal as a party to the question of sharing Ganga water with India was seen as pointing in this direction. See Muni, n. 12, pp. 391-405.
29. A paper on the Proposal for Regional Cooperation, n. 9, p. 2.
30. *Ibid.*, p. 7.
31. The paper also suggested various possible names of the organisation:

    (a) 'South Asian Association for Cooperation' (SAAC);

(b) 'Association of South Asia' (ASA);

(c) 'Association of South Asia for Cooperation' (ASAC);

(d) 'Organisation of South Asian States' (OSAS).

(For details see *The Paper on Proposal for Regional Cooperation* n. 9, p. 6).

32. *Ibid.* p. 8.
33. For details on Indian reaction to the proposal see Waterman, n.15, pp. 30-33; Muni and Muni, n. 12, pp. 31-34 ; S.D. Muni, "SARC: Building Regionalism From Below", n.12, pp. 391-405; Imtiaz Bokhari, "SARC : Progress, Problems, Potential and Prospects" *Asian Survey*, Vol. XXX, No. 4 April 1985.
34. Statement by R.D. Sathe, Foreign Secretary of India at the First Meeting, Colombo, 21-23 April, 1981 (official text) as published in Muni and Muni, n. 12, p.108.
35. *Ibid.*, p.109.
36. Author's interview with Sh. Rasgotra, n. 27, Sh. Rasgotra informed that India wanted to carefully assess the motives and response of other countries to the proposal.
37. n. 34, pp.111-12.
38. For a detailed analysis of Nepal's attitude towards SARC see Sridhar K. Khatri, "South Asian Regional Cooperation: its Implications for Nepal", *Asian Survey*, April 1985 pp.426-43; Rishikesh Saha, "Guidelines from Experience" in Pran Chopra (ed.), *Future of South Asia*, Delhi, 1986, pp.136-69; B.C. Upreti, "Nepal and SAARC" in Virender Naraina and B.C. Upreti, (ed.), *SAARC—a study of Perceptions and Policies*, New Delhi, 1991, pp.111-25.
39. For a detailed study of Sri Lankan perception see Shelton Kodaikara, "South Asian Cooperation: A Sri Lankan perspective in South Asian Regional Cooperation", in Satyamurty (ed.), *South Asian Regional Cooperation*, Institute of Asian Studies, Hyderabad, 1982, pp. 213-26; Shelton Kodaikara, "Asymmetry and Commonalities" in Pran Chopra (ed.), *Future of South Asia*, Delhi, 1986, pp.117-36; V. Kanesalingam, "Political Dimensions of South Asian Cooperation", Country paper for Sri Lanka in V. Kanesalingam (ed.), *Political Dimensions of South Asian Cooperation*, Marga Institute, Colombo, 1991.
40. For details on Maldives policy towards SARC see Daniel F. Waterman, n. 15, pp. 22; V. Kanesalingam, *Maldives and its Neighbours: The Background to Friendly Dimensions of SAARC*, Colombo, 1991, pp. 96-104; Swaroop Rani Dubey, "Maldives and SAARC" in Narain and. Upreti (ed.), n. 38, pp. 136-43.
41. For a detailed study on Bhutan's attitude towards SARC see

Kapileshwar Labh, "Bhutan and SAARC", in Narain and Upreti, n.38, pp.125-36; Waterman, n.15, p. 22.

42. For details see, "An Indian Note Regarding Areas of Cooperation", *From SARC to SAARC*, n. 9, p.17.

43. "South Asian Regional Cooperation", Report of the Committee of the Whole, Colombo, 31 August, 2 September 1981; *From SARC to SAARC*, n. 9, p. 13.

44. *Ibid.* pp.12-13. The areas identified by the Committee were Education and Training, Cultural Exchanges, Scientific and Technological Cooperation including cooperation in the field of New and Renewable Sources of Energy; Tourism, Transport, Shipping, Monetary Cooperation; Cooperation in International Economic Negotiations and Negotiations with Multinational Corporations; Information and Mass Communication; Environment including Marine Pollution Control, Postal Services (as part of the Telecommunications); Co-ordination of policies on Manpower Export and Promotion of cooperation amongst Regional Planners, Non-governmental Organisations, Academic, Research and other Institutions.

45. Joint Communique issued at the conclusion of the Second Meeting of Foreign Secretaries, *From SARC to SAARC,* n. 9, pp. 22-23.

46. Statement by R.D. Sathe, Foreign Secretary of India, at the Second Meeting of Foreign Secretaries Kathmandu, November 2, 1981, Muni and Muni, n.12, p.114.

47. Joint Communique issued at the conclusion of the Third Meeting of Foreign Secretaries, *From SARC to SAARC*, n. 9, pp.24-25.

48. Statement by M. Rasgotra, Foreign Secretary of India at the Third Meeting of Foreign Secretaries, Islamabad, August 7-9, 1982, Muni and Muni, n. 12, p. 117.

49. *Ibid.*, p. 118.

50. Report of the Committee of the Whole, South Asian Regional Cooperation, Colombo, January 1983, *From SARC to SAARC*, n. 9, pp. 26-30; For details see, Vernon L.B. Mendis, *SAARC: Origins, Organisation and Prospects*, Australia, 1991, pp. 25-28.

51. *Ibid.*, pp. 25-28.

52. Joint Communique issued at the conclusion of Fourth Meeting of Foreign Secretaries, March 28-30, 1983, Dhaka, *From SARC to SAARC*, n. 9, pp. 54-55.

53. Statement by M. Rasgotra, Foreign Secretary of India at the Fourth Meeting, Dhaka, March, 28-30, 1983, Muni and Muni, n. 12, p.121.

54. India's neighbours have pursued trade and industrial development relations with extra-regional centres. A greater regional interaction may threaten the newly developed vested interests in these countries as

also those extra-regional sources that benefit from continuing lack of cooperation in South Asia. This issue is closely connected to serious political considerations of regimes in these countries. It may be added here that some business and industrial sections in Pakistan have openly and strongly come out in favour of greater and unhindered trade with India but the Government of Pakistan has taken the opposite view. This is probably the reason why India's repeated emphasis on developing collective self reliance in the region has not found positive response; For details see S.D. Muni ".SARC: The Vilingili Ministerial Meeting", *Asian Affairs*, Vol. VI, No.1, Jan-March, 1984, pp. 76-87. T. Venkatasubbulu, *India's Trade with SAARC Countries*, New Delhi, 1996, pp.110-81.

55. For details on this meeting see Dilip Bobb, "Harbinger of Hope", *India Today*, August 31,1983; P.K. Mishra, "South Asia's Quest for an Identity and SARC", *India Quaterly*, New Delhi, 3:4, July-December 1984, pp. 314-23; Imtiaz H. Bokhari, "South Asian Regional Cooperation: Progress, Problems, Potential and Prospects", *Asian Survey*, New Delhi, Vol. XXX No. 4, April 1985, pp. 371-91.

56. Joint Communique at the conclusion of the First Meeting of Foreign Ministers, New Delhi August, 1-2 1983, *From SARC to SAARC*, n. 9, p. 61.

57. Declaration on South Asian Regional Cooperation, New Delhi, August, 1983, *From SARC to SAARC*, n. 9, pp. 58-60.

58. Declaration on SARC, n. 9, pp. 58-60.

59. Professor Bhabani Sen Gupta, a former research Professor in the Centre for Policy Research, New Delhi in an interview to the author on 8 June 2000 said that the contentious bilateral issues should not have been excluded from the SAARC agenda. He maintained that the Indian apprehensions on the 'other six' ganging up against her were 'absurd' since they could never do so in any manner.

60. Declaration on SARC, n. 9, pp. 59-60.

61. This statement of Mrs. Gandhi was a reference to the ethnic problem in Sri Lanka. For details see, Urmila Phadnis, "Ethnic tensions in South Asia - implications for regional cooperation", in Bhabani Sen Gupta (ed.), *Regional Cooperation and Development in South Asia*, Vol. II, New Delhi, pp.1-56; S.D. Muni, *Pangs of Proximity: India and Sri Lanka Ethnic Crisis*, New Delhi, 1993.

62. Inaugural Address, of Smt. Indira Gandhi, Prime Minister of India to the meeting of South Asian Foreign Ministers, New Delhi, August, 1983, *India Quarterly*, New Delhi, Vol. XI, nos. 3 and 4, January-March,1984, pp. 255-59.

63. *Ibid.*

64. Muni and Muni, n. 12, p. 184.

65. For details see Hussain, n. 15, pp. 9-10.

66. To attend the meeting at Male the Indian and Pakistani Foreign Ministers travelled together in Indian Air Force plane. This was interpreted as sign of reduced political tension in the region as a result of commitment to SARC. For further details see K.S. Ramchandran, "Our Neighbours: A Challenge for SAARC", Financial Express, 10 June 1985.

67. For details on security and economic environment see Muni, n. 12, pp. 391-405; K. Subramanyam, "Problems of International Security with special reference to South and South-East Asia", *Strategic Analysis*, New Delhi, May-June, 1985, pp.121-39; B. Uday Shankar, "Recent Major Developments in South Asia", *Strategic Analysis*, New Delhi, August 1985, pp. 431-40.

68. Second Meeting of SARC in Male—Narasimha Rao's Statement, *Foreign Affairs Record*, Vol. XXX. No. 7, July, 1984. pp. 216-20.

69. *Ibid*., p. 217.

70. While this meeting could adopt a fairly strong position on world economic situation, similar position on global, political and strategic issues was avoided. One such strategic issue which was of concern to most of the SARC members was the great power military presence in the Indian Ocean. Since the members had serious differences on what needed to be done to make Indian Ocean a zone of peace, it was not raised during SARC deliberations despite strong statements made by the Indian Foreign Minister and other delegates about it; For details see Muni, "SARC: The Villingili Ministerial Meeting", n. 54, pp. 76-87.

71. Joint Communique issued at the conclusion of the Second Meeting of Foreign Ministers, Male, 10-11 July, 1984; *From SARC to SAARC*, n. 9, pp. 70-71.

72. The Seventh NAM-Summit had made the following suggestions to foster sub-regional, regional and interregional cooperation among non-aligned and other developing countries.

    (a) Undertake the formulation of programmes and projects, including joint ventures, for collective self reliance within the context of national development plans.

    (b) Strengthen and more fully exploit the potentialities of the existing institutional framework, and where necessary, provide technical support and effective mechanism to give such programmes and projects a concrete shape.

    (c) Collectively express solidarity and political support to all non-aligned and other developing countries or groups of such countries in the exercise of their sovereign rights including their exploitation, processing, pricing and marketing.

[Seventh NAM Summit Final document, Seventh Conference of Heads of State of Government of non-aligned countries, New Delhi, March, 1983, *Strategic Digest* (IDSA, New Delhi) May 1983, pp. 301-56; For details on ECDC also see V. Kanesalingam, Collective Self-Reliance of South Asia, FES, Colombo, 1993, pp.10-18.]

73. *Ibid.*
74. Second Meeting of SARC in Male, *Foreign Affairs Record*, n. 68, p. 219.
75. Joint Communique, *From SARC to SAARC*, n. 9, p.11.
76. The regional diplomacy persuaded Sri Lanka to end its boycott of the meeting. Bangladesh contacted Sri Lanka on the issue. President Zia of Pakistan who was on a tour of the Far East, was requested by the foreign office to intervene. He contacted President Jayawardene and Prime Minister Rajiv Gandhi. The two leaders clinched the issue of Sri Lanka's participation at Thimpu; For further details see Pran Chopra, "SARC Gains From Crisis: From Male to Thimpu", *Deccan Herald*, 18 May 1985.
77. The chief delegate from Sri Lanka, Mr. Esmond Wickramasinghe, advisor to the President, made it clear that although Sri Lankan Foreign Minister could not come, his country's participation was full and unqualified, *Newstime*, 19 May, 1985.
78. SARC: Third Meeting of Foreign Ministers, Foreign Affairs Record, Vol. XXXI, No. 5, May 1985, p.130.
79. *Foreign Affairs Record*, n. 68, p. 131. While the decision regarding the Summit could be taken with consensus, no such decision could be made regarding creation of the Secretariat. Bangladesh, Sri Lanka and Pakistan seemed to give SARC an institutional shape closer to ASEAN. India was strongly opposed to this idea; For details see Muni, "SARC: the Villingili Ministerial Meeting", n. 54, pp. 76-87; Imtiaz H. Bokhari, "SARC: Progress, Problems, Potential and Prospects", n. 15, pp. 371-91.
80. n. 78.
81. Madhav Rao Scindia, "Unity in South Asia - India's Pivotal Role in the Club", M.D. Dharamdasni (ed.), Varanasi,1988, p. 107.
82. *Ibid.*, p. 109.
83. *Ibid.*, p. 108.
84. *Ibid.*, p. 111.
85. Muni, n. 12, pp. 402-03.

4

India and SAARC (1985-1990)

The Heads of the State/Government of seven South Asian countries—Bangladesh, Bhutan, India, Maldives, Nepal, Pakistan and Sri Lanka—formally established the South Asian Association for Regional Cooperation (SAARC) in their first summit meeting held in Dhaka on 7-8 December 1985.[1] They adopted a Charter for SAARC in this summit meeting. The basic objectives set forth in the Charter were, inter-alia, to promote the welfare of the people of South Asia and to improve their quality of life; to accelerate economic growth, social progress and cultural development in the region; and to promote and strengthen collective self-reliance among countries of South Asia.

During the initial formative period between 1985 and 1990 five SAARC Summits were held: Dhaka, December 1985; Bangalore, November 1986; Kathmandu, November 1987; Islamabad, December 1988 and Male, November 1990. With each Summit making a contribution the confidence of the Member States deepened, activities expanded and the SAARC became a reality.

India and other SAARC Member Countries

Formally committed to the principles of non-alignment India was extremely cautious to avoid any kind of overt political or security overtone to the regional cooperative endeavour in South Asia.[2] This attitude was borne out of past experience of political/security pacts bringing in the influence of extra-regional powers in the region in utter disregard to the objectives of non-alignment. The contents of Bangladesh proposal for a regional cooperative arrangement were thus acceptable to India since it emphasised economic, scientific, technical and cultural cooperation. India hoped that the cooperation in these fields would ultimately help in resolving political disputes in the region. The hard realities of the sub-continental politics, however, indicated otherwise as noted by a South Asian scholar as under:

(i) External powers' involvement in the region—deliberately sought, and more importantly, used to blunt the edge of Indian predominance;

(ii) India's neighbours share a few common characteristics but not borders, making for generally minimal contacts among themselves. The single most important issue for all of them is how to relate to India, the focal point of their threat perceptions.[3]

India thus becomes the most significant feature of SAARC. India's size, resources and power potential makes it implicitly predominant in the asymmetrical power structure in South Asia.[4] India accounts for 76 per cent of the region's population, 72 per cent of its land area and 76 per cent of the total national income of SAARC Member Countries in terms of US dollars (79 per cent in terms of purchasing power parity).[5] India shares a common border with other SAARC Member Countries, except the island nations of Sri Lanka and Maldives—Sri Lanka is separated from India by only a few miles of ocean waters. Significantly, no other SAARC Member Country shares a common border with another country of South Asia. The sub-continent, therefore, is quite rightly considered highly Indo-centric.

India which shares the mass misery and deprivation of SAARC Member Countries, also shows characteristics which sharply distinguish her from others. India has laid down a vast industrial infrastructure; she has a strong military machine; her scientific and technological manpower is significant in number; her achievements in certain areas of science and technology including nuclear and space research can match the best in the world; she has a relatively stable democracy with a vast, politically stabilizing middle class having a significant purchasing power.

Such an India, seeking a global role, exercising her nuclear option along with past history of cultural and civilisational influence extending far and wide in South and South-East Asia, naturally gives rise to serious misgivings about her role among smaller SAARC

Member Countries, particularly geographically contiguous State of Pakistan, Bangladesh, Nepal and Sri Lanka.[6] These Indian neighbours perhaps perceive 'Big India' as a nation in search of a regional platform for seeking a global role and in the process absorbing/assimilating them and threatening their distinct national identities. This perception of India's neighbours[7] probably impels them to make efforts to bring bilateral disputes on the agenda of SAARC. This asymmetry between India and other SAARC Member Countries is considered by some observers as the single biggest drawback that is inherent in the group's composition. A Pakistani academician thus observed:

> The most serious impediment to greater cooperation in South Asia is the lack of consensus about the future shape of the region. The smaller states favour a regional arrangement which guarantees equality to all states and does not restrict their option of conducting relations with the rest of the world. This framework comes in conflict with India's perception of South Asian Power structure.[8]

In such an environment of mistrust and suspicion of her role, India's two important pre-conditions — no bilateral and contentious issues to be discussed in SAARC and the principle of unanimity for decision making—were incorporated in the SAARC Charter as 'General Provisions'. India's objective in eliminating anti-India political issues from SAARC agenda was to ensure its smooth initial take off.

Evolution of SAARC (1985-1990)

First Summit—Dhaka, 1985

A formal beginning was thus made in the First Summit at Dhaka with the adoption of historic 'Dhaka Declaration'.[9] This declaration described the first meeting as a 'tangible manifestation of their determination to co-operate regionally'.[10] It also pointed out that poverty, underemployment and pressures of population were the grave challenges faced by the region and that the regional cooperation was the logical response to these problems. The declaration further reaffirmed the goal of optimum utilization of human and material resources for promoting the welfare and prosperity of the peoples of South Asia. It emphasized the need for people-to-people contacts at various levels. Further, it also expressed satisfaction at the progress made in the implementation of the Integrated Programme of Action in the nine agreed areas of cooperation.

The Summit leaders supported the need for an atmosphere of peace as an essential prerequisite for the realisation of the above objectives. They expressed concern over the deteriorating international political situation, the escalation of the arms race, nuclear proliferation,[11] the crisis in the global economy, the incapacity of international financial and technical institutions to respond to the needs of the poorer countries and the general inadequacy of the international economic system.

Charter of SAARC

The Charter of the SAARC signed at this Summit enunciated the objectives, principles and the institutional framework of SAARC. The principal objectives of SAARC being socioeconomic welfare and cultural development of the South Asian peoples, emphasis was laid on the achievement of the goal of collective collaboration in the economic, social, cultural, technical and scientific fields.

Institutional Framework

The Charter lays down the institutional framework of SAARC defining its administrative and operational machinery. It provides for a pyramidal structure, with Summit at the apex, supported by the Council of Ministers (Foreign Ministers of the Member States) and the Standing Committee comprising of Foreign Secretaries of the Member States. A network of Technical Committees for each of the agreed areas of cooperation provides the base structure of the administrative organisation. The Council of Ministers is to function as a cabinet, referring matters to the Summit for decisions and further, to carry them out through the Standing Committee. The Standing Committee is thus the important executive agency for the decisions taken by the Council of Ministers and the Summit. There is also a Programme Committee to monitor the performance of Technical Committees.[12]

The Charter also provides for setting up a Secretariat with the Secretary General, seven Directors and the General Services Staff.[13] The SAARC Secretariat came into existence in January 1987 at Kathmandu to co-ordinate and monitor the implementation of SAARC activities, service the meetings of the Association and serve as the channel of communication between SAARC and other international organisations. The Secretary General of the Secretariat is nominated by the Member Countries on the basis of rotation.

The most significant feature of the Charter is the provision that the Heads of State/Government would meet once a year, or more often, if necessary.

The inaugural Dhaka Summit set the precedent for procedures and modalities to be followed in future. Thus each Summit was to be preceded by a meeting of the Standing Committee and of the Council of Ministers. After the conclusion of each Summit, a declaration expounding the Summit's philosophy and thinking was issued along with a Joint Communique which contained in summary form the substantive decisions of the Summit.[14]

The Dhaka Summit not only gave the Charter of the Association but also set up two study groups — one to examine the problem of terrorism and the other of drug trafficking and abuse.[15] It further, agreed to convene conferences of Ministers to consider the issues of the New International Economic Order and the improvement of the World Trading System through GATT taking particularly into account the interest of the least developed among the developing countries and the participation of women in development.[16]

The Indian Position

The Indian Prime Minister Rajiv Gandhi in his speech in the First SAARC Summit nostalgically remembered Nehru's declaration in the Asian Relations Conference (1947) where he said that 'we meet together we hold together, we advance together'.[17] Mr Gandhi asserted that the South Asian cooperation was an important step towards realising the larger Asian consciousness.[18] But the nostalgia of the past was tempered with the pragmatism of the current realities when the Prime Minister expounded Indian policy towards regional cooperation in South Asia. He said:

> Certainly we have problems and difficulties and these do impose constraints on us. Enduring cooperation is cooperation adapted to the realities of our condition. The model we have evolved for ourselves is a model which is in accord with our realities. Our compulsions and our genius. We have not sought to melt our bilateral relationships into a common regional identity, but rather to fit South Asian cooperation into our

respective foreign policies as an additional dimension. We have evolved modalities which do not allow bilateral stresses and strains to impinge on regional cooperation. Our cooperation tempers enthusiasm with pragmatism, and initiative with consensus. At the same time, in the light of our experience of the recent past, we have every reason to hope that the practice of regional cooperation will have a beneficial impact on bilateral relationships.[19]

The Indian Prime Minister Rajiv Gandhi also emphasised involvement of the people in regional cooperation efforts when he said:

...Above all, let us involve our people in every facet of our activity, South Asian Regional Cooperation, must be a peoples movement, involving the hearts and minds of our people.[20]

Rajiv Gandhi who came to power in India by a quirk of circumstance represented a change of generation in political leadership. He was quite different from his mother, Indira Gandhi, who was associated with a tough line in India's conduct of her relations with neighbouring countries. She was also a key factor in the liberation struggle of Bangladesh and emergence of a strong India after 1971 war with Pakistan. Unlike her mother, Rajiv Gandhi was an apolitical person and seemed open to ideological re-orientation of India's policies. He could establish a good equation with President Jayawardene of Sri Lanka and Ms. Benazir Bhutto who came to power in Pakistan after a long spell of military dictatorship. The two young Prime Ministers of India and Pakistan provided a welcome change from the past and generated great hopes of striking cordial relations between the two countries. Pran Chopra noted the change in India's policy behaviour since Mrs. Indira Gandhi's days in power when he said:

...Instead of tactics of intimidation associated with the politics of Mrs. Gandhi, both in domestic politics and in relations with neighbours, tactics of reassurance and reconciliation took over under Rajiv Gandhi.[21]

This augured well for the newly born regional grouping in South Asia.

India considered launching of SAARC as an historic opportunity to overcome the contentious bilateral, political disputes with her neighbours through regional cooperation in economic and cultural fields. This approach of India was summed up by the Minister of External Affairs B.R. Bhagat in his statement on First SAARC Summit in Indian Parliament where he said:

> While the Summit Conference has ushered in a new era of cooperation among the South Asian countries, we should not under-estimate the difficulties that we are going to encounter in this ambitious venture. We have still to overcome the bitterness of the past and satisfactorily resolve some of the current problems in our relations. There are also, inevitably differences in our perception of both national interests and global issues. SAARC provides both a challenge as well as opportunities to overcome these difficulties.[22]

The First SAARC Summit generated high hopes and expectations. The launching of SAARC was seen as not only a logical outcome of a global process of regionalism but also holding promise of a wider Asian grouping in future. Dinesh Singh, a former Indian Minister for External Affairs speaking in Indian Parliament after the Summit meeting said:

> The Summit at Dhaka fills the gap in the global chain of regional organisations.This was the only area in the world that did not have a regional organisation.... Now that we have a South Asian Association, I hope it would be possible for a larger group to participate in a wider dialogue. I am happy that China has welcomed SAARC—it gives the hope of the possibility of that wider Asian organisation.[23]

Dinesh Singh even suggested inclusion of other Asian countries in a larger Asian grouping when he said:

> ... Now, with the meeting of SAARC, I hope, we shall also have an Asian Council of Ministers apart from the Council of Ministers of SAARC and that they will make a positive contribution of Asia in the process of disarmament and peace. May I also hope that we shall have in this organisation three other countries which have so far been left out, namely, Afghanistan, Burma, and Iran. With their inclusion, we would have completed the chain.[24]

There was a sense of cautious optimism among a large section of South Asian observers. One newspaper in its editorial termed SAARC a people's movement but dependent on the political will of the leaders of the seven countries. The editorial further observed that India's neighbours with some reservations about 'dominant' India, have taken "the first step to overcome an ingrained fear and a polite excuse of being swamped by a larger India which had only tended to stultify the potential for mutual cooperation of a generally homogenous set of people."[25]

It was indeed quite creditable and extremely positive outcome of the SARC process that despite deterioration in Indo-Pak and Indo-Sri Lankan relations during 1984, the SAARC Summit could launch the regional association in 1985.[26] In fact, Sri Lanka's attitude at Male Foreign Ministers' meeting and later its initial refusal to join Thimpu meeting of Ministers in 1984, had threatened to derail the SARC process.[27]

However, the provision to exclude the bilateral contentious issues from SARC agenda came in handy and SARC spirit withstood these initial shocks. Likewise, the provision to take decisions on the basis of unanimity provided confidence to the smaller member countries that they had an equal stake and opportunity in the regional cooperation process. The Indian insistence on these two provisions as the basic ground rules thus proved to be useful in pushing the SARC process and forging the South Asian association. Pran Chopra considers the unanimity principle in SAARC as a positive outcome so long as trust-evoking policies are followed by the member states of SAARC. He observed:

> ... the sheer size of India in comparison with other countries of the region and its centrality in relation to all of them... does not stand in the way of inter-country cooperation in this region; nor does the fear and suspicion about India which India's neighbours are supposed to entertain about it. So long as trust-evoking policies are followed towards each other by India and its neighbours, there is as good a chance of trustful relations developing in this region as in any other.[28]

The fear of India's neighbours that she would dominate and act in pursuance of her ambition to be a South Asian hegemon proved to be unfounded during initial years of SARC. Likewise, there were no indications of India's neighbours 'ganging-up' against her as apprehended. However, there were voices of dissent as well. An analyst termed SAARC a fragile venture and a futile search for a mirage in the context of severe limitations on regional economic cooperation on account of linkages of South Asian countries with the developed economies of the West. He observed:

> ... it should not be difficult for them [SAARC member countries] to put aside their political differences and seriously get on with the urgent business of promoting economic cooperation that would benefit all the peoples of the region. This mutual cooperation would certainly strengthen their bargaining position in the international markets where the developed Western countries dictate terms.
>
> But this does not happen. All the countries of the region without exception, have turned their faces away from their neighbours and have embarked upon a futile search for a mirage—to be able to prosper with the blessings of their exploiters. This search goes on because each one of them is more closely integrated with the developed capitalist countries of the West than with each other.[29]

One of the objectives set forth by SAARC was probably to reverse this very trend and achieve collective self-reliance in a more equitable international order.

Second Summit—Bangalore, 1986

The Second Summit held on 16-17 November, 1986 at Bangalore (India) pushed the institutionalisation of SAARC further by endorsing the Memorandum of Understanding[30] on the establishment of the SAARC Secretariat signed by the Council of Ministers. It also decided to locate the Secretariat at Kathmandu.[31]

The Bangalore Declaration

The Bangalore Declaration adopted by the Summit called for more concrete and action oriented projects within the Integrated Programme of Action. It emphasized the need for greater people-to-people contacts through such action as regular and frequent interchange of scholars, academics, artists, authors, professionals and businessmen as well as facilitation of tourism. The Declaration welcomed the setting up of Technical Committees on Women in Development and on the Prevention of Drug Trafficking and Drug Abuse. It directed the undertaking of annual reviews on the needs of children. It also condemned all acts of terrorism as criminal and reiterated the desire of promoting peace, stability, amity and progress in the region through strict adherence to the principles of United Nations Charter and the non-aligned movement.

On global issues, the Summit called for an end to the nuclear arms race and early conclusion of a Comprehensive Nuclear Test Ban Treaty. It called for the adoption of a regional approach for obtaining favourable terms of trade and assistance from the developed world and the revival of the North-South dialogue. It emphasised closer SAARC consultation and cooperation in relevant international economic conferences and institutions.[32]

The summit leaders considered[33] several new ideas for expanding and strengthening the cooperative programmes under SAARC.[34] They approved following ideas in principle and directed that these be elaborated and concretized through expert level examination to be completed by March 1987 for the consideration of the Council of Ministers in their next meeting:

(i) A South Asian Broadcasting Programme covering both radio and television be launched;

(ii) Concrete steps be taken to facilitate tourism in the region, including facilities for limited convertibility of national currencies for tourists from SAARC countries;

(iii) A SAARC Documentation Centre be set up for students, scholars and researchers to have ready access to reliable and up-to-date information on technical, scientific and developmental matters;

(iv) A concerted programme of exchange of scholars be formulated and action taken for an early institution of SAARC scholarships. SAARC Fellowships and SAARC Chairs in order to promote increasing cross-fertiiization of ideas through greater interaction among students, scholars and academics in SAARC countries;

(v) A Youth Volunteer Programme be established in SAARC under which volunteers from one country would be able to work in other countries in the fields of agriculture and forestry extension work (The idea behind this directive was to harness the idealism of youth for regional cooperative programme).[35]

The Indian Position

Bangalore Summit again provided an opportunity to the Indian Prime Minister Rajiv Gandhi to reiterate the Indian policy objectives in SAARC when in his speech he said:

> Ours is not a political association. We have much to gain from peace, progress and stability in our neighbourhood. This is the logic of our working together.

> Bilateral relations have their difficult moments. SAARC reminds us that at such moments we should seek what unites us and not what divides us. We have consciously decided not to burden SAARC with our bilateral concerns, yet, by providing a framework for forging a cooperative set of relations among our countries, SAARC can help us positively in growing out of these problems.[36]

To reinforce Indian objective of a non-controversial cooperative framework, the Indian Prime Minister Rajiv Gandhi emphasized the role of sports and culture to raise the peoples' consciousness of their identity as South Asians. In his concluding remarks in the Summit Meeting he said:

> Sports is a ready medium for mass participation as the sports events in Kathmandu and Dhaka have already testified. During the year to come, let us explore how we might use culture and the mass media, as vehicles for enhancing our awareness of each other without detracting in any way from our individual national identities.[37]

The Indian Prime Minister while talking of non-political nature of SAARC, also mentioned the logic of South Asian nations working together as the 'gains' to be achieved through peace, progress and stability. There seemed to be an apparent contradiction in these assertions since peace and stability could not be achieved without political harmony and shared strategic perceptions. It is indeed a unique feature of SAARC that the official process has been immunised from bilateral contentious issues but at the same time the provision for regular annual summit meetings provides an excellent informal opportunity to discuss and sort out bilateral political disputes.

The Bangalore Summit proved this point beyond doubt when intense and detailed discussion took place between India and Sri Lanka on the vexed ethnic problem in Sri Lanka. An Indian newspaper emphasising the importance of bilateral issues during SAARC Summit at Bangalore, noted that Sri Lankan President Jayawardene's arrival some three hours ahead of others made it possible for him and Prime Minister of India to exchange views on the airport itself.[38] The discussions were reported to be 'very pointed and even maps were referred during discussions indicating boundaries of Tamil ethnic province in Sri Lanka.[39] A commentator in a Colombo newspaper observed as under:

> SAARC has kept out bilateral issues out of its deliberations. It is naive to imagine that there are no bilateral conflicts among the countries concerned. SAARC is not attempting to gloss over these and bilateral consultations do take place among the countries to overcome these differences.... This is important as in the final analysis cohesiveness and regional identity depend on minimising or elimination of differences among the countries concerned.[40]

The consensus on general formulation on terrorism in the Bangalore Summit was yet another evidence that the SAARC agenda could not be confined to mere economic, technical and cultural issues as envisaged. This consensus committed the members to a strong denunciation of all forms of terrorist activities as also to the UN resolution requiring the member countries to co-operate in combating terrorism, refrain from instigating it or allowing their territories to be used for terrorist activities.

Indian anxiety and concern in pushing this issue was obvious in the light of allegations of Pakistani sponsorship of Sikh separatism in the Indian state of Punjab during this period. Even the informal contact between Indian Prime Minister Rajiv Gandhi and his Pakistani counterpart Mohammad Khan Junejo was far from cordial. Pakistan Foreign Secretary Abdul Sattar initiated a diplomatic offensive against India at SAARC media centre on several issues hampering normalisation of relations between the two countries. Sattar maintained that the principle of bilateralism did not exist in the Simla Agreement signed between the two countries after the 1971 war. He thus invited sharp Indian reaction since the principle of bilateralism was the most important item of this agreement.[41] The regional political problems and issues were thus creeping into SAARC agenda at the outset.

India at the same time was keen to expand the scope of cooperation by inclusion of trade and industry among the areas of cooperation but was strongly opposed by Pakistan presumably due to fears of Indian domination. Pakistan's opposition was more to do with politics than economics of trade. A news report thus commenting on Summit Declaration noted:

> The declaration will be silent on the issue of expanding the scope of SAARC, on which India had set its heart, but which was strongly opposed by Pakistan (it did not want trade and industry to be included in the cooperative pattern). India did not push the point, even though it was supported by Bangladesh.[42]

The Bangalore Summit, however, will be remembered for taking an early lead in deciding to setup SAARC Secretariat and thus facilitating institutionalisation of the SAARC process.

Third Summit— Kathmandu, 1987

The Third SAARC Summit was convened in Kathmandu, Nepal on 2-4 November, 1987.The Summit Meeting witnessed signing of two important agreements—one on establishing the SAARC Food Security Reserve[43] and second for a SAARC Regional Convention on Suppression of Terrorism.[44] The Summit also decided to commission a study on the 'Protection and Preservation of the Environment and the Causes and Consequences of Natural Disasters' in a well-planned comprehensive framework. In fact, while deciding to commission this study, the Summit leaders expressed their deep concern at the fast and continuing degradation of the environment including extensive destruction of forest, in the South Asian region. They also noted that South Asia was afflicted with such natural disasters as floods, droughts, landslides, cyclones, tidal waves which have had a particularly severe impact causing immense human suffering.[45]

Kathmandu Declaration

In the Kathmandu Declaration, the Summit leaders called for greater participation of the Non-Government Organisations (NGOs) in promoting socioeconomic and cultural development under the aegis of SAARC. They emphasised the need to further consolidate and streamline the process of implementation of the Integrated Programme of Action. On international issues the leaders welcomed the understanding reached between the United States and the Soviet Union on Intermediate Nuclear Forces (INF) and called for the early conclusion of the Geneva Conference on disarmament in respect of Comprehensive Test Ban Treaty and Convention to Ban Chemical Weapons.[46]

The Summit leaders expressed satisfaction at the launching of the SAARC Audio Visual Exchange Programme[47] which coincided with the opening of this Summit. Further, taking note of the dates for institution of the SAARC Chairs, Fellowships and Scholarships and commencement of organised tourism among SAARC Member Countries, they directed that the Schemes for the SAARC Documentation Centre and the SAARC Youth Volunteer Programme be implemented at the earliest.

The Kathmandu Declaration also stressed the need for increased resource flows to the least developed countries, resumption of the North-South dialogue, early conclusion of the International Conference on Money and Finance for development and liberalisation of the multilateral trading system with the renewed efforts from within and outside the GATT Uruguay Round of Multilateral Trade Negotiations.

The Indian Position

india in the Third Summit wanted to expand the scope of cultural cooperation and bring on SAARC agenda the issue of cooperation in trade.[48] The Indian Prime Minister in his address to the Summit expressed these ideas in following words:

> There is also much more we can do in the area of culture, especially forms of culture which draw in large number of people as participative spectators. We might consider a South Asia Festival which brings together from all parts of our region a diversity of arts and crafts, poetry and songs, dance and drama, and traditional sports.

He further said :

> Our planning experts have foreseen the advantages of cooperation in trade and industry, money and finance. It would be useful to authorise studies on the scope and modalities of cooperation in these sectors. We could make an objective determination later as to whether the balance of advantage lies in our entering these fields.' [49]

India at the same time wanted to underline the political dimension of the regionalism in South Asia when the Prime Minister Rajiv Gandhi explained India's viewpoint on the implications of regional cooperation beyond the stipulated areas. He said:

> ...Foremost it fosters a sense of regional identity, a sense of shared destiny. This adds a second common dimension to our respective foreign policies. The first, of course, is the membership of each of our countries in the non-aligned movement. SAARC is thus taking shape as a factor in determining our place in the world, collectively as a region and individually as independent countries. In a broad perspective, such regional understanding is a positive political development.[50]

The Indian protestations and assertions of keeping bilateral political issues out of the SAARC agenda notwithstanding, the political dimension of interstate relations among SAARC Member

Countries, determine to a great extent the behaviour of these countries in SAARC deliberations.

Pakistani scholar Ross Masood Hussain points out debatable political issues sought to be discussed by India in the Third Summit Meeting.[51] These issues were— India's move to support Afghanistan's application for membership of SAARC and to welcome the Indo-Sri Lanka Accord in the Summit declaration. The application for Afghanistan's entry into SAARC was opposed by most SAARC countries so long as Soviet forces were present in that country. Pakistan objected to the second move as well questioning on principle as to "whether SAARC under the provisions of the Charter, could discuss a bilateral and contentious issue and, in the context of the presence of Indian Forces in Sri Lanka [and] also drew a parallel between Afghanistan and Sri Lanka".[52] Both moves failed due to lack of unanimity, but the SAARC Standing Committee was directed to look into the matter of admission of new members since the Charter contained no such provision.

Fourth Summit— Islamabad, 1988

The Fourth SAARC Summit held in Islamabad on 29-30 December, 1988 was very significant on two counts: one, it was being held against the background of worldwide trend of lessening of tensions between the US and the Soviet Union and the restoration of democracy in Pakistan; and two, a sense of unease and frustration was creeping into to the deliberations at the slow growth of SAARC process.

The Indian Position

The Indian Prime Minister Rajiv Gandhi in his address to the Summit pointed towards the 'momentous events' which had taken place and were "fundamentally altering the world and the world order".[53] He pointed out in this regard following events:

(i) the Treaty concluded between the US President Reagan and the Soviet President Gorbachev on dismantling of nuclear weapons systems;

(ii) Geneva Accord on Afghanistan which could lead to the establishment of a government based on national consensus, ensuring a sovereign, independent and non-aligned Afghanistan;

(iii) end of the Iran-Iraq war;

(v) proclamation of Palestinian State by Yasser Arafat and commencement of dialogue between the United States and the PLO;

(v) possibilities of a solution to the conflict in Kampuchea, promise to the Namibian people for implementation of the Independence Plan adopted by the Security Council ten years ago;

(vi) revival of cooperation between India and China in working towards a new world order based on the Panchsheel, the Five Principles of peaceful co-existence;

(vii) progressive defusion of the tension between the Soviet Union and China; and

(viii) Indian response to the request for assistance from the Maldives to thwart the invasion by foreign mercenaries aimed at subverting the democratic will of the people; and democratic elections in Pakistan leading to the installation of a new government in that country.[54]

The frustration at the slow pace of growth of cooperation in SAARC was also manifested in the Indian Prime Minister's speech when he termed the Association as 'laggards' and asked:

> Can it, however, be said that South Asian regional cooperation has grown at a pace commensurate with these developments of fundamental significance to the international community and the emerging world order.[55]

One of the basic reasons for Indian frustration probably was lack of cooperation in the core economic areas, particularly 'trade'. This was reflected in the Prime Minister's statement when he reiterated:

> We also need to strengthen linkages between ourselves to give us strength, individually and as a region. This calls for increased economic exchanges within our region, covering the gamut of economic activities from agriculture to industry—infrastructure, technology and human resource development. Economic cooperation must lie at the heart of a regional cooperation. There has to be a degree of harmonization to ensure that complementarities in our economies are matched to give strength to our respective economies and strength to our voice and influence in world forums....

Yet we shy away from trade and economic cooperation....[56]

The Indian Prime Minister tried to reassure and assuage the apprehensions of the smaller SAARC Member Countries, regarding India's undue advantage on account of size and economic potential when he said:

> Given the disparity in size, levels of development and degrees of diversification in the economies of the countries constituting our association, there will, of course, have to be special measures and safeguards built into any scheme of regional cooperation to protect the interests of each of us and to promote the common interests of all. India has no hesitation in declaring at the outset that it is fully conscious of its special obligations and special responsibilities. We will not seek to secure any unfair advantage at the expense of any of our partners. Indeed, the interests of none of us can be secured by damaging the interests of any one else.[57]

The economic cooperation and particulariy 'trade' among SAARC Member Countries is a sensitive issue which is not confined to mere economic arguments. While the proponents[58] of South Asianism suggest that there might be some small costs in the short and medium term but all countries of the region, including India, would stand to gain from trade and economic cooperation; there are others who do not buy the argument of asymmetric gains in favour of India since India is also a poor country. A political analyst maintains that the Bangladeshi and especially Pakistani rejection of trade has symbolised political 'resistance' to Indian 'domination'[59]

Both countries use economic "asymmetries" inherent in trade between India and its smaller neighbours, but clearly both invest trade with great symbolic importance. This analyst also notes the argument of some Indians who 'see trade as a sign of diplomatic "normalisation", especially with Pakistan, which they argue discriminates against India as against no one else'. An Indian official is thus quoted as saying:

> It's true that we don't need or want trade that badly with Pakistan on economic grounds, but we think it is fundamental to a real process of normalisation - it's a principle with us... We accept imports from Pakistan on an MFN basis: they can sell us anything on our schedule of acceptable imports. But they don't treat us on an MFN (Most Favoured Nation) basis.[60]

This analysis mentions another viewpoint which argues that "trade brings non-economic benefits not just symbolically but also very concretely in the form of influence-building-benefits which make trade and economic cooperation more generally worthwhile."[61]

Islamabad Declaration

The Fourth Summit carried on with the SAARC agenda and issued the Islamabad Declaration.[62] The heads of State/Government expressed satisfaction at the progress in the implementation of the SAARC Integrated Progaramme of Action and took note of the measures to streamline and re-orient various SAARC activities to make them more action-oriented; the establishment of the SAARC Agricultural Information Centre (SAIC) was welcomed and the leaders expressed satisfaction at the operationalisation of South Asian Food Security Reserve and ratification of the SAARC Convention on Suppression of Terrorism. The Summit decided to declare the year 1989 as the SAARC Year for Combating Drug Abuse and Drug Trafficking and directed the concerned Technical Committee to examine the possibility of a Regional Convention on Drug Control.[63]

The Fourth Summit expanded the agreed areas of cooperation to twelve by including 'education' within SAARC sphere of activities. A Pakistan proposal entitled 'SAARC 2000: A Basic Needs Perspective', envisaging the development of the human resources of South Asia within a 'broad frame work of a long term perspective' for the attainment by the year 2000 AD of specific targets in areas such as food, clothing, shelter, education, primary health care. population planning and environmental protection was adopted. The year 1990 was declared the `SAARC year of the Girl Child' and the summit called for specific programmes and activities to increase public awareness of the problems of girl child. Pakistan's offer to host a Centre for Human Resource Development and the Second Ministerial meeting on 'Women and Development' was welcomed.[64]

A significant decision of this summit was a direction given to the Secretary General to convene a special meeting of the Group of Co-ordinators to identify specific areas in the core economic areas of trade, manufactures and services where cooperation would be immediately feasible. The Summit leaders also directed that the report of the Group be presented to the next session of the Standing Committee and the Council of Ministers.[65]

SAARC Summits have been supporting the involvement of NGOs and professional bodies in its activities. Islamabad Summit took it a step further and decided to exempt Supreme Court Judges and members of national Parliaments of SAARC countries from visa requirement while travelling within the region. Further, the Council of Ministers was directed to identify other categories of persons to be extended this facility.[66]

Fifth Summit—Male, 1990

The Fifth SAARC Summit was convened at Male, Maldives on 21-23 November 1990. It was originally scheduled to be held in Colombo, Sri Lanka in 1989 but had to be postponed on account of serious bilateral differences between India and Sri Lanka on the issue of withdrawal of Indian Peace Keeping Force (IPKF) which was stationed in Sri Lanka due to Tamil-Sinhala ethnic conflict.[67] IPKF continued to stay in Sri Lanka during 1989 despite Sri Lankan President's request for withdrawal of the Force. This caused a major strain in Indo-Sri Lankan relations and Sri Lanka refused to host the SAARC Summit. Later, after the withdrawal of IPKF in March 1990, Sri Lanka wanted to host the postponed Summit of 1989.[68] Sri Lanka finally relented after a prolonged dispute and the summit was held in Male. This Summit was, therefore, a significant landmark in the evolution of SAARC in the sense that the Association survived its first test to uphold the provision to keep bilateral political disputes out of the SAARC agenda. In fact, the dissent against this provision was articulated by the King of Bhutan in the inaugural Summit at Dhaka itself when in a forthright manner he declared:

> ...it may neither be possible nor desirable to limit the discussion in our meetings to issues of a non-political nature or the political climate of our region will undoubtedly cast a long shadow over our deliberations. In the geo-political realities of our region it would be unrealistic to ignore the primacy of the political factor as in the final analysis it will be the political environment of the region which will determine the shape and scope of regional cooperation in South Asia.[69]

Given the political realities of the sub-continent it seems well-nigh impossible to rule-out political issues from South Asian regionalism. Some experts maintain that the "regionalism is essentially a political phenomenon notwithstanding its usual form of economic and socio-cultural cooperative interaction."[70]

The Indian Position

The Male Summit carried on with its agenda of socio-cultural and international economic issues. The Indian Prime Minister in his address to the Summit again highlighted the slow progress of SAARC process in core economic areas. Reiterating India's position in respect of bilateral disputes on SAARC agenda, the Prime Minister Chandra Shekhar said:

> Economic cooperation among the South Asian countries has its own logic and compulsions. The framers of SAARC Charter, therefore, displayed foresight and wisdom in not making such cooperation contingent upon the solution of bilateral problems.[71]

Expressing deep concern at mass poverty in South Asia (46 per cent of the world's poor located in the region) and dismally low volume of global trade share (0.8 per cent of global exports) of South Asia, the Indian Prime Minister reminded the Summit of the regional economic integration in other parts of the world. He observed:

> Remarkable changes are taking place in the world. Competition for resources is increasing. Even the developed countries in order to maintain their technological lead and competitive edge, are moving towards greater integration - a more unified European Community, the US-Canada Common Market Agreement, the desire of East European Countries to join the West European Economic mainstream and the constitution of APEC are all pointers in this direction.[72]

In Comparison to these global developments, he underlined the failure of SAARC in not responding to the growing trend of greater regional economic cooperation.

He observed:

> The nature of cooperation among the SAARC countries that exists today is modest and limited.Through our on going activities, we have certainly benefited from each other's needs and potential. Some of the spectacular events organised have indeed helped in projecting the SAARC personality. However, there seems to be no direct impact of SAARC activities on the lives of the peoples of our countries. The low level of day to day interaction between our peoples persists. Indeed, in some areas we seem to be regressing. From 1980-1987 intra-SAARC

exports and imports, as a percentage of SAARC global trade, fell from 4.94 per cent to 2.98 percent and from 2.29 per cent to 1.39 per cent respectively.[73]

He pointed out that SAARC was one year behind schedule in completing the studies that were mandated at the Kathmandu Summit, on cooperation in the fields of trade and industry and for the prevention of environmental degradation.[74]

Male Declaration

The Male Declaration endorsed the decision of the Council of Ministers in regard to the time frame for completion of the Regional Study on the Causes and Consequences of Natural Disasters and the Protection and Prevention of the Environment. The Declaration underlined the need for expeditious action for completing the regional study within the time frame stipulated by the Council of Ministers. The Summit approved the launching of the Scheme regarding special SAARC Travel Document and called for expeditious enactment of enabling measures for the implementation of the SAARC Regional Convention on Suppression of Terrorism. It was also decided that the representatives of the national development banks of the SAARC Member Countries would get together to work out the precise modalities of setting up a Fund for regional projects and the manner in which these could be related to joint venture projects. India's offer to host this meeting was accepted.[75]

Continuing with its social agenda the Summit significantly decided to observe the years 1991-2000 AD as the 'SAARC Decade of the Girl Child', the year 1991 as the 'SAARC year of the Shelter', the year 1992 as the 'SAARC year of the Environment' and the year 1993 as the 'SAARC year of Disabled Persons.'

The Summit decided to hold the second Ministerial Meeting on International Economic issues in India in 1991.[76]

The Summit leaders in full agreement on important international political and economic issues called for immediate and unconditional withdrawal of Iraqi forces from Kuwait and the restoration of its legitimate government. They expressed support for the banning of chemical weapons and early conclusion of a Comprehensive Test Ban Treaty. They directed the Council of Ministers to prepare a strategy for mobilising regional resources which would encourage and strengthen individual and collective self-reliance in the region and supported Paris Declaration (1990) and the Programme of Action adopted by the UN conference on the Least Developed Countries.[77]

SAARC Activities: 1985-1990

During 1985-90, the activities on SAARC agenda can be summarised as below:

(i) Activities in the agreed areas of cooperation integral to IPA. The Integrated Programme of Action on agreed areas of cooperation was initiated even before formal launching of SAARC. As already pointed out in Chapter 3, the Programme was adopted by the Foreign Ministers of SAARC Member Countries in March 1983. The Technical Committees comprising of representatives from Member States formulate programmes and prepare projects in their respective fields. The Technical Committees submit their reports to the Standing Committee through the Programming Committee. The Report of the Secretary General to the Fifth Male Summit noted the current status in respect of various issues incorporated in IPA.[78]

(ii) Activities to promote people to people contact - SAARC Audio Visual Exchange (SAVE), organised Tourism, SAARC Documentation Centre, Fellowships and Scholarships and SAARC Youth Volunteers Programme.[79]

(iii) Activities relating to setting up of SAARC Regional Institutions - SAARC Agricultural Information Centre(SAIC), SAARC Meteorological Research Centre, Institute of Rural Technical and Regional Software Centre etc.

(iv) Activities regarding subjects suggested by the Planning agencies—economic cooperation in trade, manufactures and services; plan modelling techniques, establishment of data bank of socio-economic indicators; setting up a group on statistics.

(v) Areas of cooperation agreed at the Third Summit (Kathmandu, 1987) and the Fourth Summit (Islamabad, 1988)-cooperation for prevention and reduction of natural disasters and improvement of environment; impact on the region of Green House Effect; SAARC 2000 AD: A Basic Needs Perspective; establishment of a centre for human resource development.[80]

(vi) Activities on some officially claimed important achievements during the period—establishment of a SAARC Food Security Reserve of 2,21,480 metric tonnes meant for emergency situation like droughts and floods etc; ratification of the Regional Convention on Suppression of Terrorism; agreement on a SAARC travel document to enable certain categories of the people to travel without visa; and agreement on a draft Convention on Prevention of Narcotic Drugs.

Reasons for Slow Growth of SAARC

Till the Male Summit (1990) SAARC was based largely on inter-governmental activities and the Integrated Programme of Action (IPA).[81] The progress in SAARC during 1985-90 was very slow. Based on comparative study of several regional groupings some scholars have identified some basic political factors for a successful regional cooperation. These are:

(i) Common and similar (though not necessarily identical) threats either from internal or external sources, or both which provides a congruence in security perceptions;

(ii) Similar political systems which provide a congruence in ideological/political perception ;

(iii) Common foreign policy orientations regarding major issues related to the global balance of power and its regional manifestations which provide a congruence in strategic perception; and

(iv) A consensus regarding the role of pivotal power itself.[82]

Considering the SAARC and South Asian political strategic environment one cannot but observe that there was no congruence of ideological, political or security interests in the region. On the other hand, there were intra-regional tensions caused primarily by the position of the pivotal power, i.e., India. J.N. Dixit analysing the years 1985-91 observes:

> Regardless of the factual position of New Delhi's commitment to the principles of non-alignment and peaceful co-existence, regional perceptions about India were that it harboured hegemonic ambitions....[83]

Given these perceptions, there could be no consensus about the role of the pivotal power in SAARC. On the contrary India was perceived as the biggest security threat by its neighbours.

The second half of 80s, when SAARC was taking shape, was a period in transition which witnessed significant developments in world political and strategic environment. India and its neighbours had to adjust to new emerging realities of a new world order.[84] Some of these developments from the point of view of India and her neighbours were:

(i) Erosion and disappearance of cold war and consensus between US-USSR on major international issues;

(ii) Indications of Soviet withdrawal from Afghanistan and likely increase in the influence of US-Pakistan in the region;

(iii) Increasing thaw in Sino-Soviet relations;

(iv) China adopting more tactful approach towards India with the disappearance of cold war (in 1988, Indian PM paid a visit to Beijing after a gap of 25 years and Deng Xiaoiping reiterated China's desire to normalise relations with India).

India's relations with her neighbours, however, could not reap the benefits of global détente during this period. India's mediatory efforts to resolve Tamil ethnic crisis in Sri Lanka miserably failed and India's Peace Keeping Force (IPKF) in Sri Lanka was considered unjustified military intervention into a neighbouring country particularly since IPKF failed to neutralise the Liberation Tigers of Tamil Elam (LTTE), the Tamil separatist group waging war against Sri Lankan Government.[85] Indo Pak relations also did not make any headway during this period despite restoration of democracy in Pakistan in 1988.[86] The confrontation on Siachin Glacier between the two countries and Pakistan's support to terrorists in Indian states of Punjab and Jammu and Kashmir continued unabated. The newly elected government in Pakistan could not withstand the pressures of hardline segments in political and military establishments —the Islami Jamhuri Ittehad (IJI), Inter Services Intelligence (ISI) and the Pakistan Military itself.[87] Despite initial euphoria on Indo Pak relations after the restoration of democracy, these could not be normalised because the Pakistani Army still had a dominant say on Indian policy and security issues.

Nepal voiced complaints against India not providing adequate transit facilities for its trade and entered into substantial defence supplies arrangements and economic cooperation projects with China apprehending Indian dominance.[88] India's bilateral relations with her neighbours during second half of eighties were quite uneasy. Indian dilemma of reconciling her bilateralism with the objectives of SAARC were evident when Prime Minister Rajiv Gandhi in the inaugural Summit emphasised that bilateral relationships were not to be subsumed into a common regional identity.[89]

The conflict-situation between India and most of her neighbours, politico-strategic divergence in their foreign policies, exclusion of bilateral contentious issues from SAARC agenda and failure to develop any policy consensus marked slow growth of SAARC during initial years. J.N. Dixit sums up India's policy in SAARC during these years in following words:

> ...India pursued a policy of forging cooperation with its neighbours in the fields of culture, tourism, trade and transfer of technology and information. New Delhi also indicated that despite political hurdles put forward by Pakistan, India would fully activate SAARC for regional well-being. At the same time, India was firm in ensuring that SAARC was not used as an instrumentality to pressurise it to compromise on disputes with its neighbours which would affect its territorial integrity or security interests.[90]

India and SAARC-Balance Sheet (1985-1990): An Appraisal of India's Regional Policy

The balance sheet of SAARC after initial years of institutionalisation presents a mixed picture of achievements and failures. The early gains on institutionalisation and resilience to an adverse political environment seem to have been marred by continued inter-state tensions. The critics of SAARC argue that the efforts to promote greater cooperation would not make much headway if political issues are kept out of SAARC process. These critics consider holding of summits and proliferation of areas of cooperation futile if the mistrust and strategic divide continues between India and her neighbours. Lok Raj Baral makes following observations:

> ... However slow and tardy SAARC's progress may be, at least the South Asian rulers meet once a year for discussions on matters of common concern. Yet the regional cooperation process does not instil confidence nor has it been able to sustain the kind of enthusiasm that was generated at the initial stage. Obviously, this is so because the much expected change in regional strategic environment has not been evident....[91]

Strategic Divergence between India and Her Neighbours

India-Pakistan

The strategic divergence is most acutely manifested in Indo-Pak relations. In Pakistan's perception India's goals and attitudes in the region are a major hurdle to SAARC's positive progress. Any increase in defence spending by India is seen as India's pursuit of her hegemonic ambitions in the region. The SAARC process is not seen as contributing, in any manner, to diminishing fear and mistrust between India and Pakistan. There was a brief positive interlude, though, during initial years of SAARC when a representative, democratic government of Benazir Bhutto came to power in Pakistan prior to Islamabad SAARC Summit. A news analysis in an Indian daily predicted a marked shift in India's Pakistan policy before the Summit. This report filed from Islamabad observed:

> The indications here after much of the ground has been laid for the meeting of the Prime Ministers of India and Pakistan in the ministerial and official level exchanges are that the outcome of the meeting will see a substantial change in India's policy approach to Pakistan.
>
> The emphasis in the Indian diplomatic approach is likely to shift significantly from the earlier insistence that there could be no discussion on confidence-building measures until Pakistan abandoned its covert support to terrorism in Punjab.
>
> The attempt to uplift the context of Indo-Pakistani relations has been helped to a great extent by breaking out of the logjam of mutually acceptable formulations like the late General Zia-ul-Haq's suggestion of a no-war pact and India's own concept of a friendship treaty. Pakistan's new PM has made it clear that as a starting point, she would prefer the Shimla Agreement and India, for its part, is quite comfortable with this framework as a basis for the new phase.[92]

The successful conclusion of Islamabad SAARC Summit also drew positive sentiments linking SAARC process to the democratic revival in Pakistan. In a news story entitled 'Indo-Pak ties pivotal to SAARC', an Indian analyst made following assessment:

> ... This summit again proved that Indo-Pakistan relations are pivotal to the conduct of SAARC. It was the beneficiary of the dramatic upsurge of goodwill in bilateral ties as a

consequence of the re-emergence of democracy in Pakistan. If SAARC provided the opportunity and the venue for the Rajiv-Bhutto summit the bilateral exchanges moderated the tenor of proceedings of the regional forum....

One noteworthy development at Islamabad, again directly related to the radical change in Pakistan's political scenario, was stirrings of SAARC as a force that could provide moral and psychological support to the cause of democracy in the region. The leaders in greeting the new chairperson, were welcoming the new democratic order in Pakistan...[93]

The mood in Islamabad Summit was markedly different from that of previous Kathmandu Summit where sharp differences on the issues of terrorism and Afghanistan's entry into the organisation came to the fore. There were indications of some respite from ethnic conflicts within SAARC countries and its positive impact on inter-state relations among member states. An editorial comment in Indian daily captured this situation in the following manner:

> ... The dramatic change reflects realities on the ground. The end of the insurgency in Tripura following a settlement between the Government of India and the Tribal National Volunteers (TNV), which had its headquarters in the Chittagong Hills Tract district of Bangladesh, and the tapering off of the Chakma insurgency in Chittagong in Bangladesh have obviously contributed greatly to the easing of tensions between New Delhi and Dhaka. Similarly, India's action against the Liberation Tigers of Tamil Eelam (LTTE) which it had earlier been accused of aiding, and the threat posed to the Sri Lanka Government by the Janata Vimukti Perumana (JVP), have obviously brought Colombo and New Delhi closer on the issue of terrorism. Just as helpful have been Ms. Benazir Bhutto unambiguous declarations that she would not play the "Sikh Card" and that "the days of the extremists are over" as well as the ethnic conflict in Pakistan.[94]

India-Sri Lanka

However, this seeming harmonisation and easing of tensions was too good to be true in the conflict-prone South Asia. The change of regime in Sri Lanka and the insistence of its new President Premdasa on withdrawal of IPKF from the island nation plunged the region and the SAARC process into a crisis. India refused to withdraw IPKF till such time that the terms of the India- Sri Lanka Agreement were fulfilled. This resulted in Sri Lanka deciding to boycott the SAARC Foreign Secretaries' and Foreign Ministers' meetings and even refusing to host the next Summit meeting till withdrawal of IPKF from Sri Lanka. This crisis revived the debate regarding advisability of maintaining the ground rule of excluding bilateral contentious issues from SAARC agenda as also about the hypocrisy of moving ahead with regional cooperation agenda while political dissonance between India and its neighbours persisted.

The Government of India's official position was to maintain that Sri Lanka was seeking to use SAARC mechanism to bring pressure to bear on India on a bilateral matter and thus its conduct was violative of the Article X(1) of the Charter providing that bilateral and contentious issues would be excluded from the deliberations. A hard line Indian opinion maker commenting on this crisis observed:

> The consequences of political equations among member-states cannot be wished away, despite the circumspection of the SAARC constitution. Echoes of Indo-Sri Lankan differences had been heard before in the SAARC fora and, assuming that the organisation survives, political differences will cast their long shadows over future meetings.
>
> As Sri Lanka has proved, SAARC provides a sounding board to the smaller countries to dramatise their differences and quarrels with India. The question New Delhi will have to consider in depth is whether, when the major core sectors of trade and economy are kept out of the organisation's purview, it is worthwhile for India to give smaller neighbours a periodic opportunity to berate it in a regional setting. India cannot be expected to be an eager participant in this form of its public lynching because of the misfortune of its size and potential.[95]

There were, however, saner counterviews which advised Indian policy establishment to deal with neighbours with much greater sensitivity and diplomatic skill. The continued presence of IPKF in Sri Lanka against her wishes could also be seen as violative of Sri Lanka's sovereignty and hence of the SAARC's Charter which stipulates that cooperation 'shall be based on respect for the principles of sovereign equality, territorial integrity, political independence, non-interference in the internal affairs of other states and mutual benefit'. Commenting on this very crisis Venkateswaran, a former Indian Foreign Secretary expressed following views:

> ... Most regrettably, the postponement of the SAARC meeting of Foreign Ministers marks the transformation of India in the minds of other members of that regional organisation [SAARC] from a peaceful and powerful neighbour into an aggressive and self-righteous bully....
>
> On Sri Lanka, the only sensible course for India to take is to cut her losses and withdraw the IPKF, thereby preserving whatever little credibility remains of our peaceful postures vis-á-vis our neighbours. Otherwise we would have handed over a bonanza to our enemies who would capitalise on it. The stand taken by India that the IPKF cannot be withdrawn till such time that the terms of the India-Sri Lanka Agreement are fulfilled to our satisfaction can cause concern even to President Gayoom of the Maldives whose regime was saved by the timely arrival of Indian forces on his request. The President of the Maldives cannot be blamed if he is quietly worried whether the Indian battalion, which is still there, may not similarly stay on even after he asks it to leave, with India insisting on special safeguards and conditionalities to protect its own interests on the Island.[96]

The criticism of India in Sri Lankan media was on predictable lines. A representative sample was as follows:

> ... It was a matter of regret that despite the noble principles of Pancha Seela so vigorously enunciated by the Republic of India, her rulers today should give cause to a smaller neighbour to entertain misgivings as to her intentions.
>
> The event has belied that promise India has repeatedly declared her respect for this island's sovereignty. But her present reluctance to accede to the request of the President of Sri Lanka to withdraw her IPKF by a specified date, sadly contradicts her professions of sensitivity to international obligations.[97]

More than a decade later, the ethnic conflict still simmers in Sri Lanka with LTTE, the terrorist and fascist outfit, seemingly on the verge of regaining control over northern peninsula of Sri Lanka and giving a de-facto body blow to the Island nation's sovereignty. The irony of the situation is underlined in Sri Lanka's desperate desire for Indian intervention and India's severely limited options to act in spite of her firm conviction and declaration in support of Sri Lanka's sovereignty and territorial integrity. Quite obviously, the fallout of internal turmoil in South Asian countries and its implications on bilateral relations among SAARC Member Countries will need a deft and mature handling by Indian policy establishment with a view to create and maintain mutual trust and confidence with neighbours. The future of SAARC thus is dependent, to a great extent, on Indian policy orientation in the region.

Conclusion

The Indian policy during first five years of SAARC was typified by her anxiety to avoid contentious bilateral issues in order to facilitate a trouble free beginning for the regional integration process. The contentious political issues in the South Asian context inevitably imply 'India versus others' syndrome due to asymmetric power equation in the region. The Indian anxiety in ensuring exclusion of anti-India political issues, therefore, was a hard-nosed pragmatic policy prescription for regionalism to take roots in South Asia. The second Indian pre-condition regarding unanimity in decision making in SAARC, however, must have reassured all member countries of SAARC that they had an equal stake in the organisation.

India was unwilling to dilute or give-up the principle of bilateralism in resolving the political disputes with her neighbours. This explained her pronouncement regarding South Asian regionalism as an added dimension in the foreign policy objectives to help improve bilateral relationships in the region. India did not want to give up her larger objective of an Asian unity either when Indian Foreign Minister Dinesh Singh in 1985 hinted at China's participation in a future Asian organisation and expressed his desire for inclusion of Afghanistan, Burma and Iran in the regional organisation. This, however, seemed to be vain hopes of an incorrigible optimist who wanted to cling to the dreams of Nehruvian era.

India's regional policy was also marked by an apparent contradiction since it intended to achieve peace, progress and stability in the region and still called SAARC a non-political association. The objective to achieve peace, progress and stability could not be understood as anything other than an outright political objective. India's definition of 'political' in the context of SAARC presumably was only the bilateral contentious issues with her neighbours which she wanted to tackle outside the realm of SAARC.

Such a limited view of regional political situation resulted in a simmering discontent among smaller member countries of SAARC against the provision excluding bilateral contentious issues from SAARC agenda. The smaller member countries always perceived themselves at the receiving end of bilateral disputes with 'big' and 'powerful' India. This perception made these countries less than enthusiatic or even opponents of India's efforts to expand the scope of regional cooperation by including areas of 'trade' and 'industry'. Troubled by their perception of India's hegemonic ambitions in the region these countries soft-pedalled the issue of including 'trade' in possible areas of cooperation. Pakistan, in particular, opposed Indian move in this regard considering it a legitimate resistance to possible Indian domination in the region. Indian policy objectives, on the other hand, were to promote economic and cultural cooperation to ultimately overcome the contentious, bilateral disputes. India's expression of her frustration in Islamabad Summit at the slow pace of cooperation and exclusion of core economic areas from regional cooperation process made other member countries take note of Indian sentiments. This Summit made a beginning in this respect and issued directions for convening the meeting on trade, manufacture and services.

The initial years of institutionalisation of SAARC and continuation of the regional process despite the first serious challenge posed by Indo-Sri Lankan dispute on account of IPKF issue provided positive indications for the future of regionalism in South Asia. India perceived emergence of South Asian regional identity as a second common dimension in regional foreign policies after the non-alignment. This was considered a positive political development from the Indian point of view.

REFERENCES

1. Membership for Afghanistan and Burma was also considered for the organisation. Iran was offered an observer status; S.D. Muni, *Post Cold War Regionalism in Asia with special reference to the SAARC Sub-Region*, Institute of Developing Economies, Tokyo, No. 258, February 1996, p. 61.
2. For details see S.D. Muni, "SARC: Building Regionalism from Below", *Asian Survey, Vol. XXX, No. 4, April, 1985;* Also his "Political issues and South Asian Cooperation" *Mainstream*, SARC Summit Special, December, 1985; Bimal Prasad (ed.), *Regional*

Cooperation in South Asia-Some General Consideration in South Asian Regional Cooperation; Satyamurty (ed.) *SAARC*, Institute of Asian Studies, Hyderabad, 1982, pp.10-13; Amajuddin Ahmed, "Regional Cooperation in South Asia and India's role in Cooperation among South Asian Nations", M.D. Dharamdasni (ed.), *Cooperation among South Asian Nations,* Varanasi, 1988, pp.106-15; Pran Chopra, "From Mistrust to Cooperation", in Pran Chopra and others (ed.), *Future of South Asia*, Centre for Policy Research, New Delhi, 1986, pp.1-56.

3. See Nancy Jetly, "India and SAARC" in Virendra Narain and B.C. Upreti (ed.), *SAARC-A Study of Perceptions and Policies*, South Asian Centre, University of Rajasthan, Jaipur, 1991, p. 40.
4. For details on India's 'hegemonic' role in South Asia see, Leo Rose and S. Kumar, "South Asia" in W.J. Feld and G. Boyd (ed.) *Comparative Regional Systems,* New York, 1980, pp. 264-68; B. Buzan, *South Asian Insecurity and the Great Powers*, London, 1986, pp. 9-14; Mohammad Ayoob, "India in South Asia: the Quest for Regional Predominance", *World Policy Journal,* 1990, pp.107-34 ; For more on Indian pre-eminence in the region see R.W. Bradnock, *India's Foreign Policy Since 1971*, London, 1990, pp. 59-83 ; Ashok Kapur and A. Jeyaratnan, Wilson, *Foreign Policy of India and Her Neighbours*, New York, 1996, pp. 21-42.
5. For details see *SAARC Survey of Development and Cooperation,* 1998-99, RIS, New Delhi, 1999.
6. For details on asymmetrical relations between India and its neighbours see Pran Chopra, "Fact and Fiction of Inequality", *Mainstream, SAARC Summit Special,* New Delhi, December 1985, pp. 21-25; Shamsul Haq, "Problems and Promises" in Pran Chopra (ed.), *Future of South Asia*, n. 2, pp.56-87; Partha S.Ghosh, *Cooperation and Conflict in South Asia*, New Delhi 1989, pp. 214-29.
7. For a detailed study on the neighbours' perception of India's role in the region see Suneet Vir Singh, "Mutual Image Perception in South Asia" in Bhabani Sen Gupta (ed), *Regional Cooperation and Development in South Asia* Vol. I, Centre for Policy Research, New Delhi, 1986.
8. Hasan Askari Rizvi "Problems and Prospects of South Asian Regional Cooperation" *Regional Studies* Vol. II, No. 2 Spring 1984, Institute of Regional Studies, Islamabad, pp.19-20.
9. "Dhaka Declaration", *Declaration of SAARC Summits (1985-1995)* SAARC Secretariat, Kathmandu, March 1997, pp.1-6.
10. *Ibid.*, p.1.

11. For details on international and strategic situation during this period see K. Subramanayam, "Strategic Aspects of SARC", *Mainstream, SAARC Summit Special*, December 1985, New Delhi, p. 36; Also by him, "India's Relations with her Neighbours", *Strategic Analysis*, New Delhi, March 1987, pp. 1357-75.
12. For organisational chart of SAARC see *SAARC In Brief*, SAARC Secretariat, Kathmandu, 1997.
13. For organisational structure of SAARC Secretariat see *ibid.*
14. Joint Press Release issued at the conclusion of the first SAARC Summit in Dhaka on December, 8, 1985; *Declaration of SAARC Summits (1985-1995),* n. 9, p.7.
15. *Ibid.*
16. *Ibid.*, pp.7-8.
17. "South Asian Regional Cooperation: Text of Prime Minister's Address", *Foreign Affairs Record,* Vol. XXXI, No. 12, December, 1985, p. 407.
18. *Ibid.*
19. *Ibid.*, pp. 407-08.
20. *Ibid.*, p. 409.
21. Pran Chopra, "From Mistrust to Cooperation", n. 2, pp. 28-29.
22. "Foreign Minister's Statement on SARC", *Foreign Affairs Record* Vol. XXXI, No.12, December, 1985, p. 413.
23. Dinesh Singh, "Foreign Policy Positions" (Extract of the speech delivered to the Parliament on December 9, 1985), *Seminar*, New Delhi, 317, January 1986, p. 65.
24. *Ibid.,* p. 65.
25. *The Patriot,* 10 December 1985.
26. Indo-Pak relations suffered during 1984 due to hijacking of Indian Airlines plane to Pakistan by a group of Indian Sikh extremists. India suspected Pakistan's hand in the hijacking. Indo-Sri Lankan relations were soured due to Sri Lanka's assertion of Indian complicity in Tamil ethnic conflict in the island country.
27. For details see A.Hariharan, "The Seven Brothers", *The Hindustan Times,* 5 August, 1985; Also see K.S. Ramchandran, "Our Neighbours: A Challenge for SAARC", *The Financial Express*, 10 June, 1985.
28. Pran Chopra, "From Mistrust to Cooperation", n. 2, pp. 43-44.
29. Saral Patra, "SAARC: A Fragile Venture", *The Patriot*, 10 September 1985.

30. For full text of the MOU see From *SARC to SAARC* Vol. 1, SAARC Secretariat, Kathmandu,1988, pp.179-81.

31. The function of the Secretariat was envisaged to be co-ordination and monitoring of the implementation of the SAARC activities. It was to be a servicing role rather than a policy making executive role. See Janaka Nakkawita, "Second SAARC Summit to Minimise Differences", *Daily News,* Colombo, 17 November 1986.

32. *Declaration of SAARC Summits (1985-1995)*, n. 9, pp.11-19.

33. Joint Press Release issued on 17 November 1986 at the end of the second SAARC Summit, Bangalore Declaration of SAARC Summits, n. 9, p. 20.

34. For details on Bangalore Summit See Shamsul Haq, "Beyond Bangalore", in *South Asia Journal*, Vol. I, No.1, July-September 1987, pp.7-19; Also see B. Mohanan, *The Politics of Regionalism* in South Asia, New Delhi, 1992, pp. 68-69; E Sudhakar, *SAARC : Origin, Growth and Future*, New Delhi, 1994, pp.160-162; Nasir A Naqash, *SAARC: Challenges and Opportunities*, New Delhi,1994, pp. 61-84.

35. *Declaration of SAARC Summits (1985-1995)*, n. 9, pp.11-19.

36. Inaugural Address by Rajiv Gandhi, PM of India at the Second Meeting of Heads of State or Government of the South Asian Association for Regional Cooperation, Bangalore, 16 November 1986. Source: Ministry of External Affairs, Government of India.

37. Concluding Statement by Rajiv Gandhi, Prime Minister of India at the Second Meeting of Heads of State or Government of the SAARC, Bangalore, 17 November 1986, Source: Ministry of External Affairs, Government of India.

38. K.K. Katyal, "Bilateral Disputes to the Fore on SAARC Eve", *The Hindu*, 16 November 1986.

39. *The Indian Express,* 16 November, 1986; Also see "President Extols Path of Non-Violence", *The Daily News*, 17 November 1986.

40. Janaka Nakkawita, "Second SAARC Summit to Minimise Differences", *The Daily News*, 17 November 1986.

41. For details see B. Mohanan, *The Politics of Regionalism in South Asia,* New Delhi, 1992.

42. K.K. Katyal, "Bilateral Issues to Fore on SAARC Eve", *The Hindu*, 16 November 1986.

43. For the text of the agreement establishing the Food Security Reserve, see *From SARC to SAARC*, n. 30, pp. 289-93. The Food Security Reserve was meant to be utilised for member countries in

the event of emergencies and was initially sought to be created with the following contribution:

Bangladesh (21000), Bhutan, (180), India (153000), Maldives (20), Nepal (3600), Pakistan (19100), and Sri Lanka (2800); Figures in brackets metric tonnes.

44. The finalisation of this Convention was an important breakthrough in the light of the historical legacy of the region, the long porous inter-state frontier, cross border ethnic overspill and various technical and legal complexities. For text of the SAARC Convention on Suppression of Terrorism, See *From SARC to SAARC*, n. 30, pp. 294-97.

45. Kathmandu Declaration of the Heads of State or Government of the Member Countries of SAARC issued on November 4, 1987 *Declaration of SAARC Summits (1985-1995)*; n. 9, p. 30.

46. *Ibid.*, pp. 25-34.

47. SAARC Audio Visual Exchange Programme (SAVE) comprises both radio broadcast and telecast. The programmes from each member country are now being regularly broadcast/telecast on the first and fifteenth of every month by rotation.

48. For an extensive study on the need to include trade in SAARC agenda see Sumathi Nimal Fernando, "Regional Cooperation in Trade: An urgent necessity in South Asia", in *SAARC Perspective,* SAARC Secretariat, Vol. 2 No.3, May, 1988, pp. 26-36, Tarlok Singh "Perspectives after the Third Summit", Bimal Prasad (ed), *Regional Cooperation in South Asia: Problems and Prospects*, New Delhi 1989, pp.149-63; Arif A. Waqif, "Exploring Potential Areas of Industrial Cooperation in South Asia, *South Asia Journal* Vol. I, No. I, July-September 1987, pp. 51-65.

49. Address by the Prime Minister Rajiv Gandhi at the Third SAARC Summit held at Kathmandu on November 2, 1987. The Third SAARC Summit Kathmandu, Nepal November 1987, Source: Ministry of External Affairs, Government of India, p. 5.

50. *Ibid.*, pp. 5-6.

51. Ross Masood Hussain, SAARC : *Evolution and Prospects: A View from Pakistan*, FES, Islamabad, 1991, p.15.

52. *Ibid.*, p.15.

53. Prime Minister's Address at Fourth SAARC Summit, at Islamabad on December 29, 1988; *Foreign Affairs Record*, Vol. XXXIV, No. 12, December 1988, pp. 423-27.

54. *Ibid.*, 423-24.

55. *Ibid.*, p. 424.

56. *Ibid.*, p. 426.

57. *Ibid.*, p. 426.

58. For details see Tarlok Singh, "A Perspective on Development Cooperation in South Asia" in U.S. Bajpai (ed.), *India and its Neighbourhood*, New Delhi, 1986.

59. Kanti Bajpai, "Discord and Collaboration : Domestic Politics and Indian Diplomacy in SAARC", in Baladas Ghoshal, (ed.) *Diplomacy and Domestic Politics in South Asia*, Regional Centre for Strategic Studies, Colombo, Sri Lanka, 1996.

60. *Ibid.*, p. 78.

Indra Nath Mukherjee in "Economic Constraints and Potentialities" in *Regional Cooperation in South Asia: Problems and Prospects,* Bimal Prasad (ed.), New Delhi 1989, (p.119) notes that 'although both India and Pakistan are members of GATT, Pakistan's trade policy with respect to India (together with Israel and South Africa) has been discriminatory. Although Pakistan has placed as many as 400 products on its free list, only 40 products may be imported by Pakistan traders through the Trade Corporation of Pakistan.

61. *Ibid.*, p. 78.

62. The Islamabad Declaration of the Heads of State or Government of the Member Countries of SAARC issued on 31st December, 1988, *Declaration of SAARC Summits (1985-1995)*, n. 9, pp. 39-49 .

63. For details see "The SAARC Record: Retrospect and Prospect", *Report by Ambassador K.K. Bhargava, Secretary General of SAARC on Activities of the Association and Secretariat,* Kathmandu, November 1990, pp. 11-16.

64. *Ibid.*, p. 44.

65. Joint Press Release issued on 31st December, 1998 at the end of Fourth SAARC Summit, Islamabad, Declaration of SAARC Summits n. 9, p. 53.

66. Islamabad Declaration, n. 9, p. 44.

67. A.P. Venkateswaran, "SAARC in Crisis", *The Indian Express*, 23 July, 1989; Also *The Newstime*, 29 July, 1989; For the Sri Lankan point of view see, Editorial, *The Daily News*, 3 July 1989.

68. In May 1990 Sri Lanka insisted on hosting the SAARC Summit and even threatened to boycott it, if held elsewhere. On the other hand Maldives was not prepared under any circumstances to forego its claim to host the 1990 Summit because it coincided with silver jubilee of its independence. Under these circumstances Sri Lanka mooted the proposal of two meetings —one in Colombo in the first

half of the year to dispose of SAARC agenda and the other in December in Male to consider the impact of the momentous global developments on the region. However, the consensus emerged for one summit to be held in the third week of November 1990 in Male; For further details see, K.K. Katyal, "Crisis over SAARC Summit Deepens", *The Hindu*, 5 May 1990; Also Partha S. Ghosh, "An Experiment Worth Pursuing", *The Financial Express*, 18 November 1990.

69. *SAARC Summits* (1985-1995), n. 9, SAARC Secretariat, Kathmandu, 1988, p. 10.
70. Nicel Davidson (ed.), *Regionalism and New International Economic Order*: A UNITAR Study (New York, 1981), p. 25.
71. "An Ambitious Path of Economic Cooperation", speech at the SAARC Summit, Male, 21st November, *Chandra Shekhar, Selected Speeches 1990-91*, 1990 Publications Division, Ministry of Information and Broadcasting, Government of India, p. 12.
72. *Ibid.*, p.13.
73. *Ibid.*, p.14.
74. *Ibid.*, p.16.
75. Male declaration, *Declaration of SAARC Summits*, n. 9, pp. 57-58.
76. *Ibid.*, pp. 58-59.
77. *Ibid.*, pp. 63-66.
78. Report by Ambassador K.K. Bhargava, n. 63, pp.1-37.
79. For details see Bimal Prasad, "People to People Contacts in South Asia: Pre-requisites and Mechanisms", *SAARC Perspective*, Kathmandu, Vol. 2, No. 3, May 1988, pp. 15-19.
80. For details see K.K. Bhargava, "Human Resource Development: A SAARC Approach", *SAARC Perspective*, Kathmandu, Vol, 4, No. 6, November 1990, pp. 69-73.
81. For details see, *Report by Ambassador K.K. Bhargava,* n. 63, pp. 1-37.
82. Mohammad Ayoob, " The Primacy of the Political: South Asian Regional Cooperation (SARC) in Comparative Perspective": a paper presented at the international conference on South Asian Regional Cooperation, organised by BIISS, Dhaka, January 14-16, 1985.
83. J.N. Dixit, *Across Borders: Fifty years of India's Foreign Policy*, New Delhi, 1998, p.171.
84. For details see Partha S. Ghosh, *Cooperation and Conflict in South Asia*, Delhi, 1989, pp. 214-29.

85. For details see, S.D. Muni, *Pangs of Proximity: India and Sri Lanka's Ethnic Crisis*, New Delhi, 1993; J.N. Dixit, "IPKF in Sri Lanka", *The USI Journal*, Vol. XIX, No. 497, July-September 1989, New Delhi, pp. 248-62; Shelton U. Kodikara, "The Indo-Lanka Agreement of July 1987: Retrospect", in Shelton U. Kodikara (ed.) *Indo-Sri Lanka Agreement of July 1987*, Dehiwala, 1989, pp. 54-70.

86. There was an initial euphoria on Indo-Pak relations after the restoration of democracy in Pakistan. See Bhabani Sen Gupta, "Perestroika in South Asia", *The Hindustan Times,* 6 January, 1989; Malini Parthasarthy, "Marked Shift Likely in India's Pakistan Policy", *The Hindu,* 29 December,1988.

87. For details see Navnita Chadha, "Linkages between Domestic Politics and Diplomacy: Case of India and Pakistan", in Baladas Ghosal (ed.), *Diplomacy and Domestic Politics in South Asia*, Regional Centre for Strategic Studies, Colombo,1996, pp. 89-125.

88. For Indian and Nepali perspectives on the crisis of Indo-Nepal relations in late 1980s see Druba Kumar and S.D. Muni, *Indo-Nepal Relations: Views from Kathmandu and New Delhi*, CNAS FORUM: Current Issues Series, No. 10, Tribhuvan University, Kathmandu, October, 1989.

89. Text of PM's Address at Dhaka, *Foreign Affairs Record*, n. 17.

90. J.N. Dixit, *Across Borders*, n. 83, p. 202.

91. Lok Raj Baral, "Constraints on South Asian Regionalism", in *South Asia Journal* 2,1(1988), p. 18.

92. *The Hindu*, 29 December 1988.

93. L.K. Sharma, "Indo-Pak Ties Pivotal to SAARC", *The Times of India*, 6 January 1989.

94. *The Indian Express*, 3 January 1989.

95. S. Nihal Singh, " The SAARC Crisis", *The Hindustan Times*, 10 July 1989.

96. A.P. Venkateswaran, "SAARC in Crisis", *The Indian Express*, 23 July 1989.

97. *The Daily News*, Colombo, 3 July 1989.

5

Post Cold War Developments and India's Role in SAARC (1990 Onwards): Economic Implications

The period roughly corresponding to the beginning of the last decade of the twentieth century marks the beginning of a new epoch in international political and economic landscape. The economic implications of the demise of cold war made a serious impact on the process of regionalism in South Asia. India attained a new role and significance in the light of economic policy liberalisation and the phenomenon of globalization and further played a greater role in promoting regionalism in South Asia. The post-cold war developments facilitated Indian push for greater economic cooperation in South Asia.

Post-Cold War Context: Economic Dimension

The beginning of the second phase of cold war[1] with the occupation of Afghanistan by the Soviet forces brought the Super-Power conflict on the doorsteps of South Asia and significantly also saw the emergence of the idea of South Asian regional cooperation. Only a decade later, dramatic developments in international politics brought about the East-West détente and demise of the cold war. The South Asian regionalism during this period evolved into the reality of SAARC.

With an impressive institutional framework in place and a slow but positive process of sociocultural cooperation, SAARC after five summits was ready to embark on an enhanced and more meaningful mode of regional cooperation in 1990 when the demise of the cold war ushered in historic developments in international politics.

Neo-Liberal Washington Consensus

The beginning of 1990s is generally considered to be the time of the end of the cold war between the East and the West. With the end of the cold war rivalries we seem to have been engulfed, in a very short time span, by an altogether different world view. The events after the end of the cold war have been described by some as the transformation of the 'geo-politics' of forty years of cold war into 'geo-economics', i.e., into competitive areas of deregulation and free-trade.[2] The world's largest economic and military power, the United States of America, emerged as a clear hegemon in the global geo-politics. This hegemony reinforced the influence of the political-economic ideology of the countries of the North. With the collapse of the competitive power bloc of Soviet Union, the capitalist ideology became fiercely assertive. We thus saw the ascendance of the neo-liberal[3] 'Washington Consensus' which changed the political and economic paradigm of international relations.

The virtual unipolar global situation that emerged with the ascendance of neo-liberalism, relegated the concern and development issues of developing countries to insignificance. This was complete negation of what the countries of South had articulated in their modest reform proposals on the world economy in the form of the concept of New International Economic Order (NIEO) on the forum of the United Nations. Compelled by the 'oil shock' in the 70s, the countries of the North had tactically agreed to the objectives of the NIEO as the future agenda of North-South relations.

In the post-cold war period all tactical hurdles which compelled the North to accept the objectives of the NIEO, have disappeared and the rich North enjoys complete control on international politics and economics. As Chomsky rightly observes:

> The, 'principal architects' of the neo-liberal 'Washington consensus' are the masters of the private economy, mainly huge corporations that control much of the international

economy and have the means to dominate policy formation as well as the structuring of thought and opinion.[4]

Widening Global- Inequity

The most significant and marked feature of North-South relations is the inequity of the system. The divide is very real and ever increasing. The United Nations Development Programme (UNDP)'s Human Development Report (HDR), 1999 notes that the income gap between the fifth of the world's people living in the richest countries and the fifth in the poorest was 74 to 1 in 1997, up from 60 to 1 in 1990 and 30 to 1 in 1960. It further notes that in the nineteenth century, too, inequality grew rapidly during the last three decades, in an era of rapid global integration: the income gap between the top and bottom countries increased from 3 to 1 in 1820 to 7 to 1 in 1870 and 11 to 1 in 1913.[5] Continuing with the legacy, the last decade, almost corresponding with the period after the end of the cold war, whether by coincidence or design, is reported to have shown increasing concentration of income, resources and wealth among people, corporations and countries.[6]

Globalization

It seems, as if, the global rich are positioning themselves in anticipation of a framework of global governance by augmenting their strength, capturing the levers of power, defining the rules of the game to their advantage and obliterating the sovereignty of the people and of the States and undermining the role of the United Nations Organisation. Their attempt is to create one world with uniform standards in respect of consumption patterns, social norms, cultural expression, the nature of the State (particularly in its relation to the market) and model of economic development. Globalization is the new catchword given to this attempt and propagated to mythical proportions by the powerful media owned and controlled by the rich of the world.

Decline of the UN and the 'State'

The post cold war paradigm shift has significant implications for both national and international politics and development agendas of the North and the South.[7] The role of the State in economic development, as defined and prescribed by the neo-liberal ideology, is sought to be reduced and replaced by the free play of market forces. The neo-liberal 'free market' prescriptions, however, are restricted to free movement of trade, finance and investment but not of unskilled labour and the people.[8] There is increased deregulation and liberalisation of economies in the developing countries to facilitate their integration into the world-economy. The sovereign national space of developing countries is thus being infringed in respect of major economic policy decisions. The objective is to launch a comprehensive programme of privatization and roll back the government to downsize it to a minimalist state.[9] Simultaneously, the role of the United Nations has been eroding[10] - the efforts of the UN agencies to promote the ideology of the NIEO which was included in the North-South agenda with a painstaking, prolonged struggle, is being superseded by the new market fundamentalism (the so-called 'Washington Consensus') operationalised by the Bretton Woods institutions (IMF and the World Bank) and the World Trade Organisation (WTO).[11]

With the primacy of the neo-liberal economics and successful crafting of the U.S. dominated phenomenon of globalization in the psyche of the people, the developing world seems to be losing their political and economic development agenda. There is a sense of inevitability and powerlessness, particularly among the elite and the middle classes in the developing countries with respect to the 'inexorable' march of the market forces.

Policy of Economic Liberalisation in India and Other SAARC Member Countries

In the beginning of 90s, almost coinciding with the end of cold war India faced a serious external debt crisis due to economic profligacy during 1980s. In 1991, India was close to default in meeting its external debt obligations. India's credit rating was downgraded by some reputable international agencies which resulted in non-availability of commercial borrowings. The flow of foreign exchange from the Indians in the gulf also dried up due to Gulf-War. In January 1991, India was left with only US dollar one billion in the reserves—equivalent to only two weeks' imports.[12] This balance-of- payment crisis triggered the reforms in the external sector of the economy.

India thus declared adoption of market friendly reforms in respect of tariffs, import licensing, export subsidies, exchange rate and foreign direct investment.[13] It must, however, be noted that these reforms were the consequence of the fiscai deficits (the gap between central government spending and receipts) being met by borrowing at home and mounted steadily during 1980s. This was coupled with the balance of payments crisis in the external sector. Some economists consider that the BOP crisis of 1991 in India was on account of import substitution policy of the government and the adoption of market friendly, liberalised economic policies as an inevitable necessary consequence of the failure of the state regulated economy.[14]

The change in Indian economic policies in the context of an emerging global capitalist framework was a significant development in South Asia. The size and potential of Indian economy, an English speaking middle class, working democracy with some semblance of the rule of law - all this aroused great interest about India and its future economic prospects among the developed countries of the world. An Indian scholar perceives India's pursuit of economic might through the new economic policy (NEP) as possibly implying a more collaborative and subservient role vis-á-vis the major States of the North in a replay of the decades long post-war German and Japanese experiences.[15] The rationale for India's adoption of NEP is thus interpreted in the following words:

> India has embarked on the NEP on the assumption that imperialism is an irrelevant notion and a wrongful characterisation of the global economic system. The claim that India, as a whole, not just a more substantial minority (comprising its middle and upper classes) can catch up with Western standards of prosperity, is the declared rationale for adoption of the NEP. Whether this is correct or not has obvious repercussions on future Indian foreign policy-its rationale, its future prospects, and its likely challenges and pre-occupations.[16]

Apart from India, the new logic of globalization impelled the governments of other SAARC Member Countries to embark on a process of economic policy change to open up their markets and economies to the outside world.[17] With the exception of Sri Lanka where this process started much earlier, the decade of 90s represents a turning point for all countries of South Asia where major political parties of these countries committed themselves to the path of economic liberalisation and globalization and renewed interest in regionalism.[18]

Post-Cold War SAARC Process and India

The globalized economic context and a common economic policy re-orientation compelled a "growing recognition that regional cooperation in South Asia is no longer an option but a necessity".[19] How did India and other members of SAARC respond to this necessity in order to give desired direction to the process of regionalism in South Asia? This can be best assessed by an appraisal of the major decisions taken at SAARC Summits and the progress of economic cooperation among SAARC Member Countries during 1990s. Five SAARC Summit meetings were held during 1991-98 in different capitals of SAARC Member Countries after the Fifth Male Summit in 1990.

Indo-Sri Lankan Discord over 'IPKF' Issue and SAARC

The postponement of the Fifth SAARC Summit when it was originally scheduled to be held in Colombo due presumably to the likely absence of the King of Bhutan because a proper invitation was not issued to him by Sri Lanka, vitiated regional harmony.[20] India took a position that an accredited representative could not represent a head of the State/ Government and hence meeting could not be held in the absence of the King of Bhutan. President Premadasa of Sri Lanka blamed India for the postponement of the Summit. The official media in Sri Lanka took a strident anti-India position on this issue. An editorial in *The Daily News* published from Sri Lanka observed:

> That no power however big or powerful, should regard an association founded as an instrument of regional cooperation, as a means of delivering, diplomatic snub of one kind or another.[21]

Premadasa went to the extent of suggesting that the unanimity clause in the SAARC charter should be scrapped.[22] News reports from Colombo mentioned that Sri Lanka Government was keen to start a campaign among the member countries of SAARC to get the unanimity clause removed from the SAARC charter. The rationale for such a move was that the clause enabled one member to jeopardize plans and programs of the entire organisation.[23] The approach of Sri Lanka Government was put in right perspective by Prof. S.D. Muni in an assessment of Sri Lanka's policy in SAARC. He observed:

> ... [Sri Lanka's] approach towards SAARC has always been coloured by its prejudices and petty political calculations. Within months of hosting the First Foreign Secretary level meeting in Colombo in 1981, Sri Lanka approached ASEAN for membership only to show its scant regard for SAARC. If not snubbed by ASEAN then, Sri Lanka would have joined ASEAN long back....
>
> Under President Premadasa, the old approach has been revived with even greater aggressiveness. In 1989, Premadasa refused to hold the SAARC Summit in Colombo because of the IPKF presence in his country. Even afterwards, Sri Lanka did not send its delegation at the Islamabad SAARC Ministerial meeting to express its displeasure with India. In 1990, it wanted to deny the privilege to Maldives, of holding the Summit on the occasion of the silver jubilee of Maldives national day. What President Premadasa and his country experience today in the form of a stalled Summit, therefore, is nothing else but the culmination of its own distorted and shortsighted approach to SAARC.[24]

Democratisation in South Asia: A Positive Step Forward for Regional Cooperation

SAARC process, however survived this turmoil and the Sixth Summit was held in Colombo in 1991. There was, in fact, a renewed hope for regional cooperation in this Summit on account of the victory of democratic movements in Nepal and Bangladesh. In Nepal the multiparty democratic movement resulted in installation of K.P. Bhattarai and later J.P. Koirala as Prime Ministers. This change also significantly led to improvement in Indo-Nepal relations in 1991 with the signing of several agreements including on 'trade' and 'transit' between the two countries.[25]

In Bangladesh, Begum Khaleda Zia was voted to power in 1991 after a dark phase of political oppression and economic crisis in that country. The former ruler General Ershad had earlier in 1986 engineered an election in a bid to give legitimacy to his government.[26] The development in Nepal and Bangladesh favouring democratic form of government were welcome as they, sort of, completed the process of democratic change in the sub-continent after the revival of democracy in Pakistan in 1988. Some analysts consider similar political perceptions as an important pre-requisite for regional cooperation.[27] Democratization of South Asia, therefore, triggered a debate on better prospects of regionalism in this part of the world. The proposition of democrats in this regard was put forth by an academic observer in 1996 in following words:

> The global wave of democratization, particularly in most countries of the sub-continent, gave new hopes to the decade and a halı quest for South Asian regional cooperation. Relying on an old axiom that democracies do not go to war, it was assumed that with the proper nurturing of the democratic process in the member countries, regional cooperation would be automatically enhanced.[28]

However, relying on the findings of a research by two Columbia University professors who challenge the axiom that no two democracies had ever gone to war with each other,[29] this analyst assesses South Asian situation in a realistic manner and makes following conclusions:

(i) Despite the growing similarity of ideology in the region, the democratization process in South Asia would tend to encourage conflict rather than cooperation during the transitional period. The near military conflict between India and Pakistan in 1987 and 1990 and the rising tide of nationalism (seen mostly in its anti-India content) in both Bangladesh and Nepal, particularly within the last half-decade confirm this contention.

(ii) The endemic political instability inherent during the transitional phase of democratization tends to weaken rather than strengthen the enthusiasm towards regional cooperation as political leaders in individual countries are forced to be more introspective of the domestic situation before grappling with regional issues. This applies to not only the newly democratizing countries like Bangladesh, Pakistan and Nepal, but also for a relatively old democracy like India which is engaged in a transitional period of political and party leadership building processes as well.

(iii) It is harder for newly established democratic governments to deal with one another, as the domestic constraints imposed by the new system in terms of both the constitutional limitations and the competition among political forces for populist measures are likely to create newer

> obstacles until political leaders learn to appreciate the intricacies of the new environment.[30]

The conclusions above, however, need to be carefully understood and perhaps qualified in the light of the nature of polity in Pakistan and India's relations with her other neighbours. The democratic change in Pakistan never meant a complete sway of representative institutions over the levers of power. The armed forces in Pakistan have enjoyed a special status in the political decision making process even under democratic regimes.[31] Further, the fact that an institution like Inter-Services Intelligence (ISI) enjoying considerable power and influence, has not been accountable to the elected representatives, also points to the limitations of democracy in Pakistan.[32]

Moreover, the power elite in India and Pakistan whether as a matter of policy or compulsion have kept the people of two countries apart thus stifling the genuine democratic contact among the people. Likewise, the anti-India sentiment among the people of India's smaller neighbours has more to do with the asymmetry between India and her smaller neighbours, the behaviour pattern of India's power elite and myopic vision of the ruling establishments in India's neighbourhood, rather than to any transitional phase of the democratic process. A free expression of people's will in the subcontinent, an unhindered people to people contact, foreign policies shaped by mass public opinion—in short a genuine play of democratic forces would facilitate rather than inhibit the regional cooperation even during transitional phase of democracy. The cure South Asia needs is exactly what Columbia University researchers working on democratization and war concluded: more democracy not less.[33]

SAARC Summits and India 1991-1998

Sixth Summit-Colombo, 1991

The fast changing international scenario after the end of the cold war enabled India to impress upon fellow members of SAARC to close rank, anticipate the dangers of a decisive shift of power to the West and embark upon economic cooperation without any further delay. P.V. Narsimha Rao the Indian Prime Minister addressing the sixth Summit in Colombo observed:

> ...Our world is being transformed before our eyes. South Asia may, geographically, seem at the periphery of this change,

> but cannot allow itself to become peripheral. Opportunities for a more peaceful and prosperous world are within our grasp; yet the danger of a return to the acquisitive politics of the nineteenth century cannot be ruled out. This makes imperative our effort for a world in which relations among nations will be based on equity, justice and the rule of law, within the frame work of a more democratised United Nations.[34]

Indian policy of pushing forward regional economic cooperation as the fulcrum of achieving all round harmony in South Asia was underlined by Narasimha Rao when he said:

> Our cooperation must ascend to the truly regional as distinct from a mere sum total of bilateral arrangements. We should not be diffident of newer forms of cooperation. Collective economic security can assure benefits not necessarily confined to the economic field. What we need is confidence between our peoples, and between our governments, to set in motion a benevolent cycle wherein cooperation strengthens confidence which in turn, makes for closer cooperation.[35]

He also put forth the specific Indian agenda on the future of cooperation in SAARC when he asserted:

> The long-term vision of SAARC must undoubtedly include the removal of internal barriers and the free movement of goods, capital and peoples throughout SAARC. Sheer necessity dictates that we do more in the area on intra regional commercial and economic exchange. Pooling of our resources can ensure their optional utilisation. We must not deny ourselves the advantages of geographical proximity.[36]

Responding to the sheer necessity and persistent pursuit by India, the Sixth Summit made a beginning by setting up a Committee for Economic Cooperation.

The Summit Declaration

This Summit marked an important change in the composition of Heads of State/Government since all Heads, with the exception of Bhutan, were democratically elected. Bhutan was represented by its Monarch. The implications of the end of the cold war on international situation were noted by the Summit leaders at the outset:

> They noted the changing power structures in international relations and the reduction of confrontations and tension particularly among the Super Powers. These have contributed

to the receding of the threat of nuclear confrontation and to agreements on disarmament measures. The Heads of State or Government hoped that these developments would restrain the pursuit of military power in all areas of world. They expressed the hope that the peace dividend would be used for promoting further development of developing countries.[37]

The Summit Declaration emphasised the vital importance of assessing the nature and extent of international economic inter-dependence and of the need for reviving the North-South dialogue as well as for vigorously promoting South-South economic cooperation to offset the negative consequences of international economic developments. It accorded the highest priority to the alleviation of poverty in all South Asian countries and realised that the poor are required to be empowered and irreversibly linked to a mainstream of development in order to transform them to a huge potential resource to create economic growth.[38]

The Summit leaders decided to establish an Independent South Asian Commission on Poverty Alleviation (ISACPA) consisting of eminent persons from each SAARC member state to conduct an in-depth study of diverse experiences of the seven countries on poverty alleviation and to report to the Seventh Summit their recommendations on the alleviation of poverty in South Asia. They also set up a Committee for Economic Cooperation as an important outcome of the Regional Study on Trade, Manufactures and Services. An Inter-Governmental Group (IGG) was to be set up on the recommendations of this Committee. IGG in turn would examine the specific measures through which trade liberalisation would take place among the member countries[39] and also examine the Sri Lankan proposal to establish SAARC Preferential Trade Arrangement (SAPTA) by 1997.

The leaders were of the view that the question of cooperation between SAARC and appropriate international and regional organisation needs to be studied, taking into account the evolution of SAARC activities in the core economic areas. It was also decided to work towards the global objective of 'Shelter for all by the year 2000'.

The Summit welcomed the setting up of the SAARC Fund for Regional Projects (SFRP)[40] and requested the Secretary General of SAARC to set up a panel of experts to examine the proposal of His Majesty the King of Bhutan to undertake a pre-feasibility study for the establishment of a South Asian Development Fund (SADF) taking into account the views of all member states.

SAARC Crisis prior to Seventh Summit and India's Response

A uniform economic policy orientation, compelling global developments and democratic governments— it all seemed an ideal conducive environment for SAARC to consolidate on the initial gains (in terms of an institutional structure in place) and embark on the core areas of economic cooperation. However, the primacy of conflictual politics in South Asia again raised its head when the Seventh SAARC Summit was postponed twice on account of political developments in India leading to serious communal strife in the sub-continent. In December 1992 Hindu fundamentalists owing allegiance to 'Sangh Parivar'[41] in Indian politics demolished an old, unused mosque structure (The Babri Masjid) in Ayodhya, UP. This led to serious communal clashes among Hindus and Muslims in India and violent protests tacitly endorsed by the governments in Pakistan and Bangladesh.

The SAARC Summit was first postponed in December 1992 in the light of killings in India as well as killings and other violent acts in Pakistan and Bangladesh. The second, indefinite postponement in January 1993 was done presumably due to inflamed passions in Bangladesh where some fundamentalist outfits declared that they would resort to a 'Long March' and vowed to transgress into the Indian territory to construct the demolished Masjid at its original site.[42] There was also an assessment that the security situation in Bangladesh was not safe for the Indian Prime Minister to participate in the SAARC Summit.

The second postponement of the Seventh SAARC Summit led to widespread reports in the media casting doubts on the future of the association. One report noted:

> The South Asian association for regional cooperation appears to have been struck by the proverbial seven-year itch with the second postponement of the ill fated seventh summit, which was to be held at Dhaka, putting the very future of the seven nation alliance in jeopardy.
>
> While the postponement of the Summit per se would not have caused much worry except for a delay in implementation of the SAARC agenda, what is of concern is the acrimonious exchanges among the big three—India, Pakistan and Bangladesh—with the continued political exploitation of the

situation after the demolition of the Babri structure at Ayodhya on December 6.[43]

India blamed Pakistan and Bangladesh of interfering in her internal affairs while the two countries did not loose any opportunity to utilize the situation to their advantage. The Indian Prime Minister late Indira Gandhi in 1983 while inaugurating SAARC Foreign Ministers' meeting had obliquely referred to the ethnic conflict in Sri Lanka and asserted that 'it would be idle to pretend that we are not affected by what happens elsewhere'.[44] An Indian analyst drawing an analogy to this 'Indira doctrine' observed that Pakistan and Bangladesh appeared to be invoking a politically perverse version of this doctrine. He observed:

> ... the Indira doctrine is now being applied in a rather perverse fashion by Pakistan and Bangladesh. Their apparent aim is to interfere in India's internal affairs. Both these countries have, in effect, claimed that they cannot pretend that they are not "affected by what happens elsewhere". In fact, it requires no great intelligence to recognize that Islamabad and Dhaka are capitalizing on the tragic events in Ayodhya-the destruction of Babri Masjid.[45]

In a forthright assessment of India's failure to handle the fallout of the communal events on SAARC, Professor S.D. Muni blamed India for lacking diplomatic maturity and courage to face criticism from neighbours and demonstrating a panic-stricken aggressiveness in getting the summit postponed twice.[46] In this process India seemed to have played into the hands of fundamentalist forces in the subcontinent. However, these forces do not enjoy mass support in any country in the region. The orchestrated communal frenzy soon died down and the summit could be held in Dhaka in April 1993. However these events underlined the fragile nature of regional cooperation process in the absence of a political design to bring in harmony in the region.

Seventh Summit—Dhaka, 1993

The demise of the cold war and the Super-Power rivalry between the United States and erstwhile Soviet Union not only changed the basic political context of the international relations but also witnessed, simultaneous emergence of significant regional economic integration across the globe.[47] The Western Europe consolidated its economic integration by establishing a single common market and European Union (EU) in 1992/93; the United States along with Canada and Mexico created a North American Free Trade Area (NAFTA)— the US-Canada free trade area was earlier founded in 1988; Argentina, Brazil, Chile, Paraguay and Uruguay in 1991 came together in 1991 as MERCOSUR to set up a common market by 1995; the successful regional Association of South East Asian Countries (ASEAN) agreed to create a free trade area; a new type of inter-bloc regional cooperative arrangement emerged to link the Asian and NAFTA regions on the Pacific Rim with the formation of Asia Pacific Economic Forum (APEC) with the objective of promoting GATT-consistent trade liberalisation.

The Indian Prime Minister, Narasimha Rao, in his address to the Seventh SAARC Summit voiced India's anxiety and willingness to adapt to the emerging political and economic landscape of the post-cold war world. He said:

> ...qualitative changes have taken place in the world around us in the last few years. These have inevitably affected our region. All of us have to adjust to transformed equations in terms of economic influence, political and military power and strategic perceptions which have emerged with the disappearance of Super Power competition and monolithic ideological confrontations... We are witness to an international situation subject to contradictory trends of centripetal and centrifugal forces at work. While established political entities and plural societies have disintegrated, there are emerging patterns of socioeconomic integration between Nation States underpinned by a unilinear structuring of global economy.
>
> Our Association must, therefore, evolve meaningful policy approaches to deal with the world wide trends in regional cooperation, economic groupings and trading blocs as witnessed in Western Europe, North and South America, ASEAN and the Asia-Pacific region.'[48]

The Indian Prime Minister also noted the slow growth of SAARC process and explained reasons for such slow growth to emphasise Indian policy of keeping out bilateral disputes for the sake of purposeful cooperation among member countries. He maintained:

> This Summit marks the beginning of the second cycle of Summit meetings of our region. This is a watershed that merits introspection. Introspection leads me to the conclusion that the

content and range of cooperation within the SAARC region has been slower than what we wished for. The reasons are the geo-demographic disparity amongst member countries and inhibitions born of problems inherited from the past. We cannot wish these away. But, we certainly can abide by the stipulation in the SAARC Charter by setting aside issues on which there are differences of opinion, issues which are essentially bilateral. We must purposefully forge cooperation in areas of common interest and which are of more profound relevance to the well being of our peoples.[49]

The Summit Declaration

This summit marked the beginning of the economic cooperation by accepting the framework of agreement on preferential trade among the SAARC Member Countries.[50] The Summit took note of the steps taken to consolidate and streamline the activities under IPA. The need for undertaking more well defined, target oriented and time bound programmes to ensure tangible benefits for the peoples of South Asia was emphasised. The report of the Independent South Asian Commission on Poverty Alleviation (ISACPA) established at the Colombo Summit, was accepted. This report provided examples of successful poverty alleviation programmes in individual member states. An agenda for Action for eradication of poverty by 2002 AD was finalised.

The finalised framework of Agreement on SAPTA was accepted by the Summit and it was stressed that all necessary steps should be taken to begin the first round of trade negotiations to exchange trade preferences among Member-States under the Arrangement.

The progress in the areas of environment, shelter-population, children, terrorism, drug trafficking, drug abuse, etc., was noted. The summit leaders expressed their satisfaction over the adoption of a common position by Member States prior to the United Nations Conference on Environment and Development.

It was hoped that the recognition of the SAARC Chamber of Commerce and Industry would contribute to enhancing cooperation in trade and economic relations [51] ; and the formation of the Association of SAARC Speakers and Parliamentarians would contribute to regional cooperation.

It was decided to establish an Inter-Government Group (IGG) on the SADF. The IGG was required to spell out the size, structure, resources and operational modalities of the proposed fund.

The Summit held wide-ranging discussion on the current global political trends and future prospects, particularly those issues that affect South Asia. In this context, a deep commitment to the purposes and principles of the UN charter was reiterated and a resolve to strengthen the UN as a central instrument for peace, security, disarmament, development and cooperation among the nations of the world, was reaffirmed.

The leaders stressed the need to develop a common South Asian perspective on the issue to be discussed in the Second World Conference on Human Rights in 1993, the World Population Conference in 1994 and 1995 World Conference on Women.

The vital importance of economic interdependence among nations and of the need for reviving North-South dialogue were reiterated. The importance of a strengthened and liberalized international trading system was underlined. It was, therefore, noted that the successful conclusion of the Uruguay Round of Multi-lateral Trade Negotiations was a matter of great importance to developing countries.[52]

Eighth Summit—New Delhi, 1995

The heads of State/Government of SAARC countries held the Eighth Summit Meeting in May, 1995 in New Delhi after the successful conclusion of the Uruguay Round of multilateral trade negotiations and the creation of World Trade Organisation (WTO). The forces of global economy and a radically changed international situation was thus taking shape. India not only pointed out the challenges and opportunities inherent in the emerging global system but also found the SAARC environment conducive to drive home the inevitability and necessity of forging regional economic identity for SAARC.[53]

Indian policy and approach were echoed by her Prime Minister at the Eighth Summit Meeting when he said:

> ...Collective self interest has been the fundamental basis of regional cooperation all over the world. Those regional groupings that have succeeded have opened doors to free flow of goods, services, capital and people. This is also the route we have to adopt.

> The external economic environment continues to be unfavourable for developing countries...the international trading system is coalescing into powerful regional trading and economic coalitions involving major economies. The successful conclusion of the Uruguay Round of multilateral trade negotiations and establishment of WTO hold forth great challenges for us but some opportunities as well. We can respond effectively to these global factors regionally, if we make preferential trading arrangements among ourselves and enhance our collective strength internationally.
>
> ...Given the unprecedented changes taking place at the global level, the imperative to bring SAPTA into operation assumes greater dimension. It is heartening that we have taken the first step in this direction by signing the SAARC Preferential Trading Arrangement at the last Summit in Dhaka. The Inter-Governmental Group has met several times and carried forward the negotiations to finalise trade concessions. It is essential for us to provide political impetus to effectively bring SAPTA into the operation by the end of this year as agreed to at the Dhaka Summit. [54]

The Summit Declaration

The Summit endorsed a proposal to convene a commemorative session of the Council of Ministers on the theme 'SAARC - Vision for the Second Decade' to identify the areas on which SAARC should focus. There was an agreement to set up a mechanism for exchange of information on poverty eradication programmes, particularly exchange of information on technologies that are relevant to efforts aimed at poverty eradication. It was decided to observe 1995 as the 'SAARC Year of Poverty Eradication'. The Summit leaders committed themselves to addressing the fundamental causes of poverty and to provide for the basic needs of all. They reaffirmed their commitment to work for guaranteeing the realisation of the rights of all, in particular those of the poor, to food, work, shelter, health, education resources and information.

The Heads of State/Government noted with satisfaction that the first round of trade negotiations to exchange trade concessions among Member-States under SAPTA was complete. They directed that all necessary steps be taken to facilitate ratification by all Member-States and operationalised SAPTA by the end of 1995 as mandated.[55]

It was noted that the SAARC Documentation Centre (SDC) at New Delhi and the SAARC Meteorological Research Centre (SMRC) at Dhaka were established in May 1994 and January 1995 respectively. The Summit leaders also noted the progress on issues of women in development, children, youth, persons with disability, shelter, literacy, environment, terrorism, drug trafficking etc. and decided to observe 1996 as the 'SAARC Year of Literacy'. The ratification of the SAARC Convention on Narcotic Drugs and Psychotropic Substances by all Member States and its entry into force in September 1993 was welcomed.

The Summit leaders hoped that SAARC LAW—an association for the legal communities of SAARC Member Countries accorded recognition by SAARC—would play an effective role in fostering closer cooperation among the legal communities of the region. SAARC Chamber of Commerce and Industry (SCCI) was commended for disseminating information on SAPTA.

The establishment of a three window South Asian Development Fund (SADF) with merger of the SAARC Fund for Regional Projects, the SAARC Regional Fund and a third fund for social and infrastructure development, was endorsed.

It was noted with satisfaction that the collective position of the SAARC countries was formulated and presented at the World Conference on Natural Disaster Reduction and the World Summit for Social Development. However, the Summit expressed deep concern at the unabated degradation of the environment and recurrence of devastating natural disasters.

The Member-States welcomed the establishment of World Trade organisation (WTO) and reaffirmed their commitment to implement fully the Final Act of the Uruguay Round of multilateral trade negotiations.[56]

Ninth Summit— Male, 1997

The operationalisation of preferential trade arrangement among SAARC Member Countries and rapid progress in regional cooperation and economic integration world over, emboldened India to make an ambitious bid to push SAARC process further.

The Indian Prime Minister Inder Kumar Gujral with his positive approach[57] towards bilateral relations with India's neighbours exhorted the leaders of SAARC in his inaugural address to the Ninth SAARC Summit at Male in 1997. He said:

> Economic cooperation has received the focus it deserves in recent years and is making rapid progress. The third round of SAPTA will be launched shortly and will further accelerate the pace of trade liberalisation in the region. However, tariff concessions have to be deepened and extended to cover all product lines and accompanied by dismantling of non-tariff barriers, so that the objective of South Asian Free Trade Area (SAFTA) by the turn of the century or very shortly thereafter, to which we are pledged, is achieved.[58]

Expressing satisfaction at the wide ranging canvas of economic cooperation the Indian PM painted an ambitious vision of a South Asian Economic Community when he said:

> The canvas of our economic cooperation is now wide ranging, covering areas such as investment promotion and protection, avoidance of double taxation, harmonisation in customs procedure and documentation, upgradation and co-ordination of standards and modalities of smooth arbitration, to name but a few. In fact, given the momentum of global economic activity and the dramatic advances which other regions have made, our vision for South Asia should reach beyond SAFTA into the contours of a South Asian Economic Community (SAEC). This project would cover crucial issues vital for our shared economic future, such as a regional investment regime, export-oriented joint ventures, easy movement of goods and capital, enhancement of our export potential by raising quality standards, and expanded regional market, human resource and skills development, scientific and technological cooperation, upgrading and augmenting of regional infrastructure, regional diffusion of financial and other services—in short the harmonisation of the economic life of the region as a whole for our common benefit.[59]

The Summit Declaration

The Summit leaders significantly decided to make a comprehensive appraisal of SAARC to further enhance the effectiveness of the Association. This Summit is considered a major milestone in evolution of regional cooperation in South Asia. Some important decisions on economic matters were taken and it was decided to set up a 'Group of Eminent Persons' to make a comprehensive appraisal of SAARC.

The Summit decided to advance the date of realizing SAARC Free Trade Area (SAFTA) by four years to 2001. Further, cooperation was initiated in the area of trade facilitation; finalisation of a Customs Action Plan was sought; proposals for a Regional Investment Treaty and a SAARC Arbitration Council were initiated; the economic agenda also included discussions for avoidance of double taxation.

The Summit directed that a Group of Eminent Persons (GEP) be constituted comprising of one representative from each Member State and SAARC Secretary General as an invitee, to undertake a comprehensive appraisal of SAARC, identify measures including mechanisms to further vitalize and enhance the effectiveness of the Association in achieving its objectives, and to develop a long range vision and formulate a perspective plan of action including a SAARC Agenda for 2000 and beyond.[60]

The social agenda received considerable attention as usual and new areas were included. Poverty eradication remained a priority sector with a focused Agenda of Action.

The year 1997 was designated as the 'SAARC Year of Participatory Governance'.

An Environment Action Plan providing for the preparation of a SAARC State of the Environment Report to monitor and share environment data and regional capacity building through cooperation in training was finalised.[61]

Tenth Summit—Colombo, 1998

The Tenth SAARC Summit was held at Colombo, Sri Lanka in July 1998 after India and Pakistan conducted nuclear tests and declared themselves as nuclear powers. This was a very significant development in South Asia which attracted global attention and the major Western powers imposed sanctions on India and Pakistan. Serious doubts were expressed on the smooth continuation of the SAARC process in the wake of overt nuclearisation of South Asia. The informal bilateral meeting between the Prime Ministers of India and Pakistan on the sidelines of SAARC Summit acquired a great deal of political significance.[62] However, the SAARC Summit went ahead with its usual business.

The East Asian Financial Crisis

The Tenth SAARC Summit met against the backdrop of a severe financial crisis that affected the newly industrializing countries (NICs) of East Asia.[63] These countries had an extraordinary record of sustained high growth over a long period of time. The increase in the standard of living and reduction in the number of people living below poverty line during the three decades before the crisis of 1997 was considered unparalleled in these countries.

The Latin American countries after experiencing fast growth during 1950-1980 suffered serious debt burden but the NICs continued their march to economic progress during 80s and 90s. The proponents of neo-liberal economics and international financial institutions extolled these economies as model for the rest of the developing world to follow. These countries had also been receiving huge private capital inflows during 1990s. Despite claims of strong 'fundamentals' and expansion of economies at a rate almost three times the world average, these countries suffered a serious financial crisis which experts maintain has damaged their real economy.

The crisis began with the devaluation of Thai Baht in July 1997 and engulfed Malaysia, Indonesia, South Korea and the Philippines whose currencies suffered huge devaluation together with plunging of stock markets. The IMF estimates that between 1994-1996 foreign private capital inflows to the five most affected countries (Indonesia, Korea, Malaysia, the Philippines and Thailand) increased from US$ 40 billion in 1994 to US$ 107 billion amounting to 10 per cent of the GDP of these countries.[64] While the economists differ on the reasons that caused this crisis, but, one important, definite factor leading to this grave situation was extensive capital account liberalization introduced by these countries in recent years. Before this liberalisation the governments of these countries maintained controls over the borrowing and lending activities of the banks and investment activities of the corporate sector.

The East Asian financial crisis did not seriously affect economies in South Asia as apprehended. India, in particular, maintained macro-economic stability since government controls over capital inflows and outflows existed. Any speculative attacks on the currencies of South Asian countries could be controlled on account of government controls in the financial sector.[65]

The relative stability of Indian financial sector in the wake of East Asian crisis made India a more attractive destination of the international financial institutions and Western governments.[66] It also reminded South Asia that the onward march of globalization is not an unqualified blessing for the developing countries. Some experts deduced relevant lessons for South Asia:

(i) Trade liberalisation is good for an economy but financial liberalisation should only be undertaken cautiously and after proper sequencing;

(ii) If 'hot flows' of capital are to be allowed, they should be monitored carefully and managed properly;

(iii) The exchange rate system whether fixed or flexible should reflect the economic fundamentals of the country;

(iv) Transparency, absence of politicisation and prudential regulation must exist in the financial sector;

(v) Proper data reporting is a must— if only to accurately assess the financial state of the economy;

(vi) Industrialisation should be diversified, decentralised and rural oriented, not urban concentrated;

(vii) An active and free domestic media is a necessity.[67]

The Indian Prime Minister referred to the East Asian crisis in his address to the Tenth SAARC Summit and hinted at appropriate SAARC response when he said:

> ...The financial crisis in many countries including in East Asia has exposed the vulnerability of even relatively dynamic developing economies as well as the weakness of the international monetary and financial system to cope with the strains of global financial liberalisation. There is need for SAARC countries to identify, understand and face up to these challenges. We have so far, not had to face similar difficulties in South Asia. We need to identify the strengths and weaknesses of our structures and policies, so as to make sure that we are able to avoid the difficulties, while taking full advantage of the globalization and liberalisation that we are determined to follow.[68]

The Indian Prime Minister reiterated commitment of his country to the on going efforts to economic cooperation in the form of SAPTA and to the goal of SAFTA and a South Asian Economic Community.[69] He alluded to the apprehensions expressed on account of Indo-Pak nuclear tests before the Summit Meeting and took this opportunity to assert once again the Indian policy to promote socio-economic cooperation with a view to ultimately smoothen bilateral political relations among the SAARC countries. He said:

> Apprehensions have been expressed in some quarters that recent developments in South Asia could cause a set back to the SAARC process. Let me say that these apprehensions are misplaced. SAARC cooperation is driven by the imperative need for all South Asian countries to accelerate socio-economic development, reduce and eradicate poverty and to enhance the quality of life of their peoples. It is in recognition of this that the founding fathers of SAARC took a conscious decision not to burden it with bilateral concerns, many of which existed even then, and to keep contentious issues out of SAARC...At the same time we have every reason to hope that building a positive frame work of cooperation in our region will have a beneficial effect on bilateral relations....[70]

Recalling the glorious South Asian past of the struggle for independence, the Indian Prime Minister called for a break from the past fifty years after independence to declare our interdependence and our essential oneness even as there are diversities among South Asian nations.[71] He concluded his address with a very meaningful food for thought when he said:

- enough of sterile ideology,
- enough of hostile nationalism,
- enough of conflict on the basis of religion and creed,
- enough of poverty and backwardness, let us grow rich to gether.[72]

The Summit Declaration

The Tenth Summit, also known as the economic summit of SAARC discussed a wide-range of issues including the position of SAARC in the changing international economic environment.[73] The Summit also dwelt at length on the regional economic agenda and as usual reviewed progress of social issues in IPA. Significantly, the Heads of State/Government while reiterating their commitment to the promotion of mutual trust and understanding agreed that a process of informal political consultations would prove useful to promote peace, stability, amity and accelerated socio-economic cooperation.

It was recognised that South Asia with a rich, complex and varied plurality of cultural and religious traditions, was heir to a profound civilisational continuum of great antiquity which constitutes a historical basis for sustaining harmonious relations among people of the region.

The Council of Ministers were directed to examine the Report of the Group of Eminent Persons with regard to the viability of its recommendations and their implementation.

It was mentioned that the SAARC Member Countries would endeavour to coordinate their decisions in respect of the series of meetings to be organised by the WTO.[74]

The Summit welcomed the declaration issued by the SAARC Commerce Ministers on the eve of the second WTO Multilateral Meeting in Geneva setting out a SAARC approach on the issues. It was noted that emerging issues related to copyright, patents and marketing franchise, including on food grains, plants and herbs indigenous to South Asia, require firm collective responses to preserve these bio-resources from unregulated commercial exploitation by extra-regional interests. The need to enhance the collective capacity of SAARC in respect of policy analysis, with specific emphasis on international financial, monetary, trade and investment issues and their domestic ramifications was stressed.

The importance of achieving SAARC Free Trade Area (SAFTA) as mandated by the ninth Summit was reiterated. The Summit directed that a comprehensive treaty regime for creating a free trade area be drafted.

The Summit also welcomed the contribution made by the SAARC Chamber of Commerce and Industry in facilitating the engagement of the private sector in regional economic interaction. A document entitled 'Road Map to SAFTA' was presented by the President of the SCCI to the Chairperson of the Twentieth Session of the Council of Ministers. The Summit took note of this document.[75]

The development of specific projects relevant to the individual needs of three or more Member States under the provisions of the SAARC Charter was encouraged with a view to enhance sub-regional cooperation.

Integrated Programme of Action(IPA): Current Status

The SAARC summit deliberations underline slow progress in

core-areas of cooperation. The activities covered by the IPA, however, continued to dominate proceedings of SAARC. Initially there were 9 Technical Committees (TCs) to pursue activities of IPA. These were expanded to 12 and later amalgamated into eleven Committees. Following a review of the functioning of the Technical Committees, the Council of Ministers at their meeting in Nuwara Eliya in March 1999 decided that the existing eleven committees should be replaced by the seven new Committees.[76] Under this new arrangement several areas of cooperation have been put together to be tackled in one committee. Thus Agriculture and Rural Development; Transport and Communications; Forestry, Environment and Meteorology; Women, Children, Health and Population have been put together under four different committees. The Technical Committee on Science and Technology has been retained as such and two more committees, one for Human Resources Development and the other on Energy have been established.[77]

There has been no independent assessment of IPA activities except two meetings of the Chairmen of the Technical Committees (MCTC) and routine review by the SAARC Secretary General. Mahendra P.Lama has noted certain trends, constraints and drawbacks in the working of IPA as indicated below:

- Technical Committees have failed to concentrate on real critical priority areas and to engage/motivate NGOs, experts, professionals and the real beneficiaries in the interactive process.
- The activities have not been sustained in a meaningful manner.
- There is lack of co-ordination and harmonization among various TCs.
- Resource crunch, lack of inter-sectoral coordination and non-implementation of decisions are major constraints. Several important joint projects including income-generating projects did not materialise due to lack of funds.[78] Table 5.1 gives the details of the commitment of funds by the SAARC Member Countries for SAARC activities.

TABLE 5.1 COMMITMENT OF FUNDS BY MEMBER STATES FOR SAARC ACTIVITIES[79]

Country	*1990-91*	*1998-99*
Bangladesh	Tk.7 m	Tk. 7 m
Bhutan	NU.2 m	Nu. 2 m
India	IRs.20 m	IRs.25 m
Maldives	Rf. 1 m	Rf. 1.5 m
Nepal	NRs. 7 m	NRs. 7 m
Pakistan	PRs. 21 m	PRs. 22 m
Sri Lanka	SRs. 5 m	SRs. 6 m

Economic Cooperation

SAARC Preferential Trade Arrangement (SAPTA)

The preferential system in intra-regional trade in the form of SAPTA entered into force in 1995 - significantly this was two years ahead of schedule as envisaged.[80] As already noted, by this time almost all SAARC countries had embarked on a programme of economic liberalisation which included trade liberalisation. Thus, reduction in tariffs, phasing out quantitative restrictions and subsidies were on regional agenda.

The commencement of SAPTA is an important landmark in SAARC calender. This was not only the first step in economic cooperation but also towards cooperation in 'core' areas. The provisions of the Arrangement provide for preferences to contracting parties through reduction in tariffs, non-tariff barriers (NTBs) and direct trade measures; and for safeguard measures in respect of balance of payments and for Least Developed Countries (LDCs) among Member-States etc. SAPTA also stipulates the most favoured nation status principle, which implies that any concessions given by one member to another has to be extended unconditionally to all other members (except preferences extended to LDCs).[81]

In the first round of preferential tariffs under SAPTA 226 items (100 for LDCs) were covered. The maximum number of concessions (106) were offered by India. These products resulted in trade liberalisation of only 6 percent of intra-regional trade.[82] However, a large number of products offered for concession by the Member States were not imported at all from the region.

The second round (SAPTA-II) resulted in a much wider

exchange of concessions - as many as 2013 products. This round was finalised to enter into force by March 1, 1997. Table 5.2 gives the number of products offered for concession for member countries of the SAARC under SAPTA II.

TABLE 5.2 NUMBER OF PRODUCTS OFFERED CONCESSION UNDER SAPTA-II[83]

Favouring/ Offered	*Bangla desh*	*Bhutan*	*India*	*Maldives*	*Nepal*	*Pakistan*	*Sri Lanka*	*Total*
Bangladesh	—	2	222	2	26	13	7	272
Bhutan	1	—	—	—	10	33	3	47
India	513	—	—	1	—	375	22	911
Maldives	3	9	—	—	3	—	2	17
Nepal	41	38	—	12	—	172	14	277
Pakistan	26	10	230	—	99	—	21	386
Sri Lanka	16	4	22	3	14	53	—	112
Total	600	54	474	18	152	646	69	2013

In the third round, concluded on November 23, 1998, SAPTA covered a total of 3456 tariff lines. The cumulative tariff lines offered country wise are given in Table 5.3.

TABLE 5.3 SAPTA -III NOVEMBER 1998[84]

Country	*Number of tariff lines offered for concession*
India	1,917
Bangladesh	481
Pakistan	295
Sri Lanka	82
Nepal	189
Bhutan	124
Maldives	368

The share of intra-SAARC exports in total SAARC exports increased from 3.2 per cent in 1990 to 4.7 per cent in 1999. The share of intra-SAARC imports like wise have shown an increase from 1.91 per cent to 4.25 per cent during 1990-1996.[85] The intra-regional exports, however, are the lowest share in SAARC among the major regional groupings in the world as shown in the Table 5.4.

TABLE 5.4 EXPORTS WITHIN GROUPINGS[86]

Exports within Regional Economic Groupings (% of Total Exports)				
Regions	*1980*	*1990*	*1996*	*1999*
NAFTA	33.6	41.4	47.5	54.6
EU	61.0	66.0	61.5	62.6
MERCOSUR	11.6	8.9	22.8	20.5
ASEAN	16.9	18.7	23.2	22.2
SAARC	4.8	3.2	4.3	4.7

Maldives' share of increase in the proportion of exports is the highest (29.46 per cent), followed by Nepal (10.98 per cent) and India (5.10 per cent).

Reports based on tripartite study undertaken by the Business, Academia and Government (BAG) groups in SAARC Member Countries indicate that the obstacles to intra-SAARC trade are weak transport infrastructure, cumbersome documentation procedures, differing product standards and quality control measures, lack of transit facilities, differences in custom valuation methods, lack of trade information about Member States.[87] The coverage of goods under SAPTA is limited and the smaller Member-States feel that trade itself will not bring prosperity unless it is accompanied by investments in industrial sector.[88]

SAARC Free Trade Area(SAFTA)

The transition from preferential trade arrangement (SAPTA) to a free trade area is already on the SAARC agenda. The Fourth Round of preferential trade arrangement is expected to focus on SAFTA. However, this process has virtually been withheld by the political stalemate on Eleventh SAARC Summit. The responsibility for negotiating the new agreement or treaty has been given to an Inter Government Expert Group (IGEG). This Group held its meeting in June 1997. The terms of reference and an action plan for transition from SAPTA to SAFTA were discussed and the Tenth SAARC Summit in Colombo (1998) decided to set up a Group of Experts to commence negotiations on SAFTA. This group is required to spell out binding schedules for freeing trade—this is expected to be put in place by 2001.[89]

Indo-Sri Lanka Free Trade Agreement

In the Tenth SAARC Summit itself, India announced that it was ready to enter into bilateral free trade agreements with each of the countries individually, if regional arrangement is difficult to finalise. Accordingly during Sri Lankan President's visit to India in December 1998, the two countries concluded a Free Trade Agreement (FTA).[90] However, the FTA negotiations have been painfully slow. Sri Lanka in mid-February 2000 announced implementation of the Free Trade Agreement after including all agricultural products, fisheries and livestock products among the 1200 items on its negative list. The Sri Lankan President while presenting the year 2000-2001 budget as Finance Minister was reported to have said[91] that the agreement would provide considerable benefits to the country's economy; the inflow of Indian raw materials on duty-free basis would assist Sri Lankan industries to reduce cost and increase profitability; and preferential access to Sri Lankan exports, including tea and garments in the Indian market would enable Sri Lanka to attract foreign investments, increase economic activities and generate employment.[92]

Expressing optimism the Chairman of Sri Lanka Board of Investment, Thilan Wijesinghe stated that the Sri Lankan exports which were estimated to be at $27 millions in 1998 could touch at least $150 millions in three years and that these could be further increased if private sector showed appropriate dynamism and Sri Lanka attract higher foreign investment to access Indian market.[93] An advantageous feature of the Agreement for Sri Lanka is that while India would increase the items not covered in the agreement over a period of three years, Sri Lanka would do so over a period of eight years. Some economists[94] and a section of the press[95] in Sri Lanka, however, expressed reservations about this agreement. Dr J.B Kelegama argued that the heavy imbalance of Indo-Sri Lankan trade in favour of India would continue and was unlikely to boost Sri Lanka's exports to India. On the other hand, he felt, that Indian imports would flood Sri Lanka - particularly in respect of agricultural products which would be disastrous for local farmers. He argued:

> It is not so much trade barriers that prevents an expansion of trade with India but the inability of Sri Lanka to produce goods that are in demand in India...
>
> The export production structure in Sri Lanka like most other ex-colonies is geared to meet the demands of developed countries whether it is agricultural production of tea, rubber, coconut and spices or industrial production like garments, jewellery and leather products and components of electronic machines...

> The obsession with Indian market may make us lose our perspective and result in complacency regarding larger and growing markets. What we need are larger and growing markets for our exports; whether they are in India or elsewhere does not matter for we want expansion of our exports and not diversion.[96]

Following Sri Lanka, Indian Finance Minister in his budget presentation before Parliament in February 2000 announced implementation of Indo-Sri Lankan FTA with certain conditions.[97] The concessions are subject to rules of origin restrictions which require manufacture in Sri Lanka. This is defined according to the substantial transformation rule which requires that the heading must change in the country of export for origin to be established.[98]

The notification issued by the Government of India divides the goods in the customs tariff into four categories:

(i) The first category consists of two lists on which the rates of exemptions per cent of the applied rates vary from 25 to 100 per cent.

(ii) The second category is the tariff rate quota (TRQ) lists covering apparel and garments which are otherwise eligible for 50 per cent duty concession.

(iii) The third category is that of the residual list arrived by the subtracting the first two categories from the universe of the goods under customs tariff other than the negative list.

(iv) The negative list excluded from the scope of the concessions. Prominent inclusions in the negative list are coconut, copra, onion, garlic, spices other than cloves and seeds.[99]

While there were adverse initial reactions to the agreement from the local Indian industry, it was nevertheless realised that the 'big brother' India should take the first steps and open her markets gracefully. India's Commerce Secretary, Prabir Sengupta in a seminar on India-Sri Lanka FTA organized by Federation of Indian Chambers of Commerce and Industry (FICCI) in association with the Ministry of Commerce, Government of India in November 2000, observed:

> The Indo-Sri Lanka Free Trade Agreement (FTA) will boost bilateral trade and consolidate the close economic, commercial

and political relations between the two countries through increased trade and investment.

Over 50 per cent of the Indian joint venture companies and wholly owned subsidiaries in the SAARC region are in Sri Lanka. The FTA would now give impetus for sourcing and buyback from Sri Lanka.[100]

Sri Lankan Foreign Minister Lakshman Kadirgamar in an interview published in an Indian fortnightly magazine in April 2001 expressed his satisfaction on the implementation of India-Sri Lanka FTA. He said:

> ...There are some procedural problems. I would say nothing more than that. Not conceptual problems. There are always procedural problems when you are implementing a new agreement, which is barely a year old in its final form. So it was agreed that we would bring to the notice of Indian Government whatever points we felt ought to be ironed out. And the response was fully cooperative.[101]

There are differing perceptions among the observers of SAARC as to the efficacy of such bilateral arrangements outside the scope of SAFTA.

Eleventh Summit Overdue

A perusal of the Summit process above would indicate intensive official activity to further institutionalize regional cooperation and vigorously pursue core economic and social agenda of regional integration. The bilateral political disputes, however, continue to bedevil the SAARC.

The eleventh Summit scheduled to be held in Nepal in the second half of 1999 had to be postponed in the aftermath of Kargil conflict between India and Pakistan and revival of military regime in Pakistan. India seems to have expressed strong reservations against participation of an 'illegitimate' military regime in the deliberations of SAARC Summit.[102] The Dhaka Summit of 1993 was also under cloud when the Indian Prime Minister had refused to participate in the Summit on account of adverse spillover of the demolition of Babri Masjid in India. The events leading to the postponement of eleventh SAARC Summit are yet another reminder that the political and security considerations cannot be ignored in regional integration process.

There is some ray of hope for resumption of pre-Summit process with the reported relaxation in Indian position on the participation of Pakistan's military regime in SAARC. A well known commentator on South Asian affairs K.K. Katyal in May 2001 noted:

> India does not intend vetoing the move for the SAARC summit nor is averse to the use of that opportunity for top-level contacts with Pakistan....
>
> New Delhi is, thus, prepared to let the SAARC process, beginning with next month's meeting of the Foreign Secretaries, take its course. This means, it is agreeable to the next two higher-level contacts—the meeting of the Foreign Ministers and then the Summit.[103]

The reasons for slow progress of SAARC are primarily a lack of favourable political context which cannot be achieved without a serious effort by all the member countries to resolve major inter-state conflicts, and failure to evolve a shared regional strategic approach towards international politics. In the absence of a conducive politico-strategic framework, there are serious limitations on achieving SAARC objectives on social and economic cooperation. India's policy so far has failed to make any significant impact on the set pattern of her uneasy relationship with the neighbours. The relevance of SAARC is, therefore, seen to be almost negligible by some observers:

> ... its very structure as an inter-government body renders it largely incapable of new thinking and new direction. It merely embodies the existing relationship of forces between member countries and the various inter-state tensions. The primary merit of SAARC meetings is that it provides for regular discussion of inter- member problems and to that extent can help occasionally to lessen tensions....[104]

While India needs to be more magnanimous, other member states should also be more realistic in their inter-state relations if SAARC is to make progress and transform itself into a genuine forum for regional development.

Conclusion

To sum up, the end of cold war generated a conducive climate for Indian policy objectives in South Asia. Détente among big powers leading to less intrusive behaviour of extra-regional powers in South Asia, emergence of economic ideology of North as the prime-moving force in international relations, setting up of World Trade Organisation prescribing rules of international trade and economic interaction in accordance with the neo-liberal ideology of the North and democratisation of South Asia - all this provided an altogether new context for Indian policy in the region. India reiterated its policy with renewed emphasis on collective economic security in South Asia.

The Indian belief was that the enhanced economic cooperation among SAARC member countries would generate confidence and closer cooperation which would in turn bring non-economic benefits for the region. The long term objective of India in favour of free movement of goods, capital and people throughout SAARC region was declared by the Indian Prime Minister Narasimha Rao in the Sixth SAARC Summit at Colombo.

The world-wide wave of regional cooperative arrangements like EU, NAFTA, MERCOSUR, declaration on ASEAN Free Trade Area, APEC etc. provided a compelling force to the Indian initiative for greater economic cooperation in the region. With her new economic policy in favour of market-friendly reforms India argued for adjusting to the emerging political and economic landscape of the post-cold war world. Sensing an ideal opportunity, India also pushed for building regional consensus on international forums including on vital economic issues affecting North-South relations.

The chinks in India's regional policy armour were, however, evident in her mishandling of the fallout of the demolition of a mosque structure in 1993. India's insistence on postponement of Dhaka Summit twice provided an opportunity to the communal elements in the region to capitalise on divisive sentiments and make efforts to derail the regional agenda. Indian policy, however, survived this crisis. The fact that initiative for setting up a South Asian Development Fund (SADF) came from Bhutan and the proposal for SAPTA was made by Sri Lanka only underlined the success of Indian perseverance in promoting regional peace and harmony through greater economic cooperation. In an assessment of Indian policy S.D. Muni in 1993 noted:

> ...Through slow and persistent efforts, South Asian countries are coming round to the view that trade and development cooperation must get priority in SAARC activities. This is evident from the broad consensus on South Asian

Preferential Trading Arrangement (SAPTA), setting up of a regional development Fund, increasing interaction among the Chambers of Commerce and Industry of the member countries and programmes for poverty alleviation.[105]

Muni, however, also noted two divergent perspectives on SAARC in Indian foreign service bureaucracy. On these perspectives he observed:

> ...One inclined to build SAARC as a multilateral instrument of harnessing the cooperative potential of the region in socio-cultural and economic fields. This in turn could moderate political and strategic divergences among the member countries and improve climate for bilateral interactions as well. The other perspective is based upon the assumption that SAARC needs India more than India needs SAARC, because the best way for India to interact with its neighbours is through the bilateral channel....[106]

The ultimate Indian policy, it seems, is a mix of these two contending perspectives and her regional policy postures are formulated in accordance with the ascendant perspective of the time.

In the post-cold war globalized context India's policy also underlined the inevitability and necessity of SAARC acquiring a regional economic identity. India's new found significance in the wake of East Asian financial crisis of 1997 also enabled her to convincingly push for an ambitious agenda of the future to evolve South Asia into an Economic Community. The Indian emphasis on taking full advantage of the process of globalization and liberalisation was sharply underlined by the call made by the Indian Prime Minister Atal Bihari Vajpayee at the Tenth SAARC Summit in 1998 for shedding sterile ideology, hostile nationalism and conflicts of the past to fight poverty and backwardness in the region. India, however, failed to convince Pakistan ruling establishment of the economic logic of regional cooperation. Pakistan, it seems, is paranoid about India benefiting the most from regional cooperation and in the process emerging as a regional hegemon. The Indian regional policy in the post-cold war phase, nevertheless, can be adjudged as modestly successful since it helped in crafting and firmly putting in place an ambitious economic agenda of the future for South Asia.

REFERENCES

1. The occupation of Afghanistan by Soviet Union unleashed a new phase of fierce East-West cold war which finally culminated in the withdrawal of Soviet forces from Afghanistan and eventual emergence of religious fanaticism in Pakistan-Afghanistan belt. In fact, South Asia is still suffering the consequences of religious fundamentalism which emerged in reaction to Soviet occupation of Afghanistan in the form of narco-terrorism and mercenary Islamic fundamentalism. The West after tacit approval and support to these forces during Soviet presence in Afghanistan, is now realising that these forces pose a grave threat to peace and stability after they spread their tentacles far and wide in other parts of the world; For details on second cold war see, Katherine A.S. Sibley, The Cold War, London, 1998; Also S.N. Misra, *India: The Cold War Years*, New Delhi, 1994.

2. For details see Gills Boquerat and Indra Nath Mukherji, *SAARC : Economic and Political Atlas*, Pondy Paper in Social Sciences (20), Pondicherry, 1996.

3. The essence of economic neo-liberalism is the contention that government intervention is not required to bring about social welfare and if it does intervene through measures, as for example, taxes and trade barriers it will make matters worse rather than better; welfare could be increased by removing those barriers. The neo-classical economists in the 1950s and 1960s propounded that the rate of growth did not just depend on increases in physical stock of capital and labour, but could also be the result of total factor productivity. The Bretton Woods economists went beyond this to assert that a country's rate of economic growth is primarily determined by the rate of total factor productivity growth which they broadly equate with technical progress. The argument thus sums that the total factor productivity growth depends in turn on domestic policy: The more competitive the product, capital and labour markets, and the more open is the economy to foreign competition, the greater would be economic efficiency and technical progress and hence the faster would be economic growth. The basic idea is that the forces of domestic and foreign competition will compel producers to become efficient and introduce new technology, if they wish to stay in business, and this process will increase economic growth. The Bank economists claimed that these theoretical propositions were borne out by the outstanding success of East Asian economies.

   For further details see, *Towards an Economic Platform for the South*, South Centre, Geneva, 1998. pp. 52-53.

4. Noam Chomsky, *Profit Over People: Neo-liberalism and Global Order*, Delhi, 1999, p. 20. Chomsky is a world renowned political activist,

writer and Professor of Linguistics at Massachusetts Institute of Technology, USA.

5. *Human Development Report*, 1999, UNDP, Oxford.
6. *Ibid.*, p. 3.
7. See Paikiasothy Saravanamuthu, "Globalism and Economic Regionalism", in *South Asia: An Unfriendly Context for An Arduous task*?, pp. 20-39; Vernon Mendis, "Regionalism in the Context of Evolving Global Transformation", in *Regional Cooperation and Integration: Perspectives from Europe and South Asia*-Edited proceedings of a seminar organised jointly by the Delegation of European Commission to Sri Lanka, the Goethe Institute, Colombo and the Sri Lanka Foundation, Colombo, 1998, pp. 39-56.
8. For details see, "Labour, Employment and Human Development" in Ashok Chandra et. al (ed.) *South Asia, Institute of Human Development*, Institute for Applied Manpower Research and Friedrich Ebert Stiftung, Delhi, 1998.
9. For details see B. Ramesh Babu (ed.) *Globalisation and the South Asian State,* New Delhi, 1998; John H. Dunning and Khalil A. Hamdani (ed.) *The New Globalism and Developing Countries*, New York, 1998.
10. For details see Bimal Chakrobarty, *The United Nations and the Third World: Shifting Paradigm*, Delhi, 1997; Gurmeet Kanwal, "Marginalisation of the United Nations: Impact of Kosovo Conflict", *Asian Strategic Review*, IDSA, New Delhi, 1998-99, pp. 128-51.
11. For details see Muchkund Dubey, *An Unequal Treaty: World Trading Order after GATT*, New Delhi, 1996.
12. Reserve Bank of India, *Report of the Policy Group and task force on External Debt Statistics of India*, Bombay, 1992.
13. For details see, "Freeing India's Economy: The Elephant Awakes", *The Economist*, 23 May 1992, pp. 21-23; J. Bhagwati and T.N. Srinivasan, *Indian Economic Reforms,* Ministry of Finance, New Delhi, July 1993; Government of India, "Economic Reforms: Two Years After and the Tasks Ahead", Ministry of Finance, New Delhi, June 1993; T.N. Srinivasan, *Eight Lectures on India's Economic Reforms,* New Delhi, 2000.
14. For details see, Montek S. Ahluwalia, "India's Economic Reforms: An Appraisal" in Jeffery Sachs, Ashutosh Varshney, Nirupam Bajpai, (ed.), *India in the Era of Economic Reforms*, New York, 1999 pp. 26-81.
15. See Achin Vanaik, *India in a Changing World: Problems, Limits and Successes of its Foreign Policy,* Orient Longman Limited, New Delhi, 1995, p. 66.

16. *Ibid.* p. 50.
17. For details see, Sugata Bose (ed.), *South Asia and World Capitalism,* Delhi, 1990; Moazzem Hossain et al (ed.), *South Asian Economic Development: Transformation, Opportunities and Challenges,* Routledge, London, 1999; Ric Shand, *Economic Liberalisation in South Asia: Performance and Prospects,* Research and Information System for the Non-Aligned and Other Developing Countries, New Delhi, 1998.
18. For details see, Shiela Page, *Regionalism Among Developing Countries*, Overseas Development Institute, London, 2000.
19. K.K. Bhargava, "Promotion and Consolidation of the Spirit of SAARC", in L.L. Mehrotra, Chopra, Kueck (ed.), *SAARC 2000 and Beyond,* International Seminar organised by IIC, JNU and Konrad Adenauer Foundation, 1995, p. 370.
20. Sri Lanka did not invite the King of Bhutan directly for the reason that no direct flight was available from Dhaka to Thimpu. Initially Bhutan gave its token acceptance to the invitation. However, later the King of Bhutan expressed his inability to attend the summit in view of ethnic disturbance in his country. For details see, S.D. Muni, "SAARC: A Summit Smothered", *The Hindustan Times*, 20 November 1991.
21. *The Daily News*, 7 November 1991; Also, "Sri Lanka Media's Tirade against India", *The Hindu*, 8 November 1991.
22. Sri Lanka Government owned newspaper '*The Daily Observer*' reported that leaders of Sri Lanka, Pakistan and Bangladesh would discuss 'unanimity clause' in SAARC charter with the then Chairman of SAARC, President Abdul Gayoom of Maldives. Further, that they would explore the possibility of amending the Charter to prevent the sudden cancellation of meetings and programmes " at the whims and fancies of a single member". For details see, *The Daily Observer*, 7 November1991.
23. *The Hindustan Times*, 8 November 1991; Also, "Pakistan, Lanka for Review of SAARC Charter", *The Economic Times*, 10 November 1991.
24. Muni, n. 20.
25. For details see, S.D. Muni, India and Nepal : A Changing Relationship, New Delhi, 1992; Also see Dhruba Kumar, "Reconsidering Nepal-India Bilateral Relations", in Dhruba Kumar (ed.), *Nepal's India Policy,* Centre for Nepal and Asian Studies, Kathmandu, 1992, pp. 17-19.
26. For details see J.N. Dixit, *Liberation and Beyond: Indo-Bangladesh Relations*, New Delhi, 1999.
27. Mohammed Ayoob, "The Primacy of the Political: South Asian Regional Cooperation (SARC) in Comparative Perspective", *Asian Survey*, Vol. XXV, No. 4, April 1985, pp. 443-58.

28. Sridhar K. Khatri, "Democratization and Regional Cooperation in South Asia", *Everest Herald*, 26 April 1996.
29. Edward D. Mansfield and Jack Synder, "Democratization and War", *Foreign Affairs,* New York, Vol. 74, No. 3, March-April 1995, pp. 79-97.
30. Khatri, n. 28.
31. For details see, Mushahid Hussain and Akmal Hussain, (ed.) *Pakistan: Problems of Governance*, New Delhi, 1993; Kalim Bahadur, *Democracy in Pakistan: Crisis and Conflicts*, New Delhi, 1998; Also see G.Parthasarthy, "Pakistan after Kargil: Jihad versus Peace and Progress", *The Times of India*, New Delhi, 4 July 2000. Parthasarthy, a former Indian Ambassador in Pakistan observes that "many Pakistanis now privately acknowledge that it is the lack of transparency and public accountability that has led to their army becoming a virtual state within a state in their country".
32. Bindanda M. Chengappa, " The ISI Role in Pakistan Politics", *Strategic Analysis*, IDSA, Vol. XXIII, No. 11, February 2000, pp. 1857-1878.
33. Mansfield and Synder, n. 29, p. 197.
34. *P.V. Narasimha Rao, Selected Speeches*, Vol. I June 1991-June 1992, Publications Division, Ministry of Information and Broadcasting, Government of India, 1993, p.354; Also "Narasimha Rao Proposes Wider SAARC Tie-ups", *The Hindustan Times*, 22 December 1991; P.S.Suryanarayana, "SAARC Summit: Focus Will Be On Economic Ties", *The Hindu*, 21 December 1991.
35. *Ibid.*, p. 355.
36. *Ibid.*, p. 356.
37. The Colombo Declaration of the Heads of State/Government of the Member countries of SAARC issued on 21st December 1991, *Declaration of SAARC Summits (1985-1995)*. SAARC Secretariat, Kathmandu, pp.73-87; Also see, "SAARC Summit: Stress on Economic Security", *The Statesman*, 23 December 1991.
38. *Ibid.*
39. During discussion on trade liberalisation the apprehensions of Nepal regarding its economic vulnerability vis-á-vis India came to the fore. The Nepalese Prime Minister Koirala demanded that a balance be struck 'between the economic interaction of some big member countries and the less developed countries' and wanted appropriate safeguards for 'special interests of economically weaker partners' when trade was liberalised. For further details see "Asymmetrical Economies and SAPTA", *The Rising Nepal*, 26 December 1994; Also "Meeting of the Inter Governmental Group (IGG) on Trade

Liberalisation", *SAARC Newsletter,* SAARC Secretariat, October-December 1992, p. 105.

40. Although the member countries welcomed the proposal to set up a $5 million SAARC fund for regional projects, India seemed to have reservations on seeking external linkages with organisations like the Association of South East Asian Nations (ASEAN) or the European Community (EC) to secure finance for projects. Keeping in view India's reservations it was decided that the Standing Committee of the Foreign Secretaries would go into the question of linkages and financial arrangement and would define certain specific terms of reference. For further details see, T. Subramanian, "Back in Colombo: The Summit at Last", *Frontline*, New Delhi, 17 January 1992.
41. Rashtriya Swayamsevak Sangh(RSS), a hard line Hindu organisation and its front organisations in different walks of life-Bhartiya Janata Party, Vishwa Hindu Parishad, Bajrang Dal etc.-are termed 'Sangha Parivar'.
42. K.K. Katyal, "Emerging Reality in South Asia", *The Hindu* (Madras), 11 January 1993; Also see, Faisal Irfan Mian, "The Failing Spirit of SAARC", *The Frontier Post,* 12 February 1993; S.D. Muni, "Save the SAARC", *The Hindustan Times*, New Delhi, 3 February 1993.
43. *The Deccan Herald*, 17 January 1993.
44. Inaugural Address by Smt. Indira Gandhi, Prime Minister of India, in the Meeting of South Asian Foreign Ministers, New Delhi, August 1, 1983, *India Quarterly*, Vol. XL. Nos. 3 and 4, July-December 1983, p. 259.
45. P.S. Suryanarayana, "Spokes in the SAARC Wheel", *The Hindu*, 17 January 1993; Also see, S.D.Muni, "Save the SAARC", *The Hindustan Times*, 3 February 1993.
46. *The Deccan Herald,* 17 January 1993.
47. For details see Percy S. Mistry, *Regional Integration and Development: Panacea or Pitfalls*? RIS, New Delhi, 1995.
48. Address by P.V. Narasimha Rao, Prime Minister of India at the inauguration of the Seventh SAARC Summit at Dhaka, Bangladesh, April 10, 1993, Ministry of External Affairs, Government of India. p. 2.
49. *Ibid.* p. 4.
50. Zaglul Chowdhury, "SAARC Summit endorses SAPTA", *The Telegraph,* 12 April 1993; Also " SAARC and Economic Co-opeartion", *The Economic Times*, 12 April 1993; "The Dhaka Summit", *The Rising Nepal*, 13 April 1993.
51. For details see, The Economic Times, 21 April 1993; *The Statesman*, 29 April 1993.

52. The Declaration of the Seventh SAARC Summit of the Heads of State/ Government of Member countries of SAARC issued on 11th April 1993, *Declaration of SAARC Summits* etc. n. 37, pp. 87-109.
53. *The Hindu*, 3 May 1995.
54. Address by P.V. Narasimha Rao, Prime Minister of India, Eighth SAARC Summit, New Delhi, Inaugural Session. *SAARC Summits Volume II (1990-1995)*, SAARC Secretariat, Dhaka, Kathmandu, Nepal, pp.133-34.
55. For details see, Venkat S.Narayan, "From SAARC to United States of South Asia", *The Times of India*, 15 May 1995; Bijendra M. Shakya, "Revitalising SAARC Much left to be done", The Rising Nepal, 19 May 1995; K.K. Bhargava, "Delhi SAARC Summit: Malaise and Progress", *Mainstream*, 24 June 1995, pp. 5-7.
56. The Delhi Declaration of the Heads of State/Government of the Member Countries of SAARC issued on 4 May 1995, *Declaration of SAARC Summits*, etc., n. 54, pp.111-30.
57. Inder Kumar Gujral as the Foreign Minister and later as the Prime Minister of India advocated and practised the doctrine of non-reciprocity with India's smaller neighbours envisaging a flexible, positive approach in resolving bilateral disputes between India and her neighbours. This approach significantly contributed to improvement of India's relations with her neighbours with the exception of Pakistan; For details sec I.K. Gujral's interview with Shubhangshu Roy, *Economic Times*, 12 May 1997.
58. Statement by I.K. Gujral, Prime Minister of India at the Inaugural Session of the Ninth SAARC Summit, Male, May 12, 1997, pp.136-37.
59. *Ibid.*, pp. 137-38.
60. For detailed analysis also see, K.K.Bhargava, "The Maturing of SAARC", *The Economic Times*, 17 May 1997; "SAARC Comes of Age" (editorial), *The Deccan Chronicle*, 17 May 1997.
61. Davinder Kumar Madan (ed.) Ninth SAARC Summit, Male (1997), *SAARC, Origin, Development and Programmes: From 1st to the 9th Summit*, pp. 221-37.
62. Indian Prime Minister Atal Bihari Vajpayee and his Pakistani counterpart Nawaz Shrif met for nearly 90 minutes in three phases on July 29, 2000 but failed to make any breakthrough in carrying forward their bilateral relations. They could only agree to direct their Foreign Secretaries to resume dialogue stalled since September 1997. The Secretaries met more than once but could not agree on the format of the talks. See, K.P. Nayar, "PMs Silver-line nuclear cloud",

The Telegraph, 30 July 1998; M.B. Naqvi, "Agree to disagree even at SAARC", *The Times of India,* 2 August 1998.

63. For details see, Ross Garnaut, " The East Asian Crisis" in Ross H. Mcleod and Ross Garnaut, *East Asia in Crisis: From being a Miracle to Needing Ones*, London, 1998, pp. 3-30; Paul Krugman, "The Myth of Asia's Miracle", *Foreign Affairs*, Vol. 73, No. 6, November-December 1994; Udai Bhanu Singh, "Economic Crisis in East Asia", *Asian Strategic Review*, IDSA, 1997-98, pp.116-43.
64. For details see *Towards an Economic Platform for the South, South Centre*, n. 3, pp.75-80.
65. For details on East Asian Crisis and its impact on SAARC Member Countries see, *SAARC Survey of Development and Cooperation 1998-99*, RIS, New Delhi, 1999, pp. 5-32.
66. For details see, Manab Majumdar, *South East Asian Crisis: Lessons for India*, FICCI, New Delhi, 1998; Sisira Jayasuriya, "India", in Ross and Ross, n. 63 , pp. 131-44.
67. *Human Development Report South Asia, 1999*, The Mahabub-ul-Haq, Human Development Centre, 1999,p.25.
68. Prime Minister's Address at SAARC Summit. (July, 29, 1998), *Foreign Affairs Record*, Vol. XLIV No.7, July 1998, Ministry of External Affairs, Government of India, pp. 62-63.
69. For details see, P.K.Balachandran, "P.M. Offers Package to Boost Trade", *Hindustan Times*, July 30, 1998; Also see, *The Telegraph*, July 30,1998.
70. n. 68, pp. 64-65.
71. n. 68, p. 65.
72. *Ibid.*
73. *Declaration of the Tenth SAARC Summit*, Colombo, A publication of the SAARC Secretariat, Kathmandu, Nepal, issued on 31 July 1998.
74. *Ibid.*
75. *Ibid.,* For a detailed analysis also see, B.G.Verghese, "A New Beginning from Colombo", *The Indian Express*, 29 July 1998; Kanwaldeep Singh, "A Positive Signal for SAFTA", *The Times of India,* 30 July 1998; "SAARC at a Dead End" (editorial), The Island, August, 1998; "SAARC Backtracks on Trade Pact", *The Kathmandu Post,* 3 August 1998; Barrister Harunur Rashid, "A Disappointing Summit", *The Frontier Post*, 5 August 1998.
76. *SAARC Newsletter*, SAARC Secretariat, Kathmandu, September and October 1999, Vol. X, No. 9 and 10.
77. *SAARC Newsletter,* SAARC Secretariat, Kathmandu, January-March, 2000, Vol. XI, No.1, 2 and 3, p. 7.
78. Mahendra P. Lama, *Integrated Programme of Action in SAARC:*

Genesis, Evaluation, Constraints and Rationale for Revamping, RIS occasional paper No. 57 RIS, New Delhi, 1999.

79. *Ibid.*

80. For details see, J.N. Mukherji, *South Asian Preferential Trade Arrangement: Assessing Trade Flows in the First Round of Trade Negotiations,* Friedrich Naumann Stiftung, New Delhi, 1996.

81. For details see, Saman Kalegama, "SAPTA and its Future", pp. 153-173, and C.D. Wadhwa, "Assessing SAARC Preferential Trading Agreement (SAPTA)", pp. 173-197, *South Asian Survey*, Vol. 3, Nos. 1 & 2, January-December 1996.

82. I.N. Mukherjee, "Indian Exports to South Asia: Identifying Products for Sustainable Development", *Foreign Trade Review,* Vol.30, Nos. 2 & 3, July-December 1995, pp.1-20.

83. I.N. Mukherjee, *South Asian Preferential Trading Arrangement: Role of India*, paper presented at National Seminar organised by IGSAC on Building Regional Cooperation: India's Role, IIC, New Delhi, 11-13, December 1998.

84. Report, 1998-99, Ministry of External Affairs, Government of India, p.16.

85. For details see *SAARC Survey of Development and Cooperation 1998-99*, RIS, New Delhi, 1999.

86. Source : World Bank, *World Development Indicators*, 2001.

    NAFTA - Canada, Mexico, USA.

    EU - 15 Countries of Western and Central Europe.

    MERCOSUR - Argentina, Brazil, Paraguay, Uruguay.

    ASEAN - Brunei, Indonesia, Malaysia, Myanmar, Philippines, Singapore, Thailand.

87. Second Meeting of the SAARC Expert Group (SEG) on SAARC Tripartite Study, Report of the National Tripartite Brainstorming Session, March 26-27, 1997, RIS, New Delhi.

88. *Ibid.*

89. Annual Report, 1998-99, Ministry of External Affairs, Government of India, p. 5.

90. Seema Guha, "India Lanka Sign Accord on Free Trade", *The Times of India,* 29 December, 1998; Also *The Deccan Herald* 29 December, *The Hindu*, 31 December 1998.

91. *The Hindu*, New Delhi, 16 February 2000

92. *The Hindu*, 3 March 2000.

93. *Ibid.*

94. Author's interview with Saman Kelegama, Executive Director, Institute of Policy Studies, Colombo on 26th December 1998. Dr. Kelegama although welcomed the Accord but expressed his apprehension that the Indian imports would flood Sri Lankan market. He further suggested that joint ventures with buy back arrangements can mitigate this problem for Sri Lanka.
95. For details see editorials in *The Island*, "On the fast track to Suicide", 18 December 1998; "No One-sided Treaties, Please!", 28 December 1998.
96. Dr. J.B. Kelegama, "Fast Track Trade Liberalisation Agreement with India",*The Daily News*, 2 Vols. 22 and 23 December 1998.
97. Text of Free Trade Agreement between the Republic of India and the Democratic Socialist Republic of Sri Lanka in the Arun Goyal's Easy Reference Customs Tariff, Budget Edition 2000-2001, CP3, pp. 1022-37.
98. *Ibid.* Domestic value addition requirements have been kept at 35 per cent. If the material/inputs are sourced from each other's country, this is reduced to 25per cent within the overall limit of 35 per cent. The criterion of 'substantial transformation' has been provided in the rules. The goods must undergo transformation at four digit level Harmonised System of product classification.
99. For details see, *The Economic Times*, 13 March 2000; Also see, *The Hindu*, 27 June 2000; I.N. Mukherji, " Indo-Sri Lankan Trade and Investment Linkages: With Special Reference to SAPTA and Free Trade Agreement", *South Asian Economic Journal*, Vol. 1, No.1, March 2000, pp. 53-78.
100. *The Hindu*, New Delhi, 21 November 2000.
101. *Frontline,* 27 April 2001.
102. For details see *The Economic Times*, 2 November 1999; *The Hindu,* 27 November 1999; C. Raja Mohan, "No Tears for SAARC", *The Hindu*, 27 November 1999.
103. K.K. Katyal, *India not to Veto Move for SAARC Summit, The Hindu,* New Delhi, 8 May 2001.
104. Achin Vanaik, *India in a Changing World*, n.15, 1995, p. 111.
105. S.D. Muni, "Save the SAARC", *The Hindustan Times,* New Delhi, 3 February, 1993.
106. *Ibid.*

6

Post Cold War Developments and India's Role in SAARC: Political and Strategic Implications

The end of the cold war could not be predicted by the international relations theory. However, the post-cold war situation of virtual 'one system' is sought to be explained by two theoretical approaches : (i) neo-realistic and (ii) traditional realism. The neo-realistic approach gives primacy to economics. This approach considers the state system important but its emphasis is on transnational economic relations which might constrain or alter state behaviour.

The traditional realism approach maintains primacy of politics in international relations even though economic globalization is considered as having created a complication.[1] For a neo-realist "in the era of increasing 'interdependence', cooperative forms of inter-state behaviour became more important than traditional realist forms of pursuit of the national interest. Those interests are now increasingly complementary rather than conflictual, which is not to say that conflicts and tensions will not exist or surface. Power will have become more 'diffused' and one will need new international institutions (set up at the initiative of the big powers perhaps) which reflect this diffusion."[2]

The end of the cold war gave a significant push to socioeconomic cooperation in South Asia. However, despite a fundamentally changed international situation, the primacy of politics, of conflict and strife is writ large on the process of regionalism in South Asia. The neo-realist postulates on the post-cold war international relations, therefore, may not adequately explain the South Asian predicament. South Asian scholar, S.D. Muni considers that political strategic factors exercise decisive influence on regionalism and to understand this phenomenon only in economic or any other context (other than political), in his opinion, would amount to understanding it only partially or inadequately.[3]

India's Post-Cold War Regional Policy

The end of the cold war, disintegration of the Soviet Union and emergence of the U.S. as the global hegemon brought about a paradigm shift in international relations. The ideological struggle gave way to economic regionalism and efforts to create a globalized economic order dictated by the neo-liberal market principles. We also saw erosion of the UN and the institution of the nation-state.

This called for an urgent need for India to rethink and reformulate some of the postulates and premises of its foreign policy, including its policy in the sub-continent taking into account the new realities of global political developments. The old trans-regional multilateral forums such as non-aligned movement, Group of '77 and UNCTAD which were the fulcrum of Indian policy were gradually losing their relevance and importance.[4] Indian Foreign Secretary in early '90s, J.N. Dixit observes:

> ...India had to, and has, changed both the ideological and operational terms of reference of its foreign policy from 1991 onwards. Such a change was necessary not only to adjust the post-cold war equations and trends of economic globalization but also to meet the challenges of economic deprivation, terrorism, mass migration and crime-global phenomena which permeate all countries unrestrained by national boundaries or by government decrees.[5]

The end of the cold war dramatically brought down inter-state conflicts. However, the intra-state conflicts caused by ethnic, communal or socioeconomic factors continued unabated. Insurgency, terrorism within the states sponsored and exacerbated from outside and by extra-regional powers; smuggling in arms and drugs, money laundering and associated criminalisation of politics; cross-border migration; dangers posed by serious environment degradation are some of the factors identified in the post-cold war period which are serious threat to the security and peace particularly in the developing world.[6]

Post-Cold War South Asia: Conflict Prone

Post-cold war, South Asia continues to be a conflict torn region with most of the countries suffering domestic violence caused by communalism, ethnic conflict, separatism, religious fanaticism and socioeconomic deprivation. Cross-border narco-terrorism with India at the receiving end has added a new dimension to the disturbed conditions in the sub-continent.[7] South Asia this way is considered 'a unique region from global perspective', with 'its problems and conflicts having their own dynamics and most, if not all of these created with in the region by its history, its geo-politics its economics and ecology'[8]. India's policy in the sub-continent has been 'to build a strategically secure, politically stable and harmonious and economically cooperative neighbourhood'[9] Accordingly India's efforts have been to keep away foreign intervention particularly, major-power intrusion, from the sub-continent; to resolve disputes with neighbours bilaterally without use of force and third party interference; and to promote regional cooperation in pursuit of collective self-reliance and development of economy.

India occupies a unique position in South Asia—her centrality primarily determines the behaviour of other member states of SAARC. A common history, culture and ethnic links between India and her neighbours makes it difficult to immunise India from the events in the neighbouring countries. The whole region is symbiotically one entity but politically divided into different nation states. It is almost impossible to separate the politics of one country from that of another—particularly that of India and her neighbours. India thus occupies a unique and peculiar position. Indian neighbours have been extremely sensitive to India's pre-eminence in the sub-continent.[10] In fact, one of their objectives, particularly of Pakistan, and Bangladesh, in SAARC was to rein in and counter 'big India' by the norms and discipline inherent in a regional forum.[11]

The sense of insecurity among India's neighbours has been impelling them to bring in extra-regional powers to countervail India's influence. There has thus been a basic contradiction between India's policy objectives and the behaviour of her smaller neighbours in this regard. Indo-Pak relations more than any other dimension in the regional politics has been a stumbling block in the evolution and growth of regionalism in South Asia. The adversial relationship between the two has the potential of disrupting the SAARC process. The overt nuclearisation of India and Pakistan in 1998 and subsequent limited war at Kargil in Jammu and Kashmir, military rule in Pakistan and renewed interest of major powers, particularly the United States, in the sub-continent are significant factors for Indian regional policy to respond to in the post-cold war international regime.

The primary purpose of India's regional policy, according to some scholars, has been 'to extract in some form or another, recognition of India's hegemonistic status in the region from both the major external powers and from its neighbours in the region'.[12] Robert Bradnock maintains that while India sought a pre-eminent leadership position in South Asia, its ultimate objective has been self-protection rather than aggressive or territorial expansionism.[13] S.D. Muni identifies three important issue areas within Indian regional policy framework of building a stable, secure and cooperative neighbourhood as follows:

(i) The evolving nature of the interactions of the Great Powers with India and its neighbours;

(ii) Bilateral tensions and conflicts and the implications of internal turmoil and turbulence in each of the South Asian countries; and

(iii) The incentives for and the compulsions of development within the individual countries as also those impinging on regional interactions.[14]

Extra-Regional Powers and India

Role of the United States in South Asia

With the demise of the cold war and disintegration of Soviet Union, the relations of the extra-regional powers, particularly the United States, with the countries of South Asia are undergoing a marked shift away from cold war paradigm. An inkling of this rethink in U.S. policy could be seen in an unapproved policy document prepared by the Pentagon in 1992. The document envisaged a world dominated by one superpower with constructive behaviour and sufficient military might to deter any nation or group of nations to challenge its primacy.[15] V.P. Dutt captures the essential policy thrust of this document as under:

> The document exhorted the U.S. to "establish and protect a new order" that accounted sufficiently for the interests of the advanced industrial nations to discourage them from challenging our leadership while at the same time maintaining a military dominance capable of deterring potential competitors from even aspiring to a larger regional or global role". The analysts preparing the document were agreed that Germany, Japan, Russia and India were among the aspirants to global power status (the omission of China was surprising). The document discussed India's "hegemonistic aspirations over the other states in South Asia and the Indian Ocean". On Asia, it advocated that the U.S. "must maintain our status as a military power of the first magnitude...acting as a balancing force" so as to prevent the "emergence of a vacuum and a regional hegemon".[16]

Even though the document was withdrawn and disowned, the U.S. policy in the 90s seemed to be following in practice the prescriptions laid down in this document.

With the breaking of ideological umbilical cord of Indo-Soviet relations and economic policy liberalisation in India, the Indo-US relations showed signs of improvement, although more in atmospherics than in the content.[17] These relations still hinged on the US's global scheme related to nuclear non-proliferation, missile development, Comprehensive Test Ban Treaty, transfer of sophisticated technology and the new global trade regime under WTO. Nevertheless, it helped India to come closer to its neighbours. As S.D. Muni notes:

> Viewed from India's point of view, the end of the Cold War has eroded the strategic differences and prejudices which had separated it from most of its immediate neighbours (as for instance, on the question of Soviet intervention in Afghanistan during most of the '80s). This gives India greater room for manoeuvre in relating its stances to those of its neighbours on a number of strategic issues.'[18]

For the U.S., Pakistan was no longer required as a counter weight to pro-Soviet India. The relative economic strength and potential of India vis-á-vis Pakistan, in the context of India breaking out of the Nehruvian socialist economy and likely to emerge as a big market, also perhaps persuaded the U.S. establishment to have a re-look at the policy of equating India and Pakistan in South Asia.[19] The American intellectual circles have been debating the deteriorating socio-political, ethnic and economic situation in Pakistan which is being projected as potential 'failed state'. A study conducted by a Task Force set up by the Council on Foreign Relations in the U.S. had this to advise on Indo-Pak policy:

> Pakistan's political system is in dire shape. The country has the potential to become a failed state. That would be a great humanitarian nightmare and threat to regional and even global peace. The United States needs to try to head off such a tragic outcome.
>
> India, on the other hand, has the potential to become a full-fledged major power. It is a democracy whose economic ties with the United States show great promise and whose strength can help promote stability across Asia. We should explore the formation of a real strategic partnership.[20]

The process of rethink in U.S. Policy on India and Pakistan suffered a setback with India's Nuclear explosions at Pokhran on May 11 and 13, 1998. These were followed by Pakistan nuclear explosions soon after at Chagai Hills.[21] The international opinion led by the U.S. came down heavily on India and Pakistan and the U.S. in pursuance of its domestic laws, imposed sanctions on India and Pakistan.[22]

Later, India's bold move to normalise relations with Pakistan through 'Bus-Diplomacy' in 1999 when the Indian Prime Minister went to Lahore, was appreciated world over including in the U.S. But a sudden nosedive in Indo-Pak relations as a result of Pakistani intrusion in Kargil sector of Kashmir, raised alarm bells, particularly since the two countries possessed nuclear weapons. The danger of two countries possessing weapons of mass destruction and going to war obviously raised the heckles of the U.S. and other major powers. But India's monumental restraint in keeping the Kargil war limited and confined to the Indian side of the Line-of-Control (LOC) in Kashmir and a decisive and determined military response earned worldwide appreciation.

The world opinion took note of Pakistan's irresponsible behaviour in Kargil coming as it did immediately after a bold attempt at Lahore to begin a new chapter in Indo-Pak relations. The military take over in Pakistan in October 1999 further put India in bold relief as a symbol of democratic and responsible behaviour in the sub-continent.[23]

The U.S. response to Kargil situation was decisively favourable to India—it virtually compelled Pakistan to seek a face saving joint declaration with the U.S. in July 1999. Post-Kargil India and the U.S. were engaged in a marathon bilateral dialogue on issues including nuclear proliferation.[24] While the differences on major issues concerning nuclear non-proliferation, Comprehensive Test Ban Treaty persist between India and the U.S., the two countries seem to be moving closer to understand each other's viewpoints.

While the desirability of India becoming an overt nuclear power and developing a nuclear arsenal for a minimum strategic deterrence in its defence could be debated, but India's exercise of the nuclear option in the context of emerging imperatives of post-cold war politics indicates Indian ruling establishment's assertion of its sovereignty in pursuit of its perceived national interests. This has further been underlined by reiteration of the Indian position during U.S. President Bill Clinton's visit to India in March 2000. A Vision statement issued during the U.S. President's visit notes:

> India and the United States share a commitment to reducing and ultimately eliminating nuclear weapons, but we have not always agreed on how to reach this common goal. The United States believes India should forgo nuclear weapons. India believes that it needs to maintain a credible minimum nuclear deterrence in keeping with its own assessment of its security needs.[25]

The historic visit of a U.S. President after the end of the cold war has the potential of changing the strategic relationship in Asia and the world at large since the two democracies decided to build a closer and qualitatively new relationship and spelled out institutional framework to realise this objective. The U.S. President's firm stand against cross-border terrorism and for maintaining the sanctity of the Line of Control in Kashmir in the context of Indo-Pak relations indicated possibility of a shift in the U.S. position in South Asia, particularly vis-á-vis its cold war-ally Pakistan.[26] The warming-up of Indo-US relations continues despite recent change of Presidency in the US. In fact, there is a significant new push to this phenomenon with India's declared support to the nuclear doctrine of the US President Bush—the fact that this new doctrine of Nuclear Missile Defence, a historic departure from conventional nuclear 'balance of terror', can have far reaching implications for global security, makes India's support to this doctrine extremely significant. This realignment of Indo-US strategic relations in the fast changing post-cold war global order can have major implications for India's regional policy. The statement of US deputy secretary of state Richard Armitage during his visit to New Delhi in May 2001 for consultations on a new global security framework, clubbed Pakistan with so called 'rouge states'. Armitage said:

> We have questions about Pakistan. It is well known....Iraq, Iran, Libya ... They are well known as states involved in proliferation. These we refer to as hard cases. You have some in this neighbourhood.... North Korea has recently announced that it would continue to export missile technology.[27]

The reference to North Korea in the statement was significant since one of the main recipients of North Korean proliferation was Pakistan.

Role of Erstwhile USSR and China

The erstwhile USSR and China as major extra-regional powers had been exercising tremendous influence on South Asia during cold war phase. Soviet occupation of Afghanistan in 1979 brought the cold war rivalries at South Asia's doorsteps when U.S. and China propped up Pakistan as a frontline state to face the Soviet threat. Even otherwise China had been supporting Pakistan to counter Indian influence in Asia (although China could not effectively support Pakistan in 1971 Indo-Pak war thus indirectly acknowledging Indian pre-eminence in South Asia)[28]. A veteran Indian Journalist Girilal Jain of the *Times of India* summed up Sino-South Asian equation during the cold war in following words:

> India has been apprehensive for a long time, certainly since the mid-sixties, that China looks upon Pakistan as a proxy for creating problem in India. China wants to deny us what we regard as our legitimate place in the sub-Himalayan region at least, if not in the larger region which could include the Gulf. As I see it, and, as I think, Indira Gandhi saw it, the problem with China is not mainly the border dispute, it's China's perception of India's role in South Asia.[29]

China's help in Pakistan's effort to acquire nuclear and missile technology was also seen as a manifestation of this Chinese policy in South Asia.[30] China was also quite uncomfortable with India's overt nuclearisation in 1998 and joined the big powers led by the U.S. in condemning the Indian actions. China's renewed warming up to Pakistan after Kargil war continues to pose a serious challenge to India's security. The Chinese Prime Minister Zhu Rongji during his visit to Pakistan in May 2001, the first after the latest military coup there, virtually endorsed the Pakistani position on Kashmir. He said:

> We appreciate the position taken by Pakistan calling for a peaceful settlement of the problem.... It is a leftover of history and a very complicated issue. We would spare no effort to our utmost to support the efforts aimed at resolving this dispute through peaceful means.[31]

However, the disintegration of Soviet Union, India's persistent pursuit of non-alignment, Gulf-war wherein Western alliance led by the US established their supremacy in technological warfare and the latest US led NATO adventure[32] in Kosovo, Yugoslavia changed international situation in a very significant manner for China to ignore. In fact, there was even a suggestion [33] for a strategic alliance between India, China and Russia to counter U.S. hegemony in Asia and the world at large. China's South Asian policy had shown signs of a shift after the end of the cold war. Its lack of enthusiasm and denial of support to Pakistan's misadventure in Kargil was a manifestation of this shift in policy.[34] India had also been making efforts to normalise relations with China—the agreement concluded with China in 1993 to maintain peace and tranquility along the Line-of-Control and India's support to China's proposed entry into WTO were indications of this effort. S.D. Muni observes:

> ...The end of the cold war and the subsequent disintegration and political confusion in what was the Soviet Union have facilitated a positive movement in India's relations with China and the United States, thereby reducing the margin of strategic manoeuvrability of India's adversial neighbours....[35]

India and Neighbours: Early 1990s

The reduction of extra-regional powers' interference in South Asia provided greater leeway to India to push its agenda for a cooperative neighbourhood. The end of the cold war generated a conducive environment for India to resolve its dilemma of 'how to be strong enough to protect its own interests without provoking the antagonism of its neighbours and how to treat their sensitivities gently without appearing to be too weak to protect its own interests.'[36] To resolve this dilemma, however, has been a great challenge for the policy makers in India. To use the terminology of the Contori Spiegel Model[37] for classification of the South Asian States, even though the 'intrusive sector' (i.e., extra-regional or outside intervention) was less intrusive in the post-cold war phase, the alienation of the 'peripheral sector' (i.e., nations other than India) from the 'core sector' (i.e., India) was real. The 'periphery' has been perceiving the 'core' as the biggest security threat. The bilateral conflicts between the 'core' and the 'periphery' have been endemic and the internal disturbance all pervasive. The bilateral stand-off between India and Pakistan on Kashmir, cross-border terrorism, proxy war by Pakistan has been most acrimonious in South Asia.[38] But India's relations with other neighbours as well are not cordial enough to successfully promote the agenda of regionalism in the sub-continent.

A significant development in the wake of the demise of cold war in South Asia had been restoration of democracy in Bangladesh and Pakistan and change of system in Nepal from Monarchy to representative democracy.[39] Taking advantage of these positive developments India made renewed efforts to normalise relations with her adversial neighbours.

Indo-Nepal Relations

In 1990 immediately after the installation of an interim government in Nepal as a result of the successful mass movement for multiparty democracy, the Prime Ministers of Nepal and India met and decided to restore status-quo-ante in bilateral relations to April 1987 when the tensions between the two countries had surfaced.

The two sides decided to respect each other's security concerns, not to allow activities in the territory of one prejudicial to the security of the other and to have prior consultations with a view to reaching mutual agreement on such defence related matters which, in the view of either country, could pose a threat to its security. There was a further serious move to co-operate in the spheres of industrial and human resource development and for harnessing of the common rivers for the benefit of the peoples of the two countries, and for protection and management of the environment.[40]

The Indian Prime Minister paid a visit to Nepal in 1991 (the last such visit was made 14 years ago) when many significant decisions were taken and work-programmes finalised for intensification of bilateral economic cooperation. The newly elected Prime Minister of Nepal paid a historic visit to New Delhi in December 1991 accompanied by a delegation of Nepalese industrialists and businessmen. A high level Task Force was set up for the first time which prepared a comprehensive programme of bilateral cooperation. This was the first time that such an approach was adopted between India and Nepal.

During this visit five important treaties and agreements were signed: a new trade treaty; a new transit treaty; an agreement for cooperation in controlling unauthorised trade; a Memorandum of Understanding for cooperation in agriculture, meant to promote rural development and rural employment in Nepal; and another Memorandum of Understanding for the establishment of the B.P. Koirala India-Nepal Foundation.[41]

There were tangible gains for Nepal as a result of increased economic cooperation with India in the '90s—the commissioning of an industrial estate at Rajbiraj and telephone exchange at Rangeli in Nepal. A new trade regime which came into force in April 1993, providing for the customs duty free access to Indian markets for manufactured articles was improved to include articles containing not less than 50 per cent Nepalese material and labour.[42]

Indo-Sri Lanka Relations

Indo-Sri Lankan relations had suffered a serious setback on the issue of the withdrawal of Indian Peace Keeping Force (IPKF) in 1989.[43]

IPKF was stationed in Sri Lanka to facilitate a peaceful resolution of the Tamil ethnic problem in Sri Lanka in pursuance of an understanding between the two governments. In fact, the IPKF withdrawal issue even threatened the derailment of SAARC process when Sri Lanka refused to host the Fifth Summit Meeting so long as IPKF continued on Sri Lankan soil.[44] The withdrawal of IPKF in March 1990 brought this controversy to an end and commenced a new phase in Indo-Sri Lankan relations.

In 1991 the two governments, decided to establish an Indo-Sri Lanka Joint Commission with sub-commissions on Trade, Investment and Finance, and Science and Technology. The year, thereafter, (1992) saw significant increase in contacts between the business communities of the two countries. The Indo-Sri Lankan Joint Business Council was convened in New Delhi in March 1991 after a gap of 11 years. Some 100 business delegates from India participated in the Expo '92 held in Colombo in November 1992.[45]

The second session of the Indo-Sri Lanka Joint Commission in 1994 resulted in a number of positive decisions. These included restoration of preferential tariff margins on Sri Lanka cloves, reduction in tariffs on select items of export interest to Sri Lanka such as ceramic tiles, glycerin, graphite and rubber and extension of a new line of dollar denominated credit. The Bank of Ceylon was granted permission to open a branch in Madras. The seat capacity for airlines were enhanced following a civil aviation dialogue in July 1994.[46] Sri Lanka President Chandrika Kumaratunga's visit to India in 1995 further consolidated the gains of cooperation between the two countries. A credit line of US$ 30 million was extended to Sri Lanka and grant of reduction in customs duty on 18 items of export by Sri Lanka was announced.[47]

Indo-Bangladesh Relations

The positive trend of bilateral interaction was revived by India in respect of Bangladesh as well when in 1991 after a gap of seven years Indo-Bangladesh Joint Economic Commission met. India announced a Rs. 30 crores government to government credit to Bangladesh. India also welcomed the restoration of democratic rights of the people of Bangladesh.[48] In 1992 the long pending, intractable 'Tin Bigha' enclave issue was resolved by its transfer to Bangladesh.[49] However, Indo-Bangladesh relations nose-dived due to spill over of the demolition of Babri Masjid structure in India by Hindu zealots, differences due to illegal immigration from Bangladesh, repatriation of refugees from Chakma hill tracts in Bangladesh and Bangladesh's efforts to internationalise the bilateral issue of river waters at the UN General Assembly in 1993 and 1995. In fact, the 1993 SAARC Summit at Dhaka was under cloud when due to Bangladesh-reaction[50] to the demolition of the mosque structure in India. The Indian PM initially refused to attend the Summit Meeting.

India-Pakistan Relations

India's relations with Pakistan during early '90s continued in the mode of dissonance with Pakistan continuing to encourage subversive activities in Kashmir. However, the two Prime Ministers, Narasimha Rao and Nawaz Sharif met six times during 1991 and 1993 to bring down hostilities between the two nations. The Foreign Secretary level talks also continued between the two countries till January 1994[51] and the two countries agreed on a number of confidence building measures (CBMs) to avoid military confrontations. These measures included development of communication links between high military officials in the two countries, adoption of a process of prior notification of military exercises, agreement on the non-attack on each other's nuclear installations, Border Security Agreement, Joint Declaration on Prohibition of Chemical Weapons etc. Foreign Secretary level talks were discontinued in 1994 when Benazir Bhutto became the Prime Minister of Pakistan.

Gujral Doctrine and its Impact

India's search for a cooperative neighbourhood and a peaceful and secure South Asia continued with a renewed emphasis when during a short period of 1996-97 Inder Kumar Gujral became the Foreign Minister and later Prime Minister of India. He advanced a concept known as Gujral Doctrine which envisaged a new approach to resolving disputes and improving relations with neighbouring countries.[52] This initiative and push for peace in the region with a history of hostility and mistrust was probably encouraged by a decline in the fear of 'big India' among its neighbours in the changed international situation. The policy prescription for India in terms of Gujral Doctrine were:

(a) Acknowledging its greater strength and larger size, India will be accommodating and generous towards her neighbours unilaterally to the maximum possible extent without demanding reciprocity;

(b) India will react to both internal and external developments in its neighbourhood from a moral high ground;

(c) India will not allow its territory to be used against the interest of any country in the region;

(d) India will not interfere in the internal affairs of other countries in the area, and would expect the others to observe this principle as well;

(e) India respects the territorial integrity and national sovereignty of all the states of the region;

(f) India is determined to settle all its disputes through peaceful bilateral negotiations.[53]

Gujral maintained that if these principles were scrupulously adhered to, the regional relationships in South Asia, including the difficult one between India and Pakistan could be fundamentally recast. He also maintained that the implementation of these principles would generate a climate of close and mutually benign cooperation in the region where the weight and size of India was regarded positively and as an asset by these countries.

The components of Gujral Doctrine were nothing new except the novelty of the principle of non-reciprocity. This principle, however, was presumably to be confined to the smaller neighbours—Bhutan, Bangladesh, Nepal and Sri Lanka. 'The non-reciprocity was also meant that solution to one bilateral problem would not be linked to concessions by the other country for India on an issue that the latter considered beneficial.'[54]

The application of this doctrine produced tangible positive results to normalise relations between India and its neighbours.[55] India and Nepal renewed the Indo-Nepal Trade Treaty for a period of five years up to 2001. This provided for the entry of articles manufactured in Nepal into the Indian market free of customs and quantity restrictions. This also provided parity to Nepalese products vis-á-vis Indian products in respect of the levy of countervailing duty on the basis of a certificate issued by the Government of Nepal.

There were further positive developments in Indo-Nepal relations when Mahakali River Agreement with Nepal (opening up the possibility of other rivers there for joint exploitation), was ratified by Gujral. He also responded to the Nepalese demand that the Indo- Nepal Treaty of Peace and Friendship of 1950 be renegotiated and revised.[56]

The treaty on sharing of Ganga Waters at Farakka signed by the Prime Ministers of India and Bangladesh in December 1996 was a significant achievement.[57] The Indian Foreign Minister Gujral maintained that finalisation of the Ganges water treaty was in no way linked to Bangladesh giving transit through its territory to India for access to North-Eastern parts of India. This was considered a landmark Treaty and attracted widespread international attention.[58] The change of leadership in Bangladesh which brought Sheikh Hasina to power was also a contributing factor for successful conclusion of Ganga Water Treaty. The improved relations between the two countries facilitated conclusion of an agreement in March 1997 on repatriation of Chakma refugees to Bangladesh (these refugees were living in Manipur and Tripura states of India).[59] This problem was finally resolved when in February 1998, the last batch of Chakmas left India for Bangladesh.

Gujral further categorically assured Sri Lanka during his visit to that country in 1997 that India would never interfere in the internal affairs of Sri Lanka. Sri Lankan President Chandrika Kumaratunga in an address at the Institute of Regional Studies, Islamabad in December 1997 maintained that in South Asia a climate of suspicion and mistrust was created because India's neighbours "sought comfort in external linkages which were perceived as a means of survival against a powerful India. India perceived these friendships as forms of extra-regional intervention inimical to her own interest".[60] However, after the adoption of Gujral Doctrine, she said:

> New Delhi has now adopted a "hands off policy regarding the internal affairs of our country for quite sometime" and moreover the Gujral administration has extended moral support to the Lankan Government in tackling the Tamil insurgency.[61]

Likewise assurances of increased economic assistance and bilateral cooperation were conveyed to Bhutan and Maldives. Bhutan agreed to augment Ganges Water from its Sankosh River and a direct land route from Nepal to Bangladesh became operational.

Gujral doctrine, however, could not melt the ice of Indo-Pak relations despite resumption of dialogue in 1997. In fact, a section of Pakistani ruling establishment considered Gujral Doctrine to be an attempt by India to isolate Pakistan and to build up relation with the other South Asian countries.[62] J.N. Dixit summed up Indo-Pak relations at this juncture in following words:

> Pakistan has remained and will remain antagonistic and

intrusive vis-á-vis India, despite the interlude of the 'Gujral Doctrine' and the restoration of the cosmetic dialogue between the two countries. What is more important is the fact that the Pakistani power structure expected the Gowda and Gujral Government in India to be vulnerable and indecisive. Such an expectation augmented adventurist trends in Pakistan's India policies. This was illustrated in Pakistan trying to sabotage the Assembly elections in Jammu and Kashmir in 1996. Pakistan-sponsored intrusive violence and terrorism in that state continues to generate instability and disaffection there as well as in other parts of India, taking advantage of the frustration and alienation in different sections of our citizenry. The Pakistani leadership will encourage controversies between India and its other neighbours.[63]

Indo-Pak Stand-off and South Asia: Post-Lahore/Kargil

I.K. Gujral and Pakistan Prime Minister Nawaz Sharif met on the sidelines of Ninth SAARC Summit held in Male in 1997 and decided to resume the Secretary level talks. However, it was for the generally perceived hard line regime led by the Bharatiya Janata Party in New Delhi to make a bold, historic move to normalise relations with Pakistan.

In February 1999 the Indian Prime Minister Atal Bihari Vajpayee paid a two day visit to Lahore, Pakistan through the land route at Indo-Pak border at Wagah. This meeting between the two Prime Ministers acquired great significance coming as it did after overt nuclearisation of India and Pakistan in 1998.

Lahore Declaration

In the historic 'Lahore Declaration'[64] that the two Prime Ministers made at the conclusion of the visit, they shared a vision of peace and stability and progress and prosperity for their people and committed themselves to the principles and purposes of the Charter of the United Nations, and the universally accepted principles of peaceful co-existence. The Declaration significantly referred to the 'bible' of Indo-Pak bilaterism, i.e., Simla Agreement and reiterated the determination of the two countries to implement this agreement in letter and spirit; reaffirmed that an environment of peace and security was in the supreme national interest of both sides and that the resolution of all outstanding issues, including Jammu and Kashmir was essential for that purpose.

The two governments agreed to intensify efforts to resolve all issues including Jammu and Kashmir; to refrain from intervention and interference in each other's internal affairs; to take immediate steps for reducing the risk of accidental or unauthorised use of nuclear weapons. They also reaffirmed their commitment to the goals and objectives of SAARC and to concert their efforts towards the realisation of the SAARC vision for the year 2000 and beyond with a view to promoting the welfare of the peoples of South Asia and improving their quality of life through accelerated economic growth, social progress and cultural development.[65]

The Kargil Conflict

The atmosphere generated by the Lahore Bus diplomacy of Indian Prime Minister was perhaps too good to be true. Soon thereafter (or perhaps even before this process began) Pakistani army made a bid to disturb peace in the Kargil Sector of Jammu and Kashmir.[66] This led to a fierce limited war on the Indian side of the Line-of-Control in Kashmir and totally destroyed the bonhomie generated by the Lahore process.

A few months later in October 1999, the elected government of Nawaz Sharif was overthrown in a military coup by General Pervez Musharraf. Nawaz Sharif was arrested and prosecuted for charges of hijacking the aeroplane in which Parvez Musharraf was returning to Pakistan and for terrorism, kidnapping and attempted murder.[67] The trial court adjudged Nawaz Sharif guilty and sentenced him to life imprisonment. Later, in a strange turn of events the military rulers in Pakistan settled for Nawaz Sharif's externment from Pakistan. He left Pakistan to settle with his entire family in Saudi Arabia.

The hijacking of an Indian Airlines plane from Kathmandu to Kandhar, Afghanistan via Pakistan further soured India-Pakistan relations. The hijackers killed one passenger and were successful in securing release of some terrorists imprisoned in Indian jails.

The deposed Prime Minister Nawaz Sharif in a statement made on 9 March 2000 before the anti-terrorist court in Pakistan where he was tried made significant disclosures.[68] Nawaz Sharif alleged that General Parvez Musharraf had got bugged various rooms of the Prime Minster's House and the Prime Minister's Office and he could not hold a meeting in the PM House or discuss any important or sensitive matter without raising the volume of the TV in order to avoid eaves dropping. Nawaz Sharif in this statement referred to Kargil episode and said:

> Kargil was one of the most serious crises in Pakistan's history, which posed a grave danger to the integrity of the country. It necessitated resolution with utmost urgency to which I responded promptly. Why did I have to respond promptly, General (Retd.) Parvez Musharraf knows... I will not for reasons of national security elaborate any further on this issue although it is necessary that the people of Pakistan must be informed of the truth about Kargil.[69]

The truth about Kargil need not be a mystery. Kargil happened because a section of Pakistan's powerful elite could not stomach peace process with India unleashed by the Lahore bus diplomacy.[70]

India-Pakistan quarrel is considered at the core of the region's troubles. In an assessment on South Asia after the cold war, Kanti P. Bajpayee and Stephen Cohen maintain that the region is less prone to conflict than outsiders believe, but less stable than regional decision makers assume.[71] Explaining the competition between the States in the form of a five strand matrix of war, cold war, détente, entente and integration they conclude:

> Paradoxically...South Asia's increased militarization may be the cause of a cautious but steady evolution towards a détente featuring CBMs, arms control as a defensive sufficiency, and eventually perhaps conflict-management agreements that would include constraints on strategies of brinkmanship, the uses of propaganda, the resort to internal subversion and economic warfare, and alliance and counter alliance manoeuvering. South Asia's near future will be neither war nor a thoroughgoing peace, but a carefully constructed middle ground that edges away from a destabilizing cold war to détente and cooperative security.[72]

In the post-cold war phase India could evolve a working bilateral relationship with its neighbours with the exception of Pakistan. This is not to say that India's relations with its neighbours are free of conflict or tension. There is though a feeling of realism and realisation that anti-India phobia would be counter-productive for peace and stability in the region. This situation was best illustrated at a recent round table[73] organised by a daily news paper in Dhaka where eight former Foreign Secretaries of Bangladesh who guided nation's foreign policy after 1975 emphasised the need to improve relations with India.[74] The Foreign Secretaries while criticizing India's 'big-brotherly attitude' and its 'unwillingness' to resolve major issues like land and maritime boundary demarcations, exchange of enclaves, water sharing, removal of trade gap and ratification of the 1974 India-Bangladesh Agreement,[75] also observed that the political parties in Bangladesh while in opposition take anti-Indian stance and make 'irresponsible' statements for temporary political gains but while in power they try their best to improve relations with India. S.D. Muni in this regard observes:

> As internal conflicts and power rivalries intensify in India's neighbourhood, the different political groups in the region tend to indulge in India-bashing. India has traditionally been a strong internal political factor for the countries in the neighbourhood. The reverse is not true except in case of Pakistan.[76]

This assessment was borne out by two events, one in Nepal and the other on Indo-Bangla border. There were fierce, violent anti-India protests in Nepal following a reported anti-Nepal statement by a popular film star in India and an anti-India campaign by a section of Bangladesh politicians following border skirmish between Bangladesh Rifles and Indian Border Security Force.

Misgovernance in South Asia

Muni also considers internal turbulence and socio-political conflicts in India and the neighbouring States a threat to regional peace and stability in South Asia. The institutions of governance in the region have suffered erosion in legitimacy and efficacy due to sharpening polarization along ethnic and sectarian lines and is mixed up with the struggle for political rights and power rivalries.[77] Ironically, the entire region is unified in its decline of the standards of governance. The Human Development Report South Asia 1999, brought out by the Mahbubul Haq Human Development Centre, Islamabad, finds that South Asia has emerged as one of the most poorly governed regions in the world, with exclusion of the voiceless majority, unstable political regimes and poor economic management. The systems of governance have become unresponsive and irrelevant to the needs and concerns of the people.[78] The report observes:

> Formal institutions of governance have often by passed the voiceless majority. These are the unfortunate many who

> suffer from multiple deprivations on account of their income, creed, gender, or religion. They have not only been excluded from the benefits of growth but have also failed to gain political empowerment. Some of the worst consequences of their exclusion are seen in the high rates of crime and violence throughout the region. From the murders and armed robberies that instill insecurity and fear to the internal conflicts that have tamed the region, from Shia-Sunni conflict in Pakistan to the caste-based crimes in India, South Asia seems to be at war with self.[79]

The report notes that all nations of South Asia face the pernicious evils of endemic corruption, social exclusion and inefficient civil services.[80] The policy direction for India in such a situation is to project itself in the neighbourhood as a bulwark of democracy and secularism- but it can do so only by improving its own governance and by fighting the forces of sectarian extremism.[81]

Being the 'core sector' of South Asian regionalism India has a special responsibility to respond to the situation in a mature manner. India's basic dilemma remains how to reconcile its preference for bilateralism as a model for building relationship with the compulsions for regionalism.[82] The trend as predicted by S.D. Muni in early '90s would be two identifiable patterns:

> One is marked by close interaction - as with Bangladesh, Bhutan, the Maldives, Nepal and Sri Lanka. Such interaction would grow in positive context and also dissent and divergence, but remain generally manageable. The thrust in this interaction would be on economic issues, requiring greater Indian initiative and push. The other pattern is characterized by distrust and intense acrimony as in the relations between India and Pakistan.'[83]

'Peace, Security and Development' Initiative in SAARC

Pakistan at the Tenth SAARC Summit in Colombo made a determined bid to suggest that SAARC Summit leaders should formally and collectively discuss the security situation in Asia in the context of nuclearisation of the subcontinent. Pakistan Prime Minister Nawaz Sharif proposed a 'peace, security and development' initiative envisaging possibility of 'mediation and conciliation' by SAARC Foreign Ministers and a conference on 'South Asian Security and Development'.[84] The task of the conference was proposed to be the preparation of an agreement on 'renunciation of the threat and the use of force' and 'peaceful settlement of disputes'. This was taken by India as yet another Pakistani attempt to bypass her 'sacred' doctrine of bilateralism and bring in a third element of mediation between Indo-Pak disputes. Invoking SAARC Charter provision Indian diplomacy went all out to defeat Pakistani move at the Summit. President Chandrika Kumaratunga of Sri Lanka gave some oblique hints that SAARC Charter would in future open up political discussion. In response to media queries after the conclusion of Tenth Summit she said:

> It is still in the outer circle. Let us wait and see. You must not forget that some of our members have problems that go back fifty years. It is only through people to people contact that bigger issues could be resolved.[85]

She also maintained that despite SAARC Charter prohibiting the discussion of contentious issues they had welcomed bilateral discussions on the sidelines of the summits.[86] The proposal of Pakistani Prime Minister for 'peace, security an development' did not make much headway. In fact, the formal Summit Declaration endorsed India's position and put the issue of peace and security in a global rather than mere South Asian context. The relevant para-78 of the Declaration read as under:

> The Heads of State or Government were of the view that stability, peace and security in South Asia could not be considered in isolation of the global security environment. Although great power rivalry, which the NAM had consistently opposed, no longer posed a serious threat and the danger of a global nuclear conflagration had abated, yet some States had sought to maintain huge arsenals of nuclear weapons. The NPT and the CTBT, to which some SAARC members were signatories had not led to any progress towards nuclear disarmament nor prevented proliferation. They underscored their commitment to the complete elimination of nuclear weapons and the need for promoting nuclear disarmament on a universal basis, under effective international control....[87]

This declaration was projected as a diplomatic victory not only for India but for the region as a whole since it took into account India's irreducible security concerns that nuclear weapons in possession of China pose a threat and that the nuclear haves must talk of the CTBT and the NPT on equal terms, not from a position of advantage.[88] Most of the media reports in India expressed great happiness at India's 'victory'. One such report noted:

> ... it was clear even before the start of the summit, that Pakistan had been stonewalled. Speaking to the press ahead of the summit, the host Foreign Minister, Mr. Lakshman Kadirgamar of Sri Lanka, made no bones about the fact the SAARC charter gave no scope for formal discussion of political issues dividing the members. At any rate, the Colombo meet was to be quintessentially, an economic summit, he said.
>
> This was a major blow to Pakistan which was hoping that the fear of a nuclear holocaust would wrench the SAARC nations from India which had set off the bomb first. Pakistan also hoped that latent fears of Indian hegemony would help rally these nations round it. Pakistan had apparently not grasped the changing perception about India in the region following the Gujral doctrine.[89]

SAARC endorsement of India's position on peace and security in the global context apart, the Summit did not resolve the regional dilemma and stalemate on contentious political issues. It is now well known that there is a general feeling among intelligentsia and well meaning non-government activists that unless political disputes are sorted out there can be no real cooperation among SAARC countries. The nuclearisation of India, as well, has not lessened the fears of Indian domination amongst smaller SAARC countries. However, the governments of these countries (with the exception of Pakistan), by and large, accept Indian view that the cooperation in economic, social and technical fields need not wait for the solution of political disputes. India's official policy thus puts severe limitations on its ability to create a harmonious political environment in the region. The geo-political reality of India's size and power potential cannot be altered. Likewise, her security concerns need to be appreciated by her SAARC neighbours. India, nevertheless, in her own interest will have to rethink its policy of bilateralism for a larger role in promoting regional and global peace and development. An Indian academician rightly observes:

> ... As the largest and stablest democratic power, India has a special responsibility in settling the tone for bilateral relationship and giving a lead in evolving an acceptable

framework of cooperative relations in the region. Indeed, if India has to rise to the challenge of true leadership it can hardly fight shy of taking steps for meaningful accommodation with its smaller neighbours. Its ability to influence regional affairs would essentially depend on how it carries neigbours with it creating a climate conducive for accelerating peace and development in the region.[90]

Quite obviously Indian policy cannot rest on the laurels of a diplomatic victory over Pakistan. It has to do much more to get its role as a pivotal power in SAARC acceptable to other member countries.

India and Sub-Regionalism

The trend towards close interaction of India with smaller neighbours (other than Pakistan) took a significant turn and concrete shape after India's adoption of Gujral Doctrine. Nepal and Bangladesh have been insisting on the need for multilateral cooperation among the countries of the region for utilisation of the hydrological resources. Prior to Gujral Doctrine, India persisted with its straitjacket bilateralism with regard to the utilisation of river waters of the eastern Himalayas. However, due to Gujral's stress on good neighbourly policy which envisaged, inter-alia, that except in matters involving vital security and economic issues, India's approach would be non-coercive, flexible, generous and accommodative, a positive atmosphere was built up for Bangladesh and Nepal to float the idea of sub-regional cooperation.

In December 1996 Nepal circulated an approach paper in the meeting of the SAARC Council of Ministers on the feasibility of sub-regional cooperation among Nepal, Bhutan, Bangladesh and India.[91] Earlier in May 1996 SAARC Council of Ministers had endorsed the idea of forming a growth triangle consisting of the north-eastern part of India, Bangladesh, Bhutan, and Nepal.[92] In April 1997, the Foreign Secretaries of these countries in a meeting in Kathmandu drew up a document containing the objectives, principles and plan of action for the growth triangle.

Sub-regional Cooperation

The idea of sub-regional cooperation was advanced in the context of a very slow growth of SAARC process in economic areas[93] and positive political climate generated among the four countries which mooted a South Asian Growth Quadrangle (SAGQ).[94] A large number of projects were identified for implementation under the aegis of SAARC Regional Project Fund. However, none could be implemented due to lack of political will and financial resources. The signing of Mahakali Treaty between India and Nepal in 1996, transit facilities for Nepal to Bangladesh via the eastern corridor of India and through Bangladesh to overseas countries in 1997,Ganga Water Sharing Agreement between India and Bangladesh in 1996 provided the appropriate catalyst for the Foreign Ministers of these countries to launch sub-regional economic cooperation in April 1997.[95] The objectives, principles and plan of action earlier decided by the Foreign Secretaries were approved. Six sectors were identified for cooperation to be undertaken outside SAARC—these were multi-modal transport and communications, energy, trade and investment facilitation and promotion, tourism, optimum utilization of natural resources endowment and environment.[96]

The concept of sub-regional cooperation outside SAARC was not acceptable to Pakistan, while Sri Lanka and Maldives were initially hesitant. Pakistan considered this an attempt to isolate the three countries and damaging for SAARC. Sri Lankan President in December '97 said:

> No, we don't need to form blocks within SAARC, there is nothing we can't resolve within ourselves through dialogue.[97]

The reaction in opposition political circles in Bangladesh to the idea of sub-regional cooperation was fierce. Leader of the Opposition Begum Khaleda Zia believed that 'the proposed grouping, called South Asian Growth Quadrangle (SAGQ) is designed to dismantle SAARC and establish Indian expansionism'.[98] The anti-India commentators tried to create a spectre of Indian hegemony. One commentator maintained:

> Militarily, the three smaller member-states of the sub-regional group might be persuaded by India into demilitarizing and cutting their defence spending with India assuming the responsibility of their defence and security...
>
> Economically, the smaller states like Bangladesh, Nepal and Bhutan will be integrated with the eastern zone of India. Because of its natural resources, industrial potential and technological advancement, India is in an advantageous position in South Asia...

> Internationally, Bangladesh's foreign policy will be hitched on to the foreign policy directions of India. This will alienate Pakistan and its friendly countries in the Muslim world and also lead to the loss of huge foreign currency remittances for Bangladesh. Moreover, the close alliance of Bangladesh with India divorcing the Islamic Republic of Pakistan will create a negative impression among the Islamic states. So in the final analysis it appears that under the proposed sub-regionalism the national interests of Bangladesh as also of the other smaller states will be jeopardized.[99]

These arguments seemed to be the handiwork of vested interests opposed to regional cooperation in South Asia since the same arguments could be advanced by them regarding regional cooperation under the aegis of SAARC.[100]

The challenge for Indian policy establishment, despite positive impact of Gujral doctrine, was, therefore, real and difficult. The issue was discussed in SAARC Summits at Male (1997) and Colombo (1998). The Male Summit declaration reiterated the 'determination to reinforce the unity and cohesion of SAARC' and further decided that 'with the objective of enhancing regional solidarity and promoting overall development within SAARC, the Heads of State or Government encouraged, under the provisions of Articles VII and X of the Charter, the development of specific projects relevant to the special individual needs of three or more Member States.'[101]

An identical declaration under the sub-heading 'Sub-Regional Cooperation' was made in the Tenth SAARC Summit Declaration.[102] Article VII of the Charter provides that "the Standing Committee may set up Action Committees comprising member states concerned for the implementation of projects involving more than two but not all member States."Article X incorporates general provision on exclusion of bilateral and contentious issues from SAARC deliberations and provision regarding decisions at all levels to be taken on the basis of unanimity. The concept of sub-regional cooperation was thus basically altered to bring the same within the purview of SAARC unanimity. The projects on sub-regional cooperation will thus have to be cleared by the Council of Ministers within the SAARC parameter.

The idea of the growth quadrangle was thus subjected to the snails-pace of SAARC process which was devoid of political will and financial resources. It merely provided an opportunity to the anti-India hate brigade to inflame passions and fears of Indian domination.

The idea of growth quadrangle is, however, based on experiences of the countries in Asia-Pacific region and envisages cooperation among three or more countries for development of a geographically contiguous zone consisting of a part, or the whole, of each of the participating countries. The concept of growth triangles is also called National Economic Territories (NETs) to emphasise the natural aspects, viz., geographical proximity, areas lying in common river basin systems, regions around the rim of the sea or bay, or areas linked and served by important ancient trade routes etc.[103] The proposed South Asian Growth Quadrangle incorporating most of these factors can prove to be an excellent testing ground for the concept as well as the will of the SAARC to promote development and welfare of the people in South Asia.

India and Trans-Regional Groupings

In the changed political and economic context after the end of the cold war India has been trying to adjust her policies to take full advantage of the newly emerging global order. One such shift in India's policy stance was much talked about 'Look-East Policy'.[104] Acknowledging the growing importance of Asia-Pacific region in international trade and industrial activities and in pursuance of its own vision of a larger role in global economy Indian Prime Minister Narasimha Rao in 1993 declared in Singapore that 'the Asia Pacific would be the springboard for our leap into the global market place...much more is possible and desirable. India therefore, wants a real and sizeable jump.'[105] It was in keeping with this policy that India started to look towards ASEAN and APEC for a closer association and participation.[106] India's move towards other regional associations and groupings could also be partly attributed to her frustration and irritation due to the attitude of her neighbours in SAARC. S.D. Muni maintains:

> For India, though SAARC is a preferred channel of integrating South Asia through cooperative interdependence, it does not promise high economic incentives. India's regional trade in South Asia is 1 per cent of its total foreign trade. Even in a strengthened SAARC when this trade increases substantially, it cannot fulfil the needs of the growing Indian

economy. India also feels frustrated in its failure to induce Bangladesh for forging comprehensive economic cooperation ties and to induce Pakistan in establishing normal trade and economic relations at the bilateral level, not to mention the irritation arising out of the communal question in these relations. Therefore, India has to look towards other economically dynamic regions for its investments, technology and trade. Hence its moves towards ASEAN, APEC and the Indian Ocean Rim.[107]

India and ASEAN

ASEAN was forged by the South-East Asian nations after the failure of Afro-Asian movement in the '50s.[108] The member countries of ASEAN shared a common perception about threat from communism. India regarded pro-US ASEAN members like Thailand, the Philippines as stooges of neo-colonialism. Their membership of security organisation - SEATO which was led by the U.S. was in negation of Indian policy of non-alignment.[109] Later, during the '70s and '80s, differences between India and some ASEAN[110] nations persisted on the issues of Indian Ocean as a zone of peace. Some ASEAN countries—Thailand, Singapore and the Philippines—wanted the U.S. to establish military base in Diego Garcia island of the Ocean to counter Soviet influence. Indo-Vietnam relations were also a source of friction between India and ASEAN.[111]

The end of the cold war, however, dramatically changed this situation.[112] India became a sectoral dialogue partner of ASEAN in the areas of trade, investment, tourism, science and technology in 1993. Later, in 1995 at the Fifth ASEAN Summit in Bangkok, acknowledging India's potential as a major power, her status in ASEAN was upgraded to full dialogue partner.[113] Some observers believe that ASEAN-India relationship will further be consolidated due to following factors:

(i) Every successive government in India since 1991 has supported the 'Look East Policy'.

(ii) In addition to geographic proximity ASEAN has strong civilisational linkages with India.

(iii) ASEAN and India have similar political value systems based on respect for the principles of sovereignty, territorial integrity, non-interference in the internal affairs of states, peaceful settlement of disputes and renunciation of the use of force. They have no territorial disputes nor any conflict of strategic interests. There is thus a convergence of political and strategic interests.

(iv) ASEAN and India share their concerns over regional political and security environments, particularly in the Korean Peninsula and South China Sea.

(v) ASEAN and India share their view that multi-polarity on a regional and global scale are the best guarantees for peace, security and stability.

(vi) The peoples and governments of ASEAN and India have faced more or less similar problems while striving for national security and economic development in the increasingly interdependent world.

(vii) There is convergence on pursuing the policies of openness and liberalisation in respect of trade and economic issues.[114]

Bangladesh, India, Myanmar, Sri Lanka, Thailand Economic Cooperation (BIMSTEC)

India has also become a member of Bangladesh, India, Myanmar, Sri Lanka, Thailand Economic Cooperation (BIMSTEC) which was formed in late 1997. This came up primarily as a result of 'Look-West Policy' of Thailand. Some observers see BIMSTEC as a link between SAARC and ASEAN which might be extended to include Japan in future. Some Indian economists advocate that BIMSTEC is a new hope for enhanced cooperative economic interaction in which large international infrastructure projects can be taken up in India's backward north-eastern states involving India, Bangladesh, Myanmar and Thailand, and even Nepal which has an observer status in BIMSTEC. One such economist maintains:

> ...if SAARC cannot grapple with trade policy issues it will remain a talking shop and slowly lose its relevance...Rather than expend energy on breathing new life into a moribund SAARC, India will be better off allowing SAARC to grow at its own pace and at a pace that Pakistan will allow it to grow by, and instead devote greater energy and more resources to BIMSTEC.[115]

In their Third Ministerial Meeting held in the first week of July 2000, the member countries of BIMSTEC decided to develop new transport links, expand energy cooperation and enhance trade. It was decided to speed up construction of trans-Asian highway, push cooperation in the field of energy and go for preferential trading arrangement. The Ministers also decided to set up an Inter Governmental Committee (IGC) to prepare a concept paper for free trade among member countries.[116]

Professor I.N. Mukherji of Jawaharlal Nehru University, New Delhi maintains that BIMSTEC, being more cohesive politically than SAARC, can take decisions quickly.[117]

Mekong Ganga Cooperation (MGC) forum

In pursuit of its 'Look East' policy India launched a new cooperative forum - The Mekong Ganga Cooperation (MGC) forum - with five of its eastern neighbours, namely, Myanmar, Thailand, Laos, Cambodia and Vietnam in November 2000 in Laotian capital Vientiane. The Vientiane Declaration issued on this occasion spelt out the parameters of this forum to include tourism, culture and education as the initial areas of cooperation.[118] Some observers see this as an Indian effort for battling Chinese influence in Indo-China. However, the Foreign Minister of India Jaswant Singh maintained that:

> This is a complete misrepresentation and misreading of the initiative. It is not the Mekong region alone, it is the grouping of nations from Ganga to Mekong.... It is an organization not directed at anyone. It is not a formal grouping of nations. It is nations bound together by these two great rivers - Ganga and Mekong. ...This is not directed against anyone. It challenges nobody.[119]

The Indian Foreign Minister viewed this as an affirmation of historical, cultural and geographical ties.

India's Failure to join APEC

India unsuccessfully tried to become a member of Asia Pacific Economic Cooperation (APEC).[120] APEC economies in 1995 accounted for 55 per cent of total global income, 40 per cent of global trade and a combined income of over 13 trillion US dollars.[121] This rich club aims to strengthen an open multilateral trading system without attempting to form a regional trade bloc and to focus on economic rather than political and security issues.

India's failure to join APEC is considered to be a failure of its 'Look East Policy' itself. Underlining India's problems in SAARC some observers feel that India has missed the bus for free trading club. One observer maintains:

> Apart from the SAARC, India is only major country in the world which is yet to become a member of a free trading club. Given the enormous political problems, especially between India and Pakistan, India's domineering position in South Asia, and a number of other economic constraints, notwithstanding the grandiose plans to create a virtual free trade area in South Asia by the year 2001, SAARC is not expected to make much headway. In any case SAARC would not accrue the kind of economic and non-economic benefits that a forum like APEC offer a country like India which has targeted large-scale foreign investments and a manifold increase in its trade volume in coming years.[122]

India's failure to join APEC is attributed to its negative image of an economy still mired in bureaucratic red tape with negative attitudes.

Indian Ocean Rim Association for Regional Cooperation (IOR-ARC)

However, India became a member of Indian Ocean Rim Association for Regional Cooperation (IOR-ARC).[123] This forum was formed in 1997 with the aim of improving trade links and inward investment throughout the Indian Ocean region stretching from Australia through South-East Asia, India, Africa and the Arabian peninsula. The membership of IOR-ARC is open to all sovereign States of the Indian Ocean rim who are willing to subscribe to the principles and objectives of its charter, i.e., non-interference in internal affairs, peaceful co-existence, non-discrimination and Most Favoured Nation (MFN) principle. Focussing on trade and investment, IOR-ARC explicitly excludes bilateral and other issues likely to generate controversy. IOR-ARC at present has nineteen members and two dialogue partners.[124] In addition to India two other SAARC countries—Sri Lanka and Bangladesh—are also members of IOR-ARC. Pakistan's request for membership was recently rejected by the forum due to its failure to grant MFN status to India.

IOR-ARC like APEC is based on the concept of 'open regionalism' which seems to be vague at this stage. The forum has yet to evolve an institutional framework and other rules and procedures for conducting its business.[125]

S.D. Muni reflecting on Indian policy on regionalism concludes:

> As India's attention and efforts are devoted more to South East Asia, Central Asia and the Indian Ocean region, SAARC would get reduced in importance in India's policy. The Indian policy making establishments have been rather uneasy with the constraints imposed on it by the South Asian neighbours in terms of its global perspective and aspirations to play a larger role in world affairs. Even some of the interested great powers were also happy seeing India locked in South Asian affairs. Now that India has got some opening in South Asia and the Indian Ocean Rim, it would like to make the best of this opportunity in projecting itself as an Asian player rather than a mere South Asian power.[126]

Civil Society/ Non-Government Initiatives in SAARC and India

India has been an ardent supporter of promoting people-to-people contact and non-government initiatives in building regional cooperation in South Asia apart from her interest in forging sub-regional and extra-regional linkages.[127] India's approach in this regard was evident at the outset when R.D. Sathe, Foreign Secretary of India, addressing the first meeting of Foreign Secretaries convened in 1981 to consider Bangladesh proposal for regional cooperation maintained:

> ...First and foremost it is important for us to remember that our present exercise has to relate to functional cooperation in areas which are most relevant for the socio-economic development of our peoples. It is basically, therefore, the involvement of our peoples in this exercise which is of cardinal importance. We have to prepare the public opinion in our respective countries. Our intelligentsia and academic community should help in this task....[128]

The Indian Minister of External Affairs Narasimha Rao further elaborated India's position in this regard in 1984 when he said:

> ...It is also necessary to ensure the involvement in this process [of regional cooperation] not only of Governments but

also the peoples of our countries, specially leaders of commerce and industry, scientists and intellectuals.[129]

The Indian Prime Minister Rajiv Gandhi in his concluding address in the inaugural SAARC Summit at Dhaka (1985) underlined Indian approach when he called for involvement of people in every facet of activity because South Asian regional cooperation must be a peoples' movement involving hearts and minds of the people.[130]

The Heads of State /Government of SAARC have been inviting the scholars, professionals, NGOs and media to help reinforce the SAARC process to move into core-areas of cooperation. This is, in fact, a unique experiment to bring together the official SAARC process and parallel independent intellectual efforts by scholars, professionals and NGOs in finding solutions to the South Asian crisis.

Pre-SAARC Initiatives

There have been significant contributions and ground work done by non-official individuals, groups and institutions in promoting the objectives of economic cooperation and conflict resolution in South Asia even before the idea of SAARC was mooted in 1980 by the President of Bangladesh. Shri H. T. Parekh, who was Managing Director of ICICI, for instance, made efforts in 1960 towards expanding the regional economic cooperation. He organised a group of Bombay based business executives and financial professionals with an objective to suggest a South Asian Common Market.[131]

Committee on Studies for Cooperation in Development in South Asia (CSCD)

The efforts made by Shri Parekh dissipated due to 1971 Indo-Pak war but later new initiatives came from Bangladesh and non-governmental efforts by Sri Lankan scholars. Some of these scholars representing research institutions in Bangladesh, India, Iran, Nepal, Pakistan and Sri Lanka met in Colombo in 1978 and established a Committee on Studies for Cooperation in Development in South Asia (CSCD).

The objectives of CSCD were to establish a network of research institutions in South Asia to promote joint studies on the prospects of cooperation among the countries of the region and to promote collective self-reliance within the framework of New International

Economic Order (NIEO).[132] Indian Minister of External Affairs Narasimha Rao appreciatively noted CSCD's efforts in his statement made in the second Meeting of SARC held at Male in 1984. He observed:

> ...The Committee on Studies in cooperation for development in South Asia in which many academic institutions of the region are taking part has almost completed the Phase I of its studies and is about to embark upon Phase II. These studies can provide useful inputs for our own work....[133]

Post-SAARC Developments

The initial lead by CSCD was followed by several important institutions in the region - prominent among them being Centre for Policy Research (CPR), New Delhi; Centre for the Study of Developing Societies (CSDS), Delhi; Research and Information System (RIS), New Delhi. These institutes have been active in the field both in terms of independent studies as well as joint venture with institutes from other regional countries.[134]

Non-Government Institutions Involved in Promoting Regional Cooperation

Marga Institute, Colombo which served as the Secretariat of CSCD is another leading institution in the efforts to promote regionalism in South Asia. Some other important non-government, non-official, independent participants engaged in regional dialogue and influencing state policies are International Centre for Ethnic Studies (ICES), Regional Centre for Strategic Studies (RCSS), South Asian Human Rights Documentation Centre, South Asian Forum for Human Rights, Independent Group on South Asian Cooperation (IGSAC) and Coalition for Action on South Asian Cooperation (CASAC).

Coalition for Action on South Asian Cooperation (CASAC) was established in 1994 and comprises of administrators, journalists, academics, business people and politicians. CASAC aims at promoting on going dialogues in SAARC by spreading awareness of the Association. It has launched several projects, seminars and publications dealing with conflicts, governance and cooperation in South Asia.[135]

Citizens' Commission for South Asia

In a major initiative CASAC was instrumental in setting up a Citizens' Commission for South Asia. The Citizens' Commission is comprised of eminent personalities from the seven SAARC nations. In their first meeting held in Kathmandu, Nepal on December 1-3, 2000 under the chairmanship of former Indian Prime Minister Inder Kumar Gujral, the Commission brought out a joint declaration.[136] The declaration deplored the interruption in SAARC Summit-level meetings and advocated that the impediments to purposeful and constructive regional cooperation should be removed through appropriate confidence-building measures, dialogue and the peaceful means. It further stressed the need to finalise and operationalise the SAFTA treaty and to take a common stand on globalization issues. It drew attention to the opportunities offered by information technology and the need for good democratic governance and recommended the measures to enhance the role of the Civil Society.[137] The objective of the Commission is to stress the role of Civil Society in creating a favourable climate for regional cooperation.

There are a number of organizations working on specific areas of co- operation in South Asia under the aegis of SAARC. These are SAARC Chamber of Commerce and Industry (SCCI), SAARC LAW, SAARC Association of Speakers and Parliamentarians and South Asian Media Association (SAMA).[138]

Initiatives Inspired by Official SAARC Agenda

The Independent Group on South Asian Cooperation (IGSAC) was the first to respond to the call of innovative partnership made by SAARC Heads of State/Government in Male Summit of 1990. IGSAC was created by South Asian Perspectives Network Association (SAPNA) under the auspices of the United Nations University in 1991. It comprised of fifteen South Asian scholars, professionals and policy-makers who had in-depth familiarity with region and the SAARC process.[139]

The IGSAC Report

The IGSAC report presented to the 1991 SAARC Summit in Colombo was unanimously endorsed and incorporated in the Summit Declaration. The report made following valuable observations:

(i) South Asia has a common history, common eco-system and shared fundamental values which could provide a vision of a South Asian Community based on unity in diversity;

(ii) Today South Asia is facing a multifaceted crisis of poverty, slow economic growth, uneven development, population pressure, natural resource erosion, high defence expenditure and an internal arms race, social polarization, religious fundamentalism, youth alienation and ethnic conflicts. These conflicts and problems are becoming unmanageable and together with external trends are pushing South Asia further and further to the margins of both the world economy and the international political arena;

(iii) A more complex sustainable human development strategy, than hitherto adopted, which includes greater decentralization and social mobilisation with empowerment of the poor could provide an answer to the region's needs and meet the challenge of human development, participatory democracy and good governance.[140]

The IGSAC Report also laid down an agenda for immediate action in the five core areas of poverty eradication, food security, trade cooperation, payments union and external resource mobilisation.

Independent South Asian Commission on Poverty Alleviation (ISACPA)

The process of seeking independent scholarly input by SAARC continued with the setting up of an Independent South Asian Commission on Poverty Alleviation (ISACPA) at the 1991 Colombo Summit in accordance with the recommendations of IGSAC. The members of this Commission comprising South Asian scholars, government officials and representatives of NGOs and organisations of poor, functioned independently in their personal capacity. The Commission was required to diagnose the failure of the past attempts at poverty alleviation, draw positive lessons from the ground where poor have been mobilized to contribute to economic growth and human development and also to identify the critical elements in a practical, but coherent overall strategy of poverty alleviation in South Asia.

ISACPA Recommendations

The Commission recommended that the overall development strategy should be unambiguously pro-poor and culturally relevant - it should move on two fronts i.e. the open economy industrialization front with pro-poor reforms and the poverty eradication front with social mobilisation and the poor as subjects of the process. The Heads of the State/Government in SAARC Summit, Dhaka in 1993 endorsed the Poverty Commission Report and reiterated their commitment to continue to accord highest priority to the eradication of poverty, preferably by the year 2002 as envisaged in the Commission Report.[141]

Group of Eminent Persons (GEP) Report

The Ninth Male Summit, held in 1997, constituted a Group of Eminent Persons (GEP) to undertake a comprehensive appraisal of SAARC. The report of the GEP submitted in June, 1998, highlighted the main issues requiring focussed attention of the SAARC leaders and identified measures needed to impart a new vitality and sense of direction to the Association. The report made an attempt to define a long range vision for SAARC and to identify the elements for a perspective plan of action including a SAARC Agenda for 2000 and beyond. This report envisaged an Economic Union of South Asia by the year 2020 to be achieved in two stages - by creating a Free Trade Area by 2010 and a Customs Union by 2015. In envisioning the future of SAARC, the report suggests that:

> .....serious cognizance must be taken of the fact, often proclaimed but rarely used as a basis for development policy and action, that South Asia is one of the world's distinctive cultural macro-regions; manifesting great variety, complexity and historical and philosophical depth. The SAARC process must identify the crucial role of culture in the contemporary economic and social formation of the region. Culture forms a vital and sensitive component of a society's regenerative processes and a major source influencing and enhancing creative energies in all fields.[142]

Track-Two Diplomacy

Apart from these non-official initiatives which were blessed by the official SAARC process, several other individuals, groups, NGOs and institutions have been sponsoring and participating in a sort of Track-Two Diplomacy in South Asia. Under the influence of external funding agencies, there has been a shift in focus from economic cooperation to the containment of political conflicts in these non-official initiatives.

The U. S. Information Agency (USIS) under its International Visitor Programme designed a programme in 1991 to enable visitors from South Asia to visit research centres and public interest groups involved in conflict resolution. Some of the visitors influenced by this experience decided to form a South Asian Network for Conflict Resolution. Likewise, USIS launched the famous 'Neemrana process' in South Asia.[143]

Two other individuals Tapan Bose from India and Mubashir Hasan from Pakistan formed a Pakistan-India Peoples' Forum.

A Mumbai based organisation, the International Centre for Peace Initiatives (ICPI) has been involving political leaders from South Asia in peace-making processes.[144]

Track-Three Process : The Non-Government Organizations (NGOs) Initiatives

The examples cited above are only illustrative of non-official processes which are actively pursuing the objectives of peace, development and security in South Asia. There are mixed feelings of hope, optimism, fear and uncertainty in the efficacy of this dialogue process.

While there is widespread frustration due to painfully slow progress of official SAARC process, there are also serious reservations and skepticism about non-official contribution due to its elite character and limited influence on policy makers. The fact that most of the funding and organisational initiative for the non-official efforts originate outside the region vitiates, to some extent, the whole process due to possible motivated external influence. It has been observed that the foreign diplomats and officials rather than the South Asians are more enthusiastic about 'Track Two' process.

However, a positive signal is the emergence of a genuine well meaning NGO sector in South Asia - not the NGOs which reflect the personal ambitions of a rich do-gooder or those which exploit the patronage of donors but the NGOs inspired by grass roots community leaders who start movements for the benefit of the poor.

The Human Development Report on South Asia (1997) notes an impressive growth in the number of Civil Society organisations in South Asia (well over 85,000 NGOs). The experience of NGO movements in Sri Lanka and Bangladesh is particularly encouraging. It has been estimated that approximately one quarter of population in Bangladesh benefit from NGO activities. In Sri Lanka out of some 30,000 NGOs, one-sixth are involved in development activities. In Pakistan half of the estimated 10,000 NGOs are engaged in programmes for women's development. An issue-based network of these NGOs in South Asia denotes 'Track-Three' of the regional cooperative effort. Dr. Mahbub ul Haq very aptly noted that 'the SAARC nations will find NGO efforts particularly useful if they decide to formulate a concrete programme to overcome the worst aspects of human deprivation in the shortest period of time. NGOs can help reduce the unit cost of future human investment as well as reach the poorest groups in society'.[145]

Conclusion

To sum up, we experienced a paradigm shift in international political and economic relations in the wake of developments following the end of the cold-war. The absence of 'great power' rivalry in South Asia provided India a greater opportunity to push its regional policy agenda through SAARC. The policy of non-alignment had lost its relevance. The ideological and operational terms of India's regional policy were accordingly modified to adapt to the imperatives of the new situation. India's objective was to build a stable, secure and cooperative neighbourhood. For this purpose India took into account the relations of extra-regional powers with her neighbours, bilateral disputes with neighbours and the parameters of new international order dominated by the WTO and the Bretton Woods institutions. India continued to maintain her policy of resolving contentious political disputes with neighbours in a bilateral framework and also to exclude such disputes from the SAARC agenda.

India's belief that greater economic and socio-cultural cooperation in South Asia can smoothen political and strategic discord in the region, enabled her to push SAARC into core areas of economic cooperation in the new context after the end of the cold war. SAARC could operationalise the preferential trading arrangement and prepare a blueprint for South Asian Economic Community in future.

However, the political factors still rein supreme in South Asian regionalism. Despite acceptance of an economic agenda by SAARC member countries, the SAARC process is captive to political discord between India and her neighbours. Indo-Pak relations, in particular, are a negative factor impeding progress towards regional harmony.

India's pursuit of sub-regional and extra-regional linkages reflects, on the one hand, her disappointment and frustration with the slow progress of cooperation in SAARC and on the other, her desire to play a larger Asian and perhaps global role in world affairs.

However, the civil-society and other non-government initiatives supported by India and other countries of the region provide a silver lining for the South Asian regionalism. The deadlock created by the clash of official establishments of the region can perhaps be broken by the non-official civil-society and peoples' initiatives.

REFERENCES

1. For detailed appraisal of two approaches see Achin Vanaik, *India in a Changing World: Problems, Limits and Success of its Foreign Policy*, Orient Longman Limited, New Delhi, 1995. Vanaik maintains that both realism and neo-realism have no place for notions of 'structured inequality' and 'exploitation' which are central to a third approach—the critical one which includes the Marxist approach.
2. *Ibid.*, p. 44.
3. S.D. Muni, "Political Imperatives", in Bimal Prasad (ed.), *Regional Cooperation in South Asia, Problem, and Prospects*, Vikas Publishing House, New Delhi, 1989, p. 37.
4. For details see M. Dubey, "India's Foreign Policy: Aims and Strategies", pp.10-26; Eric Gonsalves, "India's Foreign Policy: A Review", in Nancy Jetly (ed.) *India's Foreign Policy: Challenges and Prospects*, New Delhi, 1999, pp. 133-45; Lalit Mansingh *et al* (ed.), *Indian Foreign Policy: Agenda for 21st Century*, Foreign Services Institute, New Delhi, 1997.
5. J.N. Dixit, *Across Borders: Fifty Years of India's Foreign Policy*, New Delhi, 1998, p. 225.
6. For details see Dipankar Banerjee (ed.), *Comprehensive and Cooperative Security in South Asia*, Institute of Peace and Conflict Studies, New Delhi, 1998; Gowher Rizvi, *South Asia*

in a Changing International Order, New Delhi, 1993.

7. P.R. Chari, "National Security and Regional Cooperation: The Case of South Asia", in Iftekharuzzaman (ed.), *Regional Trends and South Asian Security*, New Delhi, 1997, p. 195; Kanti Bajpai and Stephen Cohen, "Cooperative Security and South Asian Insecurity", in Janne E. Nolan (ed.), *Global Engagement: Cooperation and Security in the 21st Century*, The Brooking Institution, Washington D.C., 1994, pp. 447-80.
8. Iftekharuzzaman, "Emerging Strategic Trends in South Asia", in Lok Raj Baral (ed), *South Asia: Democracy and the Road Ahead*, p. 171.
9. S.D. Muni, "India and Its Neighbours: Persisting Dilemmas and New Opportunities", *International Studies* 30, 2 (1993), p. 189.
10. Mohammed Ayoob, "India Matters", *Washington Quarterly*, Winter 2000, pp. 27-39; Also see K.K. Bhargava, "India and its South Asian Neighbours: Obligations and Privileges", Paper presented at the national seminar on India's Pivotal Role in South Asia: Optimising Benefits and Minimizing Apprehensions, CASAC, New Delhi, April 21, 2000.
11. See Chapter 3.
12. L.E. Rose in F. Robinson (ed.), *Cambridge Encyclopaedia of India, Pakistan, Bangladesh and Sri Lanka*, Cambridge, 1989, p. 236.
13. Robert W. Bradnock, *India's Foreign Policy since 1971*, Royal Institute of International Affairs, London, p. 59.
14. Muni, *India and its Neighbours*, n. 9, p.191.
15. A 46-page policy document known as 'Defence Planning Guidance' was prepared by Paul D. Wolfowitz, Under Secretary for Policy in the Department of Defence, USA. While this document was awaiting clearance of Defence Secretary Dick Chinney, it was disowned because of the outcry within the US and abroad against the document. It was first revealed by *The New York Times*; Also see *The International Herald Tribune*, Singapore, 9 March 1992, p.1.
16. V.P. *Dutt, India's Foreign Policy in the Changing World*, New

Delhi, 1999, p. 3.

17. For an analysis of improvement in the US-India ties since the Eighties see Nalini Kant Jha, "India and the United States: Pursuit and Limit of Accommodation", *Strategic Analysis*, New Delhi, Vol. 27, No. 2, April 1994, pp. 89-107; Also his "Reviving US-India Friendship in Changing International Order", *Asian Survey*, Berkley, Vol. 34, No.12, December 1995, pp. 1035-46; Daniel Kux, *India and United States*: Estranged Democracies, 1941-1991, 1993.
18. Muni, *India and is Neighbours*, n. 9, p. 191.
19. Nearly 75 per cent of Indo-US collaborations were established after 1980 with a marked increase during 1990s, Indo-US Joint Business Council, *US and India: Forging A New Balance*, New Delhi, 1994, p. 2; Also see C. Raja Mohan, "US sees India A Big Emerging Market", *The Hindu*, January 26, 1995.
20. Richard Haas and Gideon Rose, "A New US Policy towards India and Pakistan": *Report of the Independent Task Force*, The Council of Foreign Relations, USA,1997.
21. The US President Bill Clinton himself led the Western reaction against India's 'temerity' to defy the hegemony of nuclear powers. Washington also sponsored the UN Security Council Resolution 1172 of June 5,1998 which called upon India and Pakistan, among other things, to immediately stop their nuclear weapon development programmes. The US Assistant Secretary of States, Karl Inderfurth, reiterated the US expectation from India in this regard in the first week of July 1998. For further details see Statement by Karl Inderfurth, Sub-Committee on Near Eastern and South Asian Affairs, 13 July 1998, Official Text, US Information Service (USIS), New Delhi, 14 July 1998.
22. These sanctions were imposed under the Glenn Amendment. (For details see US Information Agency "Fact Sheet: India and Pakistan Sanctions", *Washington File*, 18 June 1998); A report of an Independent Task Force advocated considerable reduction in US economic sanctions (For details in this regard see Richard Haas and Merton H. Halperin, "After the Tests: US Policy Towards India and Pakistan": *Report of the Independent Task Force*, Council on Foreign

Relations and Brookings Institution, USA,1998).

23. The US Secretary of State Ms. Albright during an hour long meeting in July 1999 with the Indian External Affairs Minister Mr. Jaswant Singh in Singapore complemented Indian diplomacy for the handling of Kargil situation. A senior American official quoted Ms. Albright as describing the Indian handling of the crisis as 'masterful' saying, "you guys did not put a foot wrong"; For further details see *The Economic Times*, 26 July 1999; Also External Affairs Minister Jaswant Singh's interview to C. Raja Mohan, *The Hindu*, 25 July 1999.

24. A 1997 extradition treaty between India and the US came into force on 22nd July 1999. This would allow law enforcement agencies to co-operate in various areas including 'counter-terrorism'. US Secretary of States Madeline Albright condemned terrorism in Jammu and Kashmir state of India saying that "acts of terrorism must stop immediately because such actions make Kashmir conflict more not less difficult to resolve". She further added: "We condemn attacks against civilians and obviously those who perpetrate them and those who give assistance to perpetrators"; For more details see, "Post Kargil Sees a New Dawn in Indo-US Relations", *The Economic Times*, 22 July 1999; Also see Muchkund Dubey, "Kargil Crisis: Limits of Diplomacy", *Mainstream*, July 17, 1999, pp. 7-8.

25. Text of Vision Statement issued during U.S. President Bill Clinton's Visit to India on March 21, 2000. *The Hindu*, New Delhi March 22, 2000; Also see the Address by the President of the United States to the Joint Session of Indian Parliament, March 22, 2000 and Interview of the President by Peter Jennings, ABC World News, New Delhi, India, March 21, 2000 in *Strategic Digest*, IDSA, Vol. XXX, No. 4, April 2000.

26. The US President Bill Clinton while addressing the people of Pakistan during his brief stopover in Islamabad on March 25, 2000 spoke of four 'R's to improve the situation in the sub-continent - (a) Restraint, (b) Reduce tensions by standing against violence, (c) Respect for the Line-of-Control in Jammu and Kashmir, and (d) Restore the dialogue. "Clinton's TV Address in Pakistan", *Mainstream*, Vol. XXXVI, No. 18, April 22, 2000, pp. 9-11; Also see Amit Baruha, "A Lecture to

Pakistan", *Frontline*, Clinton's Yatra Special edition, Vol.17, No.7, April 1-14, 2000.

27. *Economic Times*, 12 May 2001, Armitage Clubs Pak with Rogues.
28. Swaran Singh, "Sino-South Asian Ties: Problems and Prospects", *Strategic Analysis*, Vol. XXIV, No.1, April 2000, p. 34; Also see Parshotam Mehra, "China and South Asia - Some Reflections on the Past and the Future", *China Report*, New Delhi, Vol. 30, No.3, July-September 1994; "China and South Asia in 21st Century", *Spotlight on Regional Affairs*, Institute of Regional Studies, Islamabad, Vol. XVIII, No. 10, October 1999.
29. As quoted by M. Tully and Z. Masani, *From Raj to Rajiv: Forty Years of Independence*, B.B.C. Books, London, 1988, p. 114.
30. Karan R. Sawhny, "Sino-Pakistani Nuclear Alliance: Prospect and Retrospect", *Mainstream*, Vol. XXXVIII, No.18, April 22, 2000, pp. 19-25; Also see Savita Pandey, "China's Nuclear Doctrine", *Strategic Analysis*, Vol. XXIII, No.12, March 2000, pp. 2011-37.
31. *The Hindu*, 12 May 2001.
32. The ethnic conflict between the Serbs and Albanian community in the Kosovo province of Yugoslavia led to military intervention by NATO which, claiming it a 'humanitarian intervention', indulged in a 78-day massive bombing campaign against Yugoslavia in 1999. NATO's declared objectives were to stop the repression against Kosovo's Albanian majority by the Yugoslavian Serbs, to put an end to ethnic cleansing and ensure that human rights were not violated. However, there are reports that a year after UN forces were stationed in Kosovo, there are vicious attacks against minorities (mainly Serbs and Roma Gypsies), organised crime is flourishing and an institutional void created after the war; For further details see Vaiju Narvane, "Inside Kosovo" (IV Parts), *The Hindu*, 30 March-2 April 2000.
33. During a recent visit to India, Russian Prime Minister Primakov suggested a strategic alliance between India, China and Russia to counter the emergence of a uni-polar world

dominated by one super power; For details see "Timely Proposal", *The Asian Age*, 23 December 1998; "Barely Hugs", *The Telegraph*, 24 December 1998.

34. The most important event that established the credibility of the Chinese posture of neutrality during Kargil conflict was the Chinese response to the visit of the Prime Minister Nawaz Sharief during June 28—July 3, 1999. The Chinese Premier Zhu Rongji in his meeting with Nawaz Sharief gave expression to China's policy on Kargil. He described Kashmir as a 'historical issue involving territorial, ethnic and religious elements which require to be solved through peaceful means and the initiatives for this had to come from Islamabad and New Delhi', Shao Zongwei, "Zhu Urges Quick Return to stability in Kashmir", *China Daily*, June 12, 1999, p. 1.
35. Muni, *India and its Neighbours*, n. 9, pp.191-92.
36. Srikant Pranjpaye, *India and South Asian States since 1971*, New Delhi, 1985, p. 3.
37. L.J. Cambri and S.L. Spregel, "International Regions: A Comparative Approach to Five Subordinate Systems", in *International Quarterly*, December 1969, pp 361-80; The Contori Spiegel Model described the interaction of the region in the context of a core sector, peripheral sector and intrusive sector. The core sector consists of a shared social, political, economic or organisational background or activity among a group of states which are alienated from the core sector in some degree by economic organisational, social or political factors and the intrusive sector consists of the extra regional or outside intervention in the politics of that region. India constitutes the core and the rest of the nations belong to the periphery.
38. For details see Ashutosh Varshney, "Three Compromised Nationalisms: Why Kashmir has been a Problem", in Raju G. C. Thomas, (ed.), *Perspectives on Kashmir: The Roots of Conflict in South Asia*, Boulder, 1992, pp. 191-232; J.N. Dixit, *Anatomy of a Flawed Inheritance: Indo-Pakistan Relations 1970-1994*, New Delhi, 1995, pp. 196-210.
39. For details see, Ayesha Jalal, *Democracy and Authoritarianism in South Asia: A Comparative and Historical*

Perspective, New Delhi, 1995; Vishnu Prajapati (ed.), *South Asia: Power and Politics (Vol.1, 2, 3)*, New Delhi, 1998; Sridhar K. Khatri, "Democratisation and Regional Cooperation in South Asia", *The Everest Herald*, 26 April, 1996.

40. For details see S.D. Muni, *India and Nepal: A Changing Relationship*, New Delhi, 1995; Also by the same author "India and Nepal Towards the Next Century", in Lalit Mansingh *et al* (ed.), *Indian Foreign Policy: Agenda for the 21st Century*, n. 4; Chaitanaya Mishra, "Indo-Nepal Relations: A view from Kathmandu", in Bertam Bastiampillai (ed.), *India and Her South Asian Neighbours*, S.W.R.D. Bandarnaike National Memorial Foundation, Colombo, 1992.

41. *Annual Report, Govt. of India, Ministry of External Affairs*, 1991-92, pp.1-2; Also see Mahendra P. Lama, "Indian Aid and Investment in the backdrop of Liberalisation in Nepal" in Kalim Bahadur and Mahendra P. Lama (ed.) *New Perspectives in Indo-Nepal Relations*, Delhi,1995.

42. *Annual Report, Govt. of India, Ministry of External Affairs*, 1993-94.p. 1; Also see Mahendra P. Lama, "Investment in South Asia: Issues, Constraints and Opportunities", Paper presented in the Conference on South Asia 2010, organised by CASAC, Kathmandu, 1-3 December 1999; Also paper by him, "Economic Cooperation as Confidence Building Measures: Role of India in South Asia", presented in the national seminar on India's Pivotal Role in South Asia: Optimising Benefits and Minimizing Apprehensions organised by CASAC, New Delhi, April 21, 2000.

43. A number of studies have critically analysed India's involvement in Sri Lanka. Some notable studies from Indian perspective are: S.D. Muni, *Pangs of Proximity: India and Sri Lanka's Ethnic Crisis*, New Delhi, 1993; P.S. Suryanaraynana, *The Peace Trap: An Indo-Sri Lankan Political Crisis*, New Delhi, 1988; S.C. Sardeshpande, *Assignment Jaffna*, New Delhi, 1992; P.Sahdevan, "India and Sri Lanka", in Lalit Mansingh et al (ed.), *Indian Foreign Policy*, n. 4, pp. 159-95; For Sri Lankan perspective on the issue see K.M. de Silva, *Regional Powers and Small State Security: India and Sri Lanka,* New Delhi, 1995; Shelton U.Kodikara (ed.), *Indo-Sri Lankan Agreement of July 1987*,

University of Colombo, Colombo, 1989.

44. For details of this controversy see Chapter 4.

45. An Independent Report titled "Indo-Sri Lankan Economic Cooperation - an Operational Programme" issued in 1993 by World Institute for Development Economic Research (WIDER) outlined practical steps to promote closer economic cooperation between the two countries. It also focussed on granting reciprocal preferential treatment across the board to all the commodities, except for a small limited exclusion list of items. For further details see Panchmukhi et al, Indo-Sri Lankan Economic Cooperation: an Operational Programme, WIDER Study Group Series No. 8, Helsinki, 1993; Lal Jaywardne *et al., Indo-Sri Lankan Economic Cooperation: Facilitating Trade Expansion through a Reciprocal Preference System*, WIDER Study Group Series No. 9, Helsinki, 1993.

46. For details see The Island, 21 July 1994; *The Hindu*, 2 August 1994.

47. *Annual Reports, Govt. of India, Ministry of External Affairs,* 1994-95, p. 7 and 1995-96, pp. 6-7.

48. *Annual Report*, 1990-91, n. 39, p. 5

49. Border enclaves between India and Bangladesh are a legacy of senseless partition of the sub-continent in 1947. There are some 90 enclaves belonging to Bangladesh in Cooch Behar District of West Bengal. In 1971 India signed a treaty for handing over the enclaves to Bangladesh. However, due to local resistance, litigation and the need for constitutional amendment, the transfer of enclaves at the Border has been delayed indefinitely. However, with positive political will India on June 26, 1992 transferred the Tin Bigha corridor to Bangladesh to facilitate easy movement of the local people in the country. For details see Vidya Shankar Aiyar, "Bangladesh", in Dipankar Banerji (ed.), *Comprehensive and Cooperative Security in South Asia*, Institute of Peace and Conflict Studies, New Delhi, 1998, pp. 88-120.

50. Following the demolition of Babari Masjid in India, the Parliament of Bangladesh, the Jatiya Sangsad, passed a resolution referring to the unfortunate events and also stated

that it hoped that the promises made by the Government of India on its reconstruction would be implemented soon. India considered this an interference in her internal affairs; For details on the text of the resolution passed by the Bangladesh Parliament and subsequent Indian objection to it, refer to A.S. Bhasin (ed.), *Indo-Bangladesh Relations 1971-1994*, Documents 185, 186, 187, Vol. I, Delhi, 1996, pp. 321-24.

51. For a detailed analysis of these talks see, J.N. Dixit, *Anatomy of Flawed Inheritance: Indo-Pak Relations 1970-1994*, New Delhi, 1995, pp. 196-210.
52. Former Indian Prime Minister I.K. Gujral in an interview with the author on May 13, 2000 emphatically asserted that his approach to relations with neighbours created an atmosphere of trust for amicable resolution of bilateral disputes.
53. Inder Kumar Gujral, "Post Cold War Era : An Indian Perspective", *World Affairs*, Vol. I, Janaury-March 1997 p.51; Also see his *A Foreign Policy for India*, External Publicity Division, Ministry of External Affairs, Government of India, 1998.
54. Padmaja Murthy, "The Gujral Doctrine and Beyond", *Strategic Analysis*, Volume XXIII, No.4, July 1999, p. 641.
55. For details see Bhabani Sengupta, "India in the Twenty First Century", *International Affairs*, Vol. 73, No.1, January 1997, pp. 297-314.
56. See "The Gujral Doctrine at Work in Nepal" (edit.) *The Deccan Chronicle*, 10 June 1997; Bhashyam Kasturi, "Momentum after the Meeting", *The Deccan Herald*, 19 June 1997.
57. For detailed reports on the Treaty see, *The Hindustan Times*, 14 December 1996; Pioneer, 26 December 1996.
58. For a report on the world press coverage of the Treaty see, *The Bangladesh Times*, 19 December 1996.
59. For details on repatriation of Chakma refugees see, *The Pioneer*, 6 January 1998.
60. *The Times of India*, New Delhi, December 22, 1997.
61. *Ibid.*
62. Former Prime Minister I.K. Gujral in an interview with the author strongly denied this charge. He asserted that he had

taken a number of steps to normalise relations with Pakistan and specifically mentioned about the unilateral visa-relaxation scheme which was initiated during his tenure in office.

63. J.N. Dixit, *Across Borders*, n. 5, p. 234; Also see his *Anatomy of Flawed Inheritance*,n. 49 pp. 196-210
64. Text of Lahore Declaration, *Public Opinion Trends, Analyses and News Service*, Pakistan Series, Volume XXVII, No. 66, March 1999, New Delhi, p. 827.
65. For details see, P.R. Chari, "CBMs: Post Cold War South Asia", *Regional Centre for Strategic Studies Newsletter*, July 1999, pp. 2-5.
66. For details of Kargil conflict see, Jasjit Singh, "Pakistan's Fourth War", *Strategic Analysis*, IDSA, Vol. XIII, No. 5, August 1999, pp. 685-702; Also see "Kargil: Perspectives from Pakistan", *Strategic Digest*, IDSA, Vol. XXIX, No.9, September 1999, pp. 1443-90. (It is a compilation of articles and editorials from news magazines.)
67. Bidanda M. Chengappa, "Pakistan's Fourth Military Takeover" *Strategic Analysis*, Vol. XXIII, No. 9, December 1999, pp. 1435-48.
68. Statement of Nawaz Sharif in ATC-1: Text, *The Dawn*, Pakistan, 9 March 2000.
69. *Ibid.*
70. A Pakistani commentator, M.P. Bhanda was reported to have said that it was generally accepted that Kargil was planned last year and its execution began in February just about the time of Lahore Declaration; See, *Dawn*, 21 July 1999.
71. Kanti P. Bajpai and Stephen P. Cohen (ed.), *South Asia After the Cold War: International Perspectives*, San Francisco, 1993, p.12.The authors define détente as a pursuit of strategic advantage short of hostilities and without resort to elements typifying a cold war... Entente also involves or can involve the pursuit of strategic advantage, but is conceived in economic terms. (This article was written prior to Lahore Bus Diplomacy and Kargil War between India and Pakistan).
72. *Ibid.*
73. *The Hindu*, New Delhi, 31 January 2000.

74. India's relations with Bangladesh were not as cordial after 1975 as prior to Mujib's assassination. In August 1975 Sheikh Mujibur Rahman, the architect of Bangladesh and its first Prime Minister and his entire family including politically active members of his extended family, were assassinated in a military coup organised by pro-Pakistan politicians, army officers and civil servants; For details see J.N. Dixit, *Liberation and beyond-Indo-Bangladesh Relations*, New Delhi,1999, pp. 203-18.

75. The hasty scheme of partition of Indian sub-continent created large number of enclaves in 1947. In May 1974 an agreement for demarcation of land boundary was signed. This was ratified by Bangladesh immediately. India has not yet ratified this treaty. If the border agreement is implemented Bangladesh will get 111 enclaves covering 1258 acres while India will receive 51 enclaves measuring 1174 acres. In addition 3024 acres of Indian land is in the possession of Bangladesh compared to 3006 acres of Bangladesh land with India. For details see 'Demarcation of land boundary agreement between India and Bangladesh, New Delhi, 16 May 1974, *International Relations of Bangladesh and Banglabandhu Sheikh Mujibur Rahman (Documents, Speeches and Press Comments) 1974-1975*, Volume II (compiled by Rabindranath Trivedi, 1999, pp., 145-50); Also see Vandana *Asthana, India's Foreign Policy and sub-continental Politics*, 199 pp. 80-93.

76. Muni, *India and Its Neighbours*, n. 9, p.199.

77. *Ibid.*, pp. 196-97.

78. *Human Development Report in South Asia, 1999*, Human Development Centre, Islamabad, 1999. p. 3.

79. *Ibid.*, p. 3.

80. *Ibid.*, p. 3.

81. Muni, *India and Its Neighbours*, n. 9, p. 200.

82. Nancy Jetley. "India and SAARC", in Virendra Narain & B.C. Upreti (ed.), *SAARC - A Study of Perceptions and Policies*, Jaipur,1991, p. 47.

83. Muni, *India and Its Neighbours*, n. 9, p. 205.

84. For the text of the speech see, *The Island*, 30 July 1998.

85. *The Hindustan Times*, 1 August 1998.
86. *Ibid.*
87. Declaration of the Tenth SAARC Summit, Colombo, SAARC Secretariat, 31 July 1998, p. 26.
88. *The Tribune*, 1 August 1998.
89. *The Hindustan Times*, 2 August 1998.
90. Jetly, n. 80, p. 46.
91. For details see *Concept Paper for Sub-Regional Cooperation in SAARC*, SAARC Secretariat, Kathmandu, 1996; *Approach Paper for Sub-Regional Cooperation in SAARC*, SAARC Secretariat, Kathmandu, 1997.
92. Indian PM Gujral also reaffirmed the idea of sub-regional cooperation in a lecture he delivered at London's Royal Institute of Internetional Affairs (RIIA) in September 1996. For details see Md. Nuruzzaman, "SAARC and Sub-regional Cooperation: Domestic Politics and Foreign Policies in South Asia", in *Contemporary South Asia*, Vol. 8, No. 3, November 1999, pp. 311-23.
93. For details see B.C. Upreti, "Sub-Regional Cooperation in South Asia: Perceptions, Potentials and Problems of Cooperation of the Eastern Himalayan region", Paper presented at the Seminar on *Building Regional Cooperation - India's Role*, organised by Indian Council of South Asian Cooperation, and India International Centre, 11-12 December 1998.
94. Muchkund Dubey, Lok Raj Baral and Rehman Sobhan (ed.), *South Asian Growth Quadrangle: Framework for Multifaceted Cooperation*, New Delhi, 1999, p.7.
95. *Ibid.*, p. 7.
96. *Ibid.*, p. 7.
97. *The Times of India*, New Delhi, December 22, 1997.
98. Dr. Zaglal Haider, "'South Asia Sub-regional Grouping: A Threat to Security of Bangladesh", *Regional Studies*, Islamabad, Volume XV, No. 3, Summer 1997. p. 31.
99. *Ibid.*, pp. 36-37.
100. A section of intellectuals in Nepal were also not in favour of

sub-regionalism. For details see M.R. Josse. "South Asian Sub-regional Grouping: A Block within a Bloc? A Kathmandu Perspective", *Regional Studies*, Islamabad, Vol. XV, No. 3, Summer 1997, pp. 41-52.

101. "Ninth SAARC Summit, Male (1997)", Davender Kumar Madan (ed), *SAARC : Origin Development and Programmes : From 1st to the 9th Summit*, 1992, pp. 222-23.

102. *Declaration of the Tenth SAARC Summit, Colombo, SAARC* Secretariat, Kathmandu, 1998. p.12.

103. Muchkund Dubey et al, *South Asian Growth Quadrangle: Framework for Multifaceted Cooperation*, n. 92, pp.1-2.

104. For an elaborate analysis of 'Look East Policy' see V. Suryanarayana, "Prospects for a Bay of Bengal Community", C. Raja Mohan, "The Asian Balance of Power", and A.N. Ram, "Historical Perspectives", in *Seminar*, March 2000, New Delhi; Sanjaya Baru, "India's Neighbourhood: Economic and Cultural, Not Physical", The Times of India, February 5, 2000; Muchkund Dubey and Nancy Jetley (ed.), *South Asia and its Eastern Neighbours: Building a Relationship in the 21st Century*, FES, New Delhi, 1999.

105. As quoted by Baladas Ghosal, "India, ASEAN and APEC" in Nancy Jetly (ed.), *India's Foreign Policy. Challenges and Prospects* ,1999, pp. 150-51.

106. For details see Sanjaya Baru, "India and Asian Regional Economic Groupings", in Jasjit Singh (ed.), *Cooperative Peace in South Asia*, IDSA, New Delhi, 1998, pp. 107-23; S. Kalegama, "South Asia and Other Regional Economic Groupings", Paper presented to the Conference on South Asia 2010: Challenges and Opportunities, CASAC, Kathmandu, 1-3 December 1999.

107. S.D. Muni, "Regionalism Beyond the Regions: South Asia outside SAARC", in Eric Gonsalves, Nancy Jetly (ed.), *The Dynamics of South Asia, Regional Cooperation and SAARC*, New Delhi, 1999, pp.122-23.

108. For details on the origin and evolution of ASEAN see G.S. Kushwaha, "Regional Trade Cooperation in South East Asia", Paper presented at the Indian Economic Conference on Asian Economic Cooperation, Bombay, 1972, pp. 12-24.

109. For details see Chintamani Mahapatra, *American Role in Origin and Growth of ASEAN*, New Delhi, 1990.

110. Association of South East Asian Nations (ASEAN) was founded in August, 1967 with 5 members, namely Indonesia, Malaysia, the Philippines, Singapore and Thailand. It was expanded when Brunei Darussalam joined in 1984, Vietnam in 1995, Laos and Myanmar in 1997 and Cambodia in 1999. India currently full dialogue partner of ASEAN is also a member of ASEAN's security forum ASEAN Regional Forum (ARF).

111. For details see G.N. Acharya, "India's Role in South East Asia: A Review of India's Foreign Policy 1948-61", *Far Eastern Economic Review*, September 21, 1961, pp. 555-83; Werner Levi, *The Challenge of World Politics in South and South East Asia*, New Jersey, USA, 1968, pp. 49-71; A.N. Ram, "Historical Perspectives", *Seminar*, with special focus on 'Looking Towards East', March 2000.

112. See Baladas Ghosal, "India, ASEAN and APEC", in Nancy Jetly (ed.), *India's Foreign Policy: Challenges and Prospects*, New Delhi, 1999 pp.150-71.

113. For details see S.D. Muni, "India Enters ASEAN's Strategic Equation", *The Times of India*, 17 May 1996; Also see Udai Bhan Singh, "India and ARF: The Post Pokharan II Phase", *Strategic Analysis*, January 1999, pp. 1591-1607; also by him, "Outlook for the ARF: Relevance for India", *Strategic Analysis*, September 1999, pp. 965-91; G.V.C. Naidu, "Future of Institutionalisation in the Asia-Pacific: The ARF and its Implications for India", *Strategic Analysis*, February 2000, IDSA, New Delhi, pp. 1957-70.

114. Soubanh Srithirath, *ASEAN-India Partnership: Towards the Next Millennium*, Ninth India ASEAN Eminent Persons' Lecture, RIS, New Delhi, 1999, pp. 15-16.

115. Sanjay Baru, "Trade and Security: Multilateral and Regional Opportunities", *The Times of India*, 16 November 1999.

116. *The Hindu*, 7 July 2000.

117. I.N. Mukherji, Commentary on New Proposal for Creating Preferential Trading Arrangement, All India Radio, 7 July 2000.

118. For details see V. Jaynath, "The Mekong-Ganga Initiative", *The Hindu*, 28 November 2000.
119. *The Hindu*, 9 November 2000.
120. APEC's membership includes Australia, Brunei, Hong Kong, Indonesia, Japan, Republic of Korea, Malaysia, New Zealand, The Philippines, Singapore, Taiwan, Mauritania, The United States. In 1997 at Vancouver meeting three new members- Vietnam, Russia and Peru - were admitted and India's efforts for entry into the organisation did not succeed. APEC also decided not to consider further expansion till 2007. For further details see Pranay Sharma. "Botched Campaign Fetches APEC Snub", *The Telegraph*, 28 November 1997.
121. G.V.C. Naidu, "India and APEC", *Strategic Analysis*, Vol. XXI, No.12, March 1998, p.1771.
122. *Ibid*., p.1777.
123. For details see *World Focus: Special Issue on Indian Ocean Rim*, May 1997.
124. Members of IOR-ARC: India, Australia, South Africa, Oman, Mauritius, Indonesia, Iran, Kenya, Madagascar, Malaysia, Mozambique, Seychelles, Singapore, Sri Lanka, Tanzania, Thailand, The United Arab Emirates, Yemen and Bangladesh (Japan and Egypt are dialogue partners).
125. For details see S. Kalegama, "South Asia and other Regional Economic Groupings", Paper presented at the Conference *on South Asia 2010: Challenges and Opportunities*, CASAC, Kathmandu, 1-3 December 1999.
126. S.D. Muni, *India in SAARC: A Reluctant Policy Maker*, A Paper prepared for the United Nations University Project on "Globalism and New Regionalism", directed by Professor Bjorn Hettne of Peace and Development Research Institute, Gothenburg University, Sweden, July 1996, pp. 24-25.
127. Nihal Rodrigo, Secretary General, SAARC, in a wide-ranging interview said that ' I do not believe that SAARC was meant to be an exclusively statist association. Contacts between people of South Asia at the non-governmental levels are being encouraged. There are a number of non-government institutions and groups in South Asia which are, what you call, proponents of regional cooperation.', "Attempts at

Regional Cooperation in South Asia", an interview by Nihal Rodrigo to *World Affairs Journal*, Vol. 3, No.1, 1999, p. 13.

128. Statement by R.D. Sathe, Foreign Secretary of India, at the first meeting of Foreign Secretaries in Colombo, 21-23 April, 1981, *Official Text*, S.D. Muni and Anuradha Muni, *Regional Cooperation in South Asia*, New Delhi, 1984, p. 110.
129. Inaugural address by the Minister of External Affairs - South Asian regional Cooperation *Standing Committee First Session, Foreign Affairs Record*, Vol. XXX No. 2, February 1984, p. 73.
130. Prime Minister Rajiv Gandhi's speech at the concluding session of First SARC-Summit, *Foreign Affairs Record*, Vol. XXXI, No.12, December 1985, p. 409.
131. H.T. Parekh, *India and Regional Development*, Bombay, 1969.
132. V.Kanesalingam, "Cooperation Among Scholars: The Role of CSCD", in Bimal Prasad (ed.), *Regional Cooperation in South Asia: Prospects and Problems*, New Delhi, pp. 200-201.
133. Second Meeting of SARC in Male - Sh. Narsimha Rao's statement, *Foreign Affairs Record*, Vol. XXX, No. 7 July 1984, p. 219.
134. For details see Gran Paul, Navnita Chadha and Gowher Rizvi, *Beyond Boundaries; A Report on the State of Non-Official Dialogue on Peace, Security and Cooperation in South Asia*, University of Toronto and York University, Canada, 1997; Also see, Sandeep Waslekar, "Track Two Diplomacy in South Asia", *Urbana, Illinois, ACIDIS Occasional Paper*, Program in Arms Control, Disarmament and International Security, University of Illinois and Urbana, Champaign, 1997.
135. For details see, CASAC *Discussion Paper-I: SAARC Vision for the Second Decade*, A Paper submitted to the Commemorative Session of the SAARC Council of Ministers, New Delhi, November 1995; *CASAC Policy Paper: Strengthening SAARC in its Second Decade*, Paper submitted to the SAARC Leaders on the eve of the Male Summit, May 1997.

136. For details see Annexe IVX.

137. K.K. Bhargava et. al (ed.), *Shaping South Asia's Future*, New Delhi, 1995.

138. Ponna Wignaraja and Susil Sirivardana, *Readings on Pro-Poor Planning through Social Mobilisation in South Asia*, Vol. I, SAPNA and Konrad Adenauer Stiftung, New Delhi, 1998.

139. Report of the Independent Group on South Asian Cooperation (IGSAC), SAARC: Moving Towards Core Areas of Cooperation, UN University South Asian Perspectives Project, Colombo, 1991, pp. 5-6.

140. For details see Report of the Independent South Asian Commission on Poverty Alleviation, Meeting the Challenge, SAARC Secretariat, Kathmandu, 1992; Also Report of the informal workshop, Poverty Reduction in South Asia: Promoting Participation by the Poor, co-sponsored by World Bank and SAARC, Washington DC, October 12-15, 1993.

141. Report of the SAARC Group of Eminent Persons established by the Ninth SAARC Summit: SAARC *Vision Beyond the Year 2000*, SAARC Secretariat, Kathmandu, p.12.

142. Under the Neemrana dialogue process, a group of distinguished citizens from India and Pakistan were invited to meet at Neemrana fort in Rajsthan. This group identified issues like the conventional arms race, nuclear proliferation, Kashmir and economic relations to be discussed over a long period of time. The Neemrana group, facilitated by granting of visas on priority basis by the Governments of India and Pakistan, have held several meetings in India and Pakistan.

143. Ilmas Fatehally, "Conflict Management and Confidence Building Measures in South Asia", Paper presented at the conference on *South Asia 2010: Challenges and Opportunities*, CASAC, Kathmandu, 1-3 December 1999.

144. Mahbub-ul-Haq, Human Development in South Asia, 1997, Human Development Centre, Islamabad, p. 96.

Conclusion

The Indian national movement during its final phase of struggle for independence from the British imperialism articulated a vision for free India's regional and foreign policy. The basic objective of this policy was to forge an Eastern Federation on the plank of anti-imperialism. The ultimate goal was freedom of Asia and peace in the world.

India's efforts during the period immediately after independence were to organise Asia and other regions which were colonised by Western powers. The basic idea was to come together politically for a just, secure and peaceful international order and to rebuild the nations ravaged by colonialism. This approach was marked by a lack of clarity on any specific region to be evolved into a common entity.

Developments in 1960s—wars with China and Pakistan and a severe economic crisis—and failure of India's initial efforts towards regionalism fundamentally changed the regional context in Asia. India had inherited a difficult and hostile neighbourhood as a result of the division of the sub-continent. A vicious cold war-international regime also impinged on India's policy, particularly in respect of her relations with South Asian neighbours. These neighbours had shown a distinct tendency to invite extra-regional influences in South Asia to countervail the power of 'big India'. This was in conflict with Indian policy of non-alignment. India was particularly sensitive to extra-regional powers engaged in cold-war making in-roads in South Asia and enlisting support of the nations in the region for their

their global game-plans. The war of 1971 with Pakistan resulting into the creation of another neighbour, Bangladesh, for India further changed the political context of the region. India emerged as a 'sort of' South Asian power distinct from her initial image of a dreamer for international peace and security which she sought to achieve through Asian unity and resurgence.

Indian Policy on Regional Cooperation in South Asia

The Indian policy response to the proposal for South Asian regional cooperation in 1980 reflected this change in the political context of Asia and world at large. India wanted to exclude the divisive and contentious political issues from any effort for regional cooperation. She insisted on inclusion of a pre-condition that such issues would not be discussed in the regional forum even before launching of SAARC. India's cautious approach was dictated by her belief that in the strife-torn South Asia an emphasis on unifying socio-cultural factors and cooperation in economic areas would ultimately help in ending the political conflict in the region.

Exclusion of Contentious Political Issues: Pakistan Factor

Indian policy in SAARC was spelled out by Prime Minister Indira Gandhi in 1983, even before formal launching of the organisation when in the first meeting of the Foreign Ministers, she said:

> I am glad we are making a beginning. We have our political differences but economic cooperation will give a strong impetus to closer friendship and greater stability in South Asia. With unity we can hope to move ahead to a future of freedom, peace and prosperity.[1]

India's approach in SAARC, therefore, has been to soften the political and strategic divergence through greater economic and socio-cultural cooperation. But the antithesis of Indian policy thrust in SAARC has been the attitude and policy of Pakistan as pronounced by Prime Minister Benazir Bhutto at the SAARC Summit Meeting of 1988. She called upon the SAARC leaders to take a clearer look at the aims and objectives of SAARC when she said:

> ...unresolved disputes, mutual suspicions and rivalries had divided our countries in the past. Some of us were spending too great a proportion of our national resources on defence, maintaining large military forces that face each other. It is,

> therefore, time that SAARC states should consider ways of limiting their arms expenditures and seek a regional solution for curbing the arms race and the danger of nuclear proliferation and war.[2]

In a recent interview to an Indian daily newspaper the Chief Executive of Pakistan, General Parvez Musharraf, said:

> Look at the South Asian Association for Regional Cooperation (SAARC). We cannot even discuss issues that are creating tensions in the region. We can achieve so much and we have achieved nothing. Who is obstructing SAARC? India can play a major role in moving SAARC forward. As the biggest country in the region, it should take others along. One would like to go along if India had the correct attitude.[3]

General Musharraf further confirmed his country's policy on SAARC and India while talking recently to Indian media representatives attending South Asia media conference. He called for enlarging the mandate of SAARC by inclusion of political issues for discussion under the SAARC framework. He maintained that while there should be economic relations with India, there could not be a "relationship" without political reconciliation.[4] Pakistan thus wants unresolved political disputes to be included in SAARC agenda as an essential condition for making progress on issues of socioeconomic cooperation in the region.

The Post-Cold War Phase

In the post-cold war period Indian policy orientation further sharpened its focus on economic cooperation in South Asia. This effort was facilitated by the changed international political context whence superpower rivalry came to an end and India's neighbours could not invoke the interference of extra-regional powers, as hitherto, in South Asia. A new phenomenon of the primacy of economics in international relations under the garb of 'globalization' further created a compelling situation for South Asia to come together and advance the agenda of regional economic cooperation. The 'pro-market' economic policy reforms and India's resilience in maintaining macro-economic stability in the wake of East-Asian financial crisis of 1997 catapulted India to a position of new significance in the global market place.

Globalization and SAARC

The end of the cold war provided greater leeway to India to promote her perception of South Asian cooperation through SAARC. The new economic logic of 'globalization' also impelled the SAARC Member States to adopt market-friendly macro-economic policies (in Sri Lanka this process commenced much earlier in 1970s). SAARC member countries embarked on the initial stage of economic cooperation in the form of a South Asian Preferential Trade Arrangement (SAPTA). A progressive time table to set up a free trade area (SAFTA), a Customs Union (SACU) and an Economic Union by the year 2020 was put in place as recommended by the Group of Eminent Persons.

A perceived common threat is generally considered to be a recipe for a successful regional cooperative arrangement. The examples of the ASEAN and the EU which emerged against the perceived threat of communism are cited as successful examples in this regard. The sponsorship and active support by the United States to these regional groupings, though, were important factors in their emergence and evolution. An absence of a perceived common threat in South Asia is seen to be a negative factor for SAARC. However, in recent past, particularly after the end of the cold war, there is a perceived common threat of marginalisation of the SAARC member countries in the emerging global economy. This is seen as a factor compelling SAARC countries to come together at least on economic issues in international forums, particularly WTO. Further, it now appears to be in the vested interest of the Western nations and their multinational corporations to smoothen the regional integration process in South Asia, particularly after the synchronization of macro-economic policy regimes in these countries in favour of the Market. The economic implications of post-cold war developments may, therefore, act as positive impulses favouring Indian efforts for South Asian integration .

India's Efforts to Create Regional Consensus

India as a matter of policy has been striving to build regional consensus on issues discussed on international forums. Despite Indo-Pak conflict in Kargil, SAARC took a common position on economic issues in the run up for Seattle round of WTO-negotiations in November 1999. SAARC Commerce Ministers after a meeting in August 1999 in Maldives issued a joint statement articulating

SAARC views. The joint statement made following points:

(i) Demand for reduction in import tariffs and abolition of non-tariff barriers prevailing in developed countries.

(ii) Developed world should stop piracy of traditional knowledge of the third world countries.

(iii) Opposition to the introduction of non-trade related issues such as social clause, labour standards and environment in the WTO agenda.

(iv) More time for the developing countries to provide legal cover for goods produced in industrialised countries and by Multi-National Corporations.

(v) Rejection of unilateral trade measures inconsistent with international law, the WTO pacts and basic tenets of multi-lateral trading system.

(vi) Regret that Uruguay round of trade negotiations leading to the formation of WTO did not result in better market access for developing countries.

(vii) Trade Related Intellectual Property Rights (TRIPs) be harmonized with the agreed UN Convention on Bio-diversity.

(viii) Transfer and dissemination of technology to developing and least developed nations be operationalised.[5]

Similarly, on several other issues such as human rights, environment and rights for women SAARC member countries have been taking common position in international forums.

Slow Process of Economic Cooperation in SAARC

The process of economic cooperation among SAARC countries is very slow but the SAARC decision to move into the free trade arrangement can make a significant contribution to the cause of regional cooperation in South Asia. However, on account of low levels of economic development in SAARC member countries, the benefits of trade-liberalisation or free trade may be very limited. A bilateral free trade agreement concluded between India and Sri Lanka in 1998 and operationalised in the year 2000, nevertheless, is an extremely positive development from the point of view of India's policy. This also demonstrates India's determination to pursue her policy objectives in the region.

With the 'spirit of globalization' reigning supreme among the policy establishments and marketisation of economies, SAARC objective of removal of poverty in South Asia has acquired a great significance. In South Asia, where a large mass of people is outside the market economy, the phenomenon of globalization may not bring them any relief. A critic of market economy and SAARC watcher Rehman Sobhan maintains:

> ...the market driven reform agenda has exposed the third world to a process of globalization which has been enormously inequitable and divisive for many developing countries. At the national level, globalization has created two societies—the narrow segment of society which has been co-opted into the process; and the majority which has been left in a state of political disempowerment, poverty and deprivation.[6]

The regional economic cooperation can be considered successful only if the scourge of mass poverty and deprivation in South Asia is eliminated.

Bilateral Conflicts between India and Other SAARC Members

The bilateral disputes between India and other members of SAARC, particularly between India and Pakistan, continue to impede and torment SAARC process. The overwhelming asymmetry between India and other SAARC member countries coupled with India's own image as the colossus of the region in search of a global role reinforces the fear and apprehensions of 'Big India' among her neighbours. India is seen as the major external threat. This assessment of India among SAARC member countries persists in the post-cold war period as well. In response to a recent statement by Indian Home Minister L.K. Advani in France describing South Asia as Indian sub-continent, Pakistan foreign office made strong objections and maintained:

> As India is only one of the countries of South Asia, the term 'Indian sub-continent' is entirely inappropriate as a description for the whole region. Its use betrays India's long cherished dream of exercising hegemony in the region, a dream that India has failed to realise and it will never succeed in achieving.[7]

Mr. Advani's another recent statement proposing a confederation in the sub-continent was considered by the Pakistan foreign office as "also reflective of the same unfortunate mindset"[8].

A recent 'secret' report about the anti-India activities of Pakistan's Inter-Services Intelligence in Nepal has attracted widespread attention.[9] One Indian daily in this regard observed:

> ...Although India has repeatedly apprised Nepal of Pakistan's gradual progression of its proxy war through such "encirclement of Indian territory" with ISI agents, the friendly neighbour has not been very forthcoming with cooperation to tackle the menace. Observers attribute Kathmandu's rather passive attitude to the political sensitivities that prevent it from acting against Pakistan, a friend of China, and its fear of India turning into a "big brother"[10].

India's neighbours expect her to play down the 'big-brotherly' attitude and keep a low-key but positive profile in SAARC. India, on the other hand, distrusts her neighbours, particularly Pakistan which is seen as attempting to undermine the secular basis of the Indian State and harbouring and sustaining cross-border terrorism against India. During his recent visit to Lisbon, Portugal to attend India-EU Summit, the Indian Prime Minister Atal Bihari Vajpayee was reported to have remarked that cross-border terrorism and calls for *jehad* (holy war) by Islamabad had become stumbling blocks for fulfilment of SAARC vision for peace and stability in the region.[11] The SAARC forum, nevertheless, particularly the summit meetings, has provided useful opportunity for the Heads of State/Government to informally discuss contentious bilateral issues on the sidelines of the summits. This opportunity would not have been otherwise available to SAARC leaders.

India probably feels that she has much more at stake than the smaller nations of SAARC and a mere South Asian regional status may not fulfil her global aspirations. India, therefore, has been seeking membership of APEC and has now become a dialogue partner of ASEAN and is actively pursuing her options in Indian Ocean Rim (IOR) community.

The Indian policy of insulating SAARC from contentious, bilateral issues has, at best, met with partial success only. The bilateral disputes among SAARC countries, particularly between India and Pakistan are deep rooted and defy the general global trend of post-cold war period. The core-issue of dispute between India and Pakistan is not Kashmir as such but a more fundamental difference on the nature of the State in India and Pakistan. The contradiction between the State of Pakistan created artificially on the basis of religion and the secular ideology of the Indian State is the root cause of the conflict between the two countries. However, despite Kargil border-war or because of it, a realisation might grow that military confrontation cannot resolve the territorial dispute between the two neighbours now possessing sophisticated missiles and nuclear weapons. It is quite probable that paradoxically nuclear-terror (as in the case of Europe) brings peace and an end to the conflict in South Asia. This could be an ideal ground for the sane civil society to step in and create a bond of friendship and amity in South Asia. The activities of NGOs/civil society institutions working to promote South Asianism are being encouraged by India and other SAARC member countries.

Civil Society Initiatives

There has been a groundswell of civil society initiatives to promote the process of peace and cooperation in South Asia. Some well meaning individuals and groups blessed by the Indian Government and SAARC have been augmenting this process. This provides hope for Indian policy makers in an otherwise dismal environment. The official SAARC support and sponsorship of some of these initiatives—particularly the Independent Commission on Poverty Alleviation and Group of Eminent Persons—are significant positive developments. The setting up of the Citizens' Commission for South Asia with eminent personalities from SAARC nations under the chairmanship of former Indian Prime Minister I.K. Gujral is yet another positive development for the cause of regional cooperation in South asia.

The individuals, groups and institutions which are making well-meaning efforts to promote peace and amity in South Asia, however, need to be cautious about liberal Western funding, some of which might be intended to influence official policy in SAARC countries.

Primacy of Contentious Politics in South Asia

India's efforts to promote regionalism in South Asia through the aegis of SAARC continues to be marred by the primacy of contentious politics among the nations of the region particularly between India and Pakistan. The challenge before Indian policy establishment, therefore, is daunting. Indian policy has to respond to the difficult task of smoothening the political and strategic divergence in the region. This is essential for the dynamism generated by the socioeconomic cooperation under SAARC to acquire a decisive edge to make South Asian regionalism a success story.

Being the most powerful state of the region India has to be a prime-mover in convincing her neighbours of her credentials in promoting the agenda of regionalism. India's neighbours continue to be torn by the doubts on Indian policy objectives - Pakistani ruling establishment, in particular, seems to be convinced that India harbours hegemonic ambitions in the regions. Except for a brief interlude of 'Gujral Doctrine' to resolve contentious bilateral disputes on the basis of non-reciprocity, India has not shown any significant shift in her approach for resolving bilateral disputes with her neighbours. A seemingly bold move by the new Indian government under National Democratic Alliance (NDA) in 1999 (bus journey by Indian Prime Minister Vajpayee to Lahore) to break the deadlock with Pakistan ended in the fiasco of Kargil border-war with Pakistan. This has proved detrimental to the regional cooperation process as well as to the evolving Indian policy in the region.

India's Extra-Regional Linkages

India's efforts to seek extra-regional linkages with ASEAN, APEC and IOC-ARC as well as her desire for promoting sub-regional cooperation with Bangladesh, Nepal and Bhutan are partly attributable to her frustration on account of slow growth of SAARC process. Indian policy is also pursuing a larger objective to grow out of the region for playing an Asian and perhaps global role in world affairs.

REFERENCES

1. Speech by Smt. Indira Gandhi, Prime Minister of India, in the Meeting of South Asian Foreign Ministers, New Delhi, August 1, 1983; *India Quarterly*, Vol. XL, Nos. 3 and 4, July-December 1984, p. 260.
2. Text of Prime Minister Benazir Bhutto's address to the Islamabad Summit, *Public Opinion Trends, Analyses and News Service, Pakistan Series*, Vol. 16, No. 237, December 31, 1988, p. 5316.
3. *The Hindustan Times*, New Delhi, 1 July 2000.

4. *The Hindu*, New Delhi, 3 July 2000.
5. *The Observer of Business and Politics*, New Delhi, 11 August 1999; Also see, *The Economic Times*, New Delhi, 11 August 1999.
6. Rehman Sobhan as cited by Lokraj Baral, "Globalization and Emerging Trends of Regionalism in South Asia" in Ramesh Babu (ed) *Globalization and the South Asian State*, 1998, p.185.
7. "Pakistan Objects to Advani's Description", *The Times of India*, New Delhi, 28 June 2000.
8. *Ibid*.
9. See "Kathmandu Nexus", *India Today*, New Delhi, 12 June 2000.
10. "Operation Madarasa to tackle ISI menace soon", *The Economic Times*, New Delhi, 24 June 2000.
11. *The Economic Times*, New Delhi, 30 June 2000.

8

Post Script

The surprise invitation of a summit meeting extended by the Prime Minister of India, Atal Behari Vajpayee to Pakistan military ruler General Pervez Musharraf generated political excitement and an expectation that the process of rapprochement and reconciliation between India and Pakistan might revive the SAARC process. The invitation by the Indian Prime Minister was made in May 2001 while reviewing the six month old unilateral cessation of combat operations against the terrorists and foreign mercenaries by the Indian security forces, popularly known as 'ceasefire' in the state of Jammu and Kashmir. The Government of India realising the futility and virtual failure of this unilateral measure declared an end to this 'ceasefire' and simultaneously extended an invitation of a summit meeting to the alleged 'architect of Kargil war', General Pervez Musharraf, who was desperately waiting for such a recognition by India. The Indian invitation to General Musharraf took political observers by surprise since it was made in the wake of a failed 'ceasefire' and against the backdrop of repeated Indian declaration that no dialogue with Pakistan was possible until Pakistani regime put an end to its sponsorship of cross-border terrorism in Jammu and Kashmir and other parts of India. This move by the Indian Government was appreciated world over and seen as a mature and bold initiative to instill a sense of sanity to the strife torn political situation in South Asia.

General Musharraf, in a clever political move and taking advantage of Indian recognition, usurped the Presidency of Pakistan in a highly unconstitutional manner. The summit meeting between Indian Prime Minister Atal Behari Vajpayee and President General

Pervez Musharraf took place in Agra, India on July 15-16, 2001. Prior to the summit meeting India and Pakistan maintained their oft-stated positions on issues dividing the two nations. Pakistan maintained that Kashmir was the 'core-issue' and that any forward movement towards normalisation of relations with India was incumbent on resolution of Kashmir dispute. India, on the other hand, held that the state of Jammu and Kashmir was at the core of Indian nationhood. India was keen to pursue the objectives of Simla Agreement and Lahore Declaration and willing to discuss 'Kashmir' as part of a composite dialogue process with Pakistan. There was, nevertheless, a promise by both the sides to keep an 'open mind' and show 'flexibility' before the summit meeting. In fact, General Musharraf even declared that he would change 'history'. The summit, therefore, generated unprecedented hope among saner elements on both sides of the border. These hopes, however, were belied when the summit came to an end without even a joint statement by the two countries. The two sides, maintaining a positive posture, pinned their hopes on future dialogue but, nevertheless, admitted to failure of 'Agra' by their acts and declarations. India accused General Musharraf of adopting a 'unifocal narrow and segmented'[1] approach and even of misusing media freedom in India to address fundamentalist constituency in Pakistan when he managed to telecast an informal breakfast meeting with Indian journalists in the midst of crucial negotiations with India at Agra. Alarmed by General Musharraf's continued attempt to use Agra summit to legitimise and consolidate himself in power, India declared a non existent 'Agra pact' 'dead' and maintained that any future dialogue would have to pick up threads from Simla Agreement and Lahore Declaration.[2]

The overt nuclearisation of South Asia in 1998 had revived political intrusion of major powers in the region even though such interference lost much of its relevance due to global détente after the end of the coldwar. The intrusion of major powers in South Asia further acquired added significance in the light of possible strategic relationship between India and the United States of America. Some of the statements and assertions made by important members of Bush administration underlined this new emerging situation. US Deputy Secretary of State Richard Armitage in an interview to an international news agency in July 2001 remarked that US-Pakistan relations in the past were relatively false. In his opinion the US had never had a balanced policy in South Asia. He explained the US-Pakistan relationship during last 50 years in following words:

> It has been a relationship that was not based on Pakistan. It was based against someone else-in the first instance India and its relationship with Soviet Union and later against the Soviet occupation of Afghanistan.[3]

The new emerging Indo-US relationship further acquired a sharp focus in the context of American pursuit of National Missile Defence and India's support, albeit qualified, to this concept. In an important counter move in July 2001 Russia and China signed a friendship treaty and reiterated their support to 1972 Anti-Ballistic Missile treaty. This treaty prohibits building of national missile defences. China also indicated its willingness to consider a strategic triangle with Russia and India in a bid to ensure a multipolar world and a new international political and economic order. Chinese Foreign Ministry spokesperson Ms. Zhang Qiyue on the eve of Chinese President Jiang Zemin's summit meeting with Russian President Vladimir Putin held in July 2001 said:

> On many international issues, China, Russia and India have similar or near-identical stand and concerns..... We hope to further strengthen the cooperation with Russia and India.[4]

China, Russia and India share a threat perception of Islamic fundamentalism emanating from Pakistan-Afghanistan region. Interestingly, the United States, although responsible for it to some extent, also realised the dangerous implications of Islamic fundamentalism and associated mercenary narco-terrorism for world peace and security.

The cauldron of South Asia in this larger political context presents an immense challenge for the Indian foreign policy establishment. Ms. Christina Rocca, Assistant Secretary of State for South Asia in the American administration, during her confirmation hearings referred to India 'already playing a role' beyond the region.[5] India being the largest state of South Asia and aspiring as well as acknowledged for a role larger than the regional will need to be the prime mover for peace process in the sub-continent. While the Indian policy seems to be in compulsive pursuit of a global role, it cannot afford to ignore its immediate neighbourhood. India will have to take bold, positive and decisive initiatives to establish peace and harmony in South Asia and thus revive SAARC regionalism. At the same time Pakistan will need to shed its India-fixation and acknowledge India's legitimate role and status in the new emerging geo-political order.

The newly acquired nuclear status with its associated risks and dangers, human deprivation and mass poverty in a globalizing economic order have instilled a sense of realism among policy makers in India and Pakistan. Even though the latest initiative to break Indo-Pak logjam failed at Agra, this effort, nevertheless, would revive the SAARC process. The much delayed eleventh SAARC summit is likely to be held in November 2001 in Kathmandu. How far the Indian policy establishment would be able to insulate the SAARC forum from contentious bilateral political issues, as envisaged in SAARC Charter, would be watched with keen interest. The challenges posed by the emerging international political and economic order beckon India and South Asia to transcend the narrow conflicts of history and extricate the vast populous sub-continent from quagmire of poverty and misery.

REFERENCES

1. For details see the text of statement made by the External Affairs Minister of India, Jaswant Singh, at his press conference on 17 July 2001. *Asian Age*, 18 July, 2001.
2. *The Economic Times*, 19 July 2001.
3. *The Indian Express*, 5 July 2001.
4. *The Hindu*, 16 July 2001.
5. *The Hindu*, 19 May 2001.

Appendix 1

Inaugural Address by Pandit Jawaharlal Nehru at Asian Relations Conference, 23 March 1947

Friends and fellow Asians,

What has brought you here, men and women of Asia? Why have you come from the various countries of this mother continent of ours and gathered together in the ancient city of Delhi? Some of us, greatly daring, sent you invitation for this Conference and you gave a warm welcome to that invitation. And yet it was not merely that call from us but some deeper urge that brought you here.

We stand at the end of an era and on the threshold of new period of history. Standing on this watershed which divides two epochs of human history and endeavour, we can look back on our long past and look forward to the future that is taking shape before our eyes. Asia, after a long period of quiescence, has suddenly become important again in world affairs. If we view the millennia of history, this continent of Asia, with which Egypt has been so intimately connected in cultural fellowship, has played a mighty role in the evolution of humanity. It was here that civilisation began and man started on his unending adventure of life. Here the mind of man searched unceasingly for truth and the spirit of man shone out like a beacon, which lightened up the whole world.

This dynamic Asia from which great streams of culture flowed in all directions, gradually became static and unchanging. Other peoples and other continents came to the fore and with their new dynamism spread out and took possession of great parts of the world. This mighty continent became just a field for the rival imperialism of Europe, and the Europe became the centre of history and progress in human affairs.

[Source: "Asian Relations" Report of the Proceedings and Documentation of the First Asian Relations Conference (New Delhi, Asian Relations Organization, 1948)].

A change is coming over the scene now the Asia is again finding herself. We live in a tremendous age of transition and already the next stage takes shape when Asia takes her rightful place with the other continents.

It is at this great moment that we meet here and it is the pride and privilege of the people of India to welcome their fellow Asians from other countries, to confer with them about the present and the future, and lay the foundation of our mutual progress, well-being and friendship.

The idea of having an Asian Conference is, not new and many have thought of it. It is indeed surprising that it should not have been held many years earlier, yet perhaps the time was not ripe for it and any attempt to do so would have been superficial and not in tune with world events. It so happened that we in India convened this Conference, but the idea of such a Conference arose simultaneously in many minds and in many countries of Asia. There was a widespread urge and an awareness that the time had come for us, peoples of Asia, to meet together, to hold together and to advance together. It was not only a vague desire but a compulsion of events that forced all of us to think along these lines. Because of this, the invitation we in India sent out brought an answering echo and a magnificent response from every country of Asia.

We welcome you delegates and representatives from China, that great country to which Asia owes so much and from which so much is expected; from Egypt and the Arab countries of western Asia, inheritors of a proud culture which spread far and wide and influenced India greatly; from Iran whose contacts with India go back to the dawn of history; from Indonesia and Indo-China whose history is intertwined with India's culture, and where recently the battle of freedom has continued -a reminder to us that freedom must be won and cannot come as gift; from Turkey that has been rejuvenated by the genius of a great leader; from the Soviet Republics of Asia which have advanced so rapidly in our generation and which have so many lessons to teach us; and from our neighbours Afghanistan, Tibet, Nepal, Bhutan, Burma and Ceylon to whom we look especially for cooperation and close friendly intercourse. Asia is very well represented at this Conference, and if one or two countries have been unable to send representatives, this was due to no lack of desire on their part or ours, but circumstances beyond our control came in the way. We welcome also observers from Australia and New Zealand because we have many problems in common, especially in the Pacific and in the southeast region of Asia, and we have to co-operate together to find solutions.

As we meet here today, the long past of Asia rises up before us, the troubles of recent years fade away, and a thousand memories revive. But I shall not speak to you of these past ages with their glories and triumphs and failures, nor of more recent times which have oppressed us so much and which still pursue us in some measure.

During the past two hundred years we have seen the growth of Western imperialisms and reduction of large parts of Asia to colonial or semi-colonial status. Much has happened during these years, but perhaps one of the notable consequences if the European domination of Asia has been the isolation of the countries of Asia from one another. India always had contacts and intercourses with her neighbour countries in the northwest, the northeast the east and the southeast. With the coming of British rule in India these contacts were broken off and India was almost completely isolated from the rest of Asia. The old land routes almost ceased to function and our chief window to the outer world looked out on the sea routes which led to England. A similar process affected the other countries of Asia also. Their entire economy was bound up with some European imperialism or other; even culturally they looked towards Europe and not to their own friends and neighbours from whom they had derived so much in the past.

Today this isolation is breaking down because of many reasons, political and other. The old imperialisms are fading away. The land routes have revived and air travel suddenly brings us very near to each other. This Conference itself is significant as an expression of that deeper urge of the mind and spirit of Asia which has persisted in spite of the isolationism which grew up during the years of European domination. As that domination goes, the walls that surrounded us fall near to each other again and meet as old friends long parted.

In this Conference and in this work there are no leaders and no followers. All the countries of Asia have to meet together on an equal basis in a common task and endeavour. It is fitting that India should play her part in this new phase of Asian development. Apart from the fact that India herself is emerging into freedom and independence, she is the natural centre and focal point of the many forces at work in Asia. Geography is compelling factor, and geographically she is so situated as to be the meeting point of western and northern and eastern and southeast Asia. Because of this, the history of India is a long history of her relations with the other countries of Asia. Streams of culture have come to India from the west and the east and been absorbed in India, producing the rich and variegated culture which is India today. At the same time, streams of culture have flowed from India to distant parts of Asia. If you would know India you have to go to Afghanistan and western Asia, to central Asia, to China and Japan and to the countries of Southeast Asia. There you will find magnificent evidence of the vitality of India's culture which spread out and influenced vast number of people.

There came the great cultural stream from Iran to India in remote and the Far East, notably China. In later years Southeast Asia witnessed an amazing efflorescence of Indian art and culture. The mighty stream which started from Arabia and developed as a mixed Iran-Arabia culture poured into India. All these came to us and influenced us, and yet so great was the powerful impress of India's own mind and culture that it could accept them without being itself swept away or overwhelmed. Nevertheless we all changed in the process and in India today all of us are mixed products of these various influences. An India, wherever he may go in Asia, feels a sense of kinship with the land he visits and the people he meets.

I do not wish to speak to you of the past but rather of the present. We meet here not to discuss our past history and contacts but to forge links for the future. And may I say here that this Conference, and the idea underlying it, is in no way aggressive or against any other continent or country? Ever since news of this Conference went abroad some people in Europe and America have viewed it with doubt imagining that this was some kind of a Pan-Asian movement directed against Europe or America. We have no designs against anybody; ours is the great design of promoting peace and progress all over the world. For too long we of Asia have been petitioners in Western courts and chancelleries. That story must now belong to the past. We propose to stand on our own feet and to co-operate with all others who are prepared to co-operate with us. We do not intend to be playthings of others.

In this crisis in world history Asia will necessarily play a vital role. The countries of Asia can no longer be used as pawns by others; they are bound to their own policies in world affairs. Europe and America have contributed very greatly to human progress and for that we must yield them praise and honour, and learn from them the many lessons they have to teach. But the West has also driven us into wars and conflicts without number and even now, the day after a terrible war, there is talk of further wars in the atomic age that is upon us. In this atomic age Asia will have to function effectively in the maintenance of peace. Indeed there can be no peace unless Asia plays her part. There is today conflict in many countries, and all of us in Asia are full of our own troubles. Nevertheless, the whole spirit and outlook of Asia are peaceful, and the emergence of Asia in world affairs will be a powerful influence for world peace.

Peace can only come when nations are free and also when human beings everywhere have freedom and security and opportunity. Peace and freedom, therefore, have to be considered both in their political and economic aspects. The countries of Asia, we must remember, are very backward and the standards of life are appallingly low. These economic problems demand urgent solution or else crisis and disaster might overwhelm us. We have, therefore, to think in terms of the common man and fashion our political social and economic structure so that the burdens that have crushed him be removed, and he may have full opportunity for growth.

We have arrived at a stage in human affairs when the ideal of that 'One World' and some kind of a world federation seems to be essential though there are many dangers and obstacles in the way. We should work for that ideal and not for any grouping which comes in the way of this larger world group. We therefore support the United Nations structure which is painfully emerging from its infancy. But in order to have 'One World', we must also in Asia think of the countries of Asia co-operating together for that larger ideal.

This Conference, in a small measure, represents this bringing together of the countries of Asia. Whatever it may achieve, the mere fact of its taking place is itself of historic significance. Indeed this occasion is unique in history for never before has such a gathering met together at any place. So even in meeting we have achieved much and I have no doubt that out of this meeting greater things will come. When the history of our present times is written, this event may well stand out as a landmark which divides the past of Asia from the future. And because we are participating in this making of history, something of the greatness of historic events comes to us all.

This Conference will split up into committees and groups to discuss various problems which are of common concern to all of us. We shall not discuss the internal politics of any country because that is rather beyond the scope of our present meeting. Naturally we are interested in these internal politics because they act and react on each other, but we may not discuss them at this stage, for if we do so, we may lose ourselves in interminable arguments and complications. We may fail to achieve the purpose for which we have met. I hope that out of this Conference some permanent Asian Institute for the study of common problems and to bring about closer relations will emerge; also perhaps a School of Asian Studies. Further, we might be able to organise interchange of visits and exchanges of students and professors so that we might know each other better. There is much else we can do, but I shall not venture to enumerate all these subjects for it is for you to discuss them and arrive at some decisions.

We seek no narrow nationalism. Nationalism has a place in each country and should be fostered, but it must not be allowed to become aggressive and come in the way of international development. Asia stretches her hand out in friendship to Europe and America as well as to our suffering brethren in Africa. We in Asia have a special responsibility to the people of Africa. We must help them to take their rightful place in the human family. The freedom that we envisage is not to be confined to this nation or that or to a particular people, but must spread out over the whole human race. That universal human freedom cannot also be based on the supremacy of any particular class. It must be the freedom of the common man everywhere and full of opportunities for him to develop.

We think of the great architects of Asian freedom-Sun Yat-sen, Zaghulul Pasha, the Ataturk Kemal Pasha and others, whose labours have borne fruit: We think also of that great figure whose labours and whose inspiration have brought India to the threshold of her independence - Mahatma Gandhi. We miss him at this Conference and I yet hope that he may visit us before our labours end. He is engrossed in the service of the common man in India, and even this Conference could not drag him away from it.

All over Asia we are passing through trails and tribulations. In India also you will see conflict and trouble. Let us not be disheartened by this; this is inevitable in an age of mighty transition. There is a new vitality and powerful creative impluse in all peoples of Asia. The masses are awake and demand their heritage. Strong winds are blowing all over Asia. Let us not be afraid of them but rather welcome them for only with their help can we build the new Asia of our dreams. Let us have faith in these great new forces and the things which are taking shape. Above all let us have faith in the human spirit which Asia has symbolised for these long ages past.

Appendix 2

A Paper on The Proposal for Regional Cooperation in South Asia. Government of the People's Republic of Bangladesh Ministry of Foreign Affairs Dhaka, November 1980

Introduction

The aim of this paper is to explain the ideas of a regional forum proposed by the President of Bangladesh with a view to periodical consultations among the countries of the region of South Asia on matters of mutual interest and possible cooperation in economic, social, cultural and other fields on a regional basis as may be mutually agreed upon.

The idea of regional cooperation in South Asia is not new. Countries of the region have cooperated with one another both bilaterally and regionally under the umbrella of such forums as the ESCAP, the Non-aligned Movement and the Common-wealth. These efforts have not fully exploited the vast potential of regional cooperation that exists and the consequential benefit that this will bring, collectively and individually, to the countries of this region. The feasibility of such cooperation was informally discussed in various capitals at different times, but until recently no concrete step was taken. President Ziaur Rahaman of the People's Republic of Bangladesh explained the possibility of organising regional cooperation for the common good of the people of this region in the course of his visits to Nepal, India, Pakistan and Sri Lanka during the period 1977-1980. The initial responses were encouraging. In the light of his consultations, he addressed letters to the Heads of Government of the countries of South Asia (namely, Bhutan, India, Maldives, Nepal, Pakistan, and Sri Lanka),

[*Source* : From SARC to SAARC: Milestones in the Evolution of Regional Cooperation in South Asia (1980-1988), Vol. I, SAARC Secretariat, Kathmandu.]

which were carried by special envoys. In his letter he proposed that the countries of the region should explore the possibility of establishing some institutional arrangements for regional cooperation and, to this end, a meeting at the Summit level be held. Replies to President Ziaur Rahman's letter have now been received from all the countries.

The responses from different South Asian capitals were positive and the proposal of the President was warmly welcomed. Some pointed out that adequate preparatory work would be necessary to ensure the success of the regional Summit meeting. It was also pointed out that against the backdrop of the history of the region, it would be wise to proceed on the basis of careful and adequate preparations so as to ensure a fruitful outcome of the Summit meeting.

In the course of the last few months, some of the leaders of the region have had the opportunity of discussing and consulting with one another about the proposal. Discussions at official level have also taken place to clarify the various elements of the proposed cooperation. These preliminary exchanges have brought out clearly that regional cooperation should, on the one hand reflect the spirit of mutual trust, understanding and sympathetic appreciation of the political aspirations existing among the countries of the region, and on the other, that such cooperation should be based on respect for the principles of sovereign equality, territorial integrity, non-interference in internal affairs of other nations and mutual benefit.

In the following pages an attempt has been made to spell out some of the basic ideas underlying the proposal of President Ziaur Rahman and the matters that the regional Summit may be expected to consider.

Rationale

President Ziaur Rahman in his letter addressed to the Heads of Government of the region briefly touched on the underlying factors which prompted him to take the initiative. He mentioned that while other regions had evolved institutional arrangements for consultations on matters of mutual interest and cooperation in the economic, social and cultural fields on a regional basis and had consequently benefited immensely from such cooperation, the only region which did not have any such arrangements for regional cooperation was the South Asian region which comprised one-fifth of the world population. However, he noted that recent positive developments in the region had created a better climate of understanding. For the first time, there were distinct possibilities of regional cooperation from which all South Asian countries would stand to gain. We should make the most of this opportunity.

It is not difficult to see how regional cooperation would benefit our countries. Other regions have attempted cooperation in selected fields on a regional basis and the results have been found to be extremely beneficial. Economically and industrially advanced countries in Western Europe have introduced, despite highly competitive economies, a wide ranging and well-developed system of cooperation. The emergence of Western Europe in recent years as one of the strongest economic forces in the world in an eloquent testimony to the success of the policy of cooperation which developed alongside the European economic resurgence. In other parts of the world, where the countries have been economically less developed attempts at regional cooperation have also been extensively made with varying degrees of success. The orientation and thrust of these different initiatives have not been identical; some have attempted at customs union, other have sought technical and cultural cooperation; yet others have endeavoured to attract investments from sources outside the region.

Bangladesh President in his letter tentatively indicated economic, technical, scientific, social and cultural fields as possible areas for regional cooperation. Such cooperation is not, however, intended to take the form of any new block or alliance. The institutional arrangements set up for such cooperation would strictly conform to the principles of non-alignment to which all the countries in the region are firmly committed.

Economic and technical cooperation on a regional basis is now accepted by all developing countries as a desirable and necessary strategy within the framework of ECDC and TCDC. In South Asia, as in other regions of the world, we have countries at different levels of development; some are relatively less developed than other. Any proposal for economic cooperation must consequently be formulated with the greatest care in order to ensure that the weak are not exploited and that the strong do not dominate. The areas selected should only be those in which cooperation will mutually benefit all the countries irrespective of existing economic disparities, so as to make regional cooperation meaningful, strengthen the spirit of mutual trust and understanding, and bridge the developmental gaps existing among the countries of the region. In the meantime, the uneven levels of development should, if anything, inspire on the one hand the less developed to catch up with their more fortunate neighbours, while on the other hand encourage the more developed to help to narrow the gap existing between them. The process will be one of gradual evolution that will assist the relatively less developed to overcome their existing problems so that in the long-run a system of preference becomes unnecessary.

A final argument in favour of such cooperation is that it is only through regional cohesion that South Asia can hope to have an effective voice in international forums. The UN systems has today over 150 states. It is only groups of countries-be they big or small—that can aspire to make decisive impact on the decision-making process in these forums. Indeed, one may go far as to say that it is only by establishing an institutional arrangement for consultation and coordination that the people of South Asia, constituting nearly one-fifth of the world population can play a role commensurate with their intrinsic global importance.

Shared perceptions and values are an important factor for the success of any venture for regional cooperation. The countries of South Asia share many common values that are rooted in their social, ethnic, cultural and historical traditions. Perceptions about certain specific events or political situation of the world may differ, but such differences do not seem to create a gulf between them that cannot be bridged. In fact, the beginning of cooperation on a regional basis may be a positive force in generating a climate of harmony conducive to a better perception of what the countries in the region have a common and the value of this shared heritage.

The experiences in regional cooperation elsewhere in the world indicated the possibility of such cooperation in spite of bilateral problems existing among the countries of the region. Even where bilateral disputes crop up, this should not stand in the way of regional cooperation in the economic, social, technical and cultural spheres. This too is evident from the fact that countries whose bilateral relations may be strained are still prepared to cooperate with one another within a regional framework. As regional cooperation grows, it also tends to generate a climate of mutual understanding reducing the scope for such disputes.

Regional Cooperation in South Asia as elsewhere in the world should in no way intrude on the existing bilateral and multilateral relations of the countries of the region; nor does the proposal envisage either the substitution or the disruption of existing cooperation between or amongst the countries of the region in other forums. ESCAP has organised consultative procedures for cooperation in a wide range of fields in which South Asian countries are closely involved. Regional activities of other bodies, such as the WHO Regional Centre in Delhi, are also engaged in useful activities and should continue undisturbed in their well-defined fields of operation. Every effort will be made to avoid duplication, which is wasteful of time, energy and resources, to emphasize the point that regional cooperation will supplement and reinforce the activities of the international organisations. As a matter of fact, it is expected that operating under the aegis of a regional framework, these international bodies will be able to contribute more meaningfully to the well-being of this region.

Regional cooperation in South Asia must be both pragmatic and realistic in outlook. Such cooperation is intended to grow step-by-step in the economic, social and cultural spheres. A number of possible areas of cooperation have been outlined later in the paper. Undoubtedly many more areas of cooperation can be found and will be found as we proceed. Regional cooperation is a dynamic process, it will grow, it will widen, and it will strengthen; just as global interdependence and cooperation have developed, so will regional cooperation throughout the world, for there is no better way we can strengthen global cooperation than on the bedrock of regional cooperation the world over.

The proposal for a South Asian meeting at the Summit level has been generally welcomed as a positive and constructive initiative, which could have a catalytic effect on the process of cooperation in the region. However, it may be justifiably argued that Summit meetings generate great expectations among people and therefore, a step-by-step approach would be more productive. There is undoubtedly some validity in this argument. Summit meetings need to be carefully prepared in advance to ensure their success. At the same time this point need not be stretched too far. A Summit meeting pre-supposes that there would be serious business for the Heads of Government, and that the Heads of Government would be able to apply their minds to those issues which could not be resolved satisfactorily at other levels. They would have a broader perspective and, what is equally important, the power of decision to resolve contentious issues. Thus, preparatory work to be undertaken prior to the Summit meeting would include preparation of the agenda, identification of the possible areas of cooperation. In the process of evolving a common position on all these aspects of the preparatory work, unanimity would be most desirable. However, would there be points on which complete agreement was not possible, it would be appropriate that the leaders of the region at the highest level address themselves to these issues.

Possible Areas of Cooperation

(a) Tele-communication.
(b) Meteorology.
(c) Transport.
(d) Shipping.
(e) Tourism.
(f) Agricultural/Rural Sector.
(g) Joint Ventures.
(h) Market Promotion: Selected Commodities.
(i) Scientific and Technological Cooperation.
(j) Education and Technical Cooperation.
(k) Cultural Cooperation.

The Framework

(I) Name

For the sake of convenience, one may consider proposing a name for the institutional framework, which would reflect, as nearly as possible, the purposes and nature of the cooperation on a regional basis. Among the various possible names the following are suggested for consideration:

(a) "South Asian Association for Cooperation" (SAAC)
(b) "Association of South Asia" (ASA)
(c) "Association of South Asia for cooperation" (ASAC)
(d) "Organisation of South Asian States" (OSAS)

(II) Declaration

It is proposed that in order to provide the basic guidelines for conducting all activities within the framework of (selected nomenclature to be inserted), the South Asian leaders' meeting at the Summit level for the first time may issue a Declaration which would embody the aims, objectives as well as the purposes and principles and its mode of operation.

Draft Declaration

The Government of Bangladesh Bhutan, India, Maldives, Nepal, Pakistan and Sri Lanka:

Convinced of the benefits that will accrue from greater regional cooperation among the countries of South Asia;

Seeking to promote peace and stability in the region through adherence to the principles of the United Nations Charter and of **Non-alignment**

Determined to uphold respect for the principles of sovereignty, national independence, territorial integrity, non-interference in one another's internal affairs, non-use of force, and peaceful settlement of disputes;

Recognizing the need to accelerate the process of economic, technical, scientific, and cultural development in South Asia through cooperative endeavours undertaken by the countries in the region in a spirit of good will and mutual trust and on the basis of equality and common interest;

Desirous of promoting active cooperation among countries of the region on matters of common interest in the economic, social, cultural, technical and scientific as well as in such other fields as may be agreed upon;

Seeking to explore all avenues for closer cooperation between the countries of South Asia, and the other regional and international organisations with similar aims and objectives;

Have decided to establish an organisation to be known as the (selected nomenclature to be inserted).

The mode of operation of (name of the organisation) shall be as under:

(A) Membership

The association is open to all states in the South Asian Region subscribing to the aims and objectives embodied in the declaration.

(B) Structure and Functions

(a) The Heads of Government of Member State shall meet once annually and may meet as often as necessary to give directions, provide guidelines, and review the activities of the (name of the organisation). Chairmanship of the organisation shall rotate among the member countries in an alphabetic order for a term of one year commencing from the date of the formation of the organisation. The venue of the meetings, both Summit and Ministerial, shall be the country acting as the current Chairman.

(b) There shall be a Council comprising the Foreign Ministers of member states as the principal functional organ of the (name of organisation). The council shall be responsible for:

(i) Finalizing the recommendations for submission to the Summit Meeting:

(ii) Implementing the decisions of the Summit Meeting:

(iii) Coordinating the various activities of the (name of the organisation); and

(iv) Approving the budget of the (name of the organisation) and deciding on the contributions of the member states.

The Councils shall meet as often as necessary but at least once a year.

(c) The Council of Foreign Ministers shall establish such committees, organs, institutions and agencies as may be necessary from time to time, under the directives and guidelines provided by the highest authority of the (name of the organisation). These committees, organs, institutions and agencies shall submit reports to the Council for its consideration.

(d) There shall be a Secretariat of the (name of the organisation) headed by a Secretary General, who will be appointed by the Heads of Government of member states upon the recommendation of the Council of Foreign Ministers on such terms and conditions as may be decided by the Heads of Government. The Secretary General shall be the principal executive of the organisation and shall perform which functions as are entrusted to him by the Council

Preparation for the Summit

President Ziaur Rahman has proposed that the leaders of the South Asian countries should meet at the Summit level to explore the possibilities of establishing a framework for regional cooperation. Bearing in mind the legacies of the past, it would indeed be a historic event. Barriers, both historical and emotional, will have to be scaled and lingering suspicion and distrust will have to yield place to a renewed spirit of understanding and goodwill. A meeting at the Summit level would be the most appropriate forum for such major initiative in embarking on a new and challenging venture envisaged in the proposal.

This paper, being circulated to all the Governments of the region, is intended to serve Governments of the region, is intended to serve as a working paper on South Asian regional cooperation. It is expected that ideas and proposals not covered in this paper will also be introduced by the Governments in the light of their own experience and studies of the subject. These inputs would be collected, studied and analysed. A set of documents would be prepared on the basis of this analysis. These documents would contain proposals, which, by then would have been presumably crystallized into concrete programmes.

The first preparatory meeting may be held at the level of Foreign Secretaries assisted by such technical officials as may be needed. The recommendations of the Secretaries level meeting would be considered by a meeting of the Foreign Ministers of the region. This meeting may also suggest the date and place of the Ministerial Meeting. The Foreign Ministers' meeting be the final preparatory stage for the Summit Meeting. The recommendations of the Foreign Ministers should include the following:

(a) Feasibility of regional cooperation and policy recommendation on the general approach to such cooperation.

(b) Possible areas of cooperation.

(c) The framework for regional cooperation/draft Declaration.

(d) Agenda for the Summit Meeting.

(e) Finalization of the date and venue of the Summit Meeting.

Appendix 3

An Indian Note Regarding Areas of Cooperation in South Asia

1. The Indian views in regard to possible areas of regional cooperation were spelt out in the statement made by Foreign Secretary, Shri R. D. Sathe, in the Colombo meeting of the Foreign Secretaries held last April. He had then stated that the exercise of identifying areas "has to relate to functional cooperation in areas which are most relevant for the socio-economic development of our peoples". He had observed that the involvement of peoples in the region is of cardinal importance and the need to involve the academic community, and the non-governmental organisations, in this exercise is also very desirable. He had pointed out the advisability , of the economic planners of the countries of the region to meet at regular intervals to discuss and exchange our experiences in the field of planning as also to consider long-term planning perspectives, taking into account the possibilities of regional cooperation.

2. India feels that the scope of the work of the existing study group on telecommunications should be widened so as to include cooperation in the sector of postal services. It is also suggested that the two existing study groups on agriculture and rural development may be combined as one study group.

3. Apart from the above amendments, possibility of setting up new study groups on following possible areas of regional cooperation may be examined:

1. Cultural Field-As already observed by India's Foreign Secretary in his statement to the Colombo Meeting the cultural cooperation can cover sports, education, films, theatres, production

[*Source* : From SARC to SAARC: Milestones in the Evolution of Regional Cooperation in South Asia (1980-1988), Vol. I, SAARC Secretariat, Kathmandu.]

of text books, organisation of seminars and exhibitions, regional film festivals, etc.

2. Infra-structural Field - This cooperation can extend to the following areas:

(i) Transport: In order to ensure an effective flow of movement of goods and also to facilitate inter-regional traffic, a well integrated system of communication especially in the form of road and rail lines would be invaluable for economic development of the region. An increased surface mobility will go a long way to contribute to the regional cooperation among the South Asian countries.

(ii) Shipping: In this area, too, we feel that the conditions imposed by the developed countries and the liner conference arrangements controlled by them militate against the national desire of the developing countries to increase in the course of time their tonnage capacity for a greater share in the transportation of sea cargo. Further, the frequent escalation in the freight charges adversely affects the development needs and the balance of payment position of the developing countries. In order to bring about a degree of self-sufficiency in this field and to give an additional fillip to economic development of the countries in this region, shipping seems to be a natural area for cooperation on a regional basis.

(iii) Tourism: This is another area where there exists a vast potential for infra-regional cooperation in South Asia. The revolutionary growth of air transportation in recent times has made tourism the second largest export industry in the world. It is essential that the countries of South Asia get a greater share of the world market in tourist traffic. The potential of the region to attract tourist is virtually unlimited and needs to be explored in depth.

(iv) Market Promotion: One of the richest areas for regional cooperation in our view is market promotion in selected commodities of common interest. Joint initiative in the region can reduce costs and have greater impact in the export markets of a number of commodities. The countries of the region command a significant share of the world market for commodities such as tea, jute and cotton. At present there are competitive promotional activities but these can be usefully and effectively combined to optimise results.

3. Cooperation related to International Economic Negotiations - This field for cooperation is being suggested with a view to present a common approach with respect to the development aid, trade concessions, etc. It would mean adopting a common stand, to the extent possible, as a group at the North-South Dialogue, ECDC, in the UNCTAD, and ESCAP sessions and in the World Bank and other UN forums connected with aid to developing countries and other aspects of development cooperation. The common strategy will be directed towards the achievement of the objectives of NIEO involving reforms in the international monetary system, stabilisation of prices of commodities of common interest for their joint marketing and measures for facing competition from synthetics in the world market.

4. Scientific and Technological Cooperation - Countries of South Asian region have a special need to develop effective use of science and technology for alleviating the widespread poverty that is a common characteristic of the area. Cooperation in this field is particularly significant in view of the fact that experience gained by the South Asian countries in this sphere can be shared with greater advantage than the technology borrowed from the industrialised countries of the developed world. This cooperation can be particularly beneficial in the field of conservation of energy, improvement of efficiency in use of the existing sources of energy through development of low-energy technology, and R&D aspects of new and renewable sources of energy.

5. India feels that the Committee of the Whole should also give attention to the following paths along which development of regional cooperation in South Asia can be promoted and thus are relevant for consideration by each of the study groups:

(a) Interchange of experience;

(b) Cooperative development; and

(c) Expanding economic relations.

6. South Asian countries can learn from one another in a great variety of ways, for instance, through exchange of teachers and students, through visiting delegation drawn from different walks of life, through collaboration among scholars and research institutions, and through various forms of cultural and scientific cooperation. Much progress can be made by encouraging lateral contracts between corresponding groups of institutions like professional associations in different fields, universities, academies of arts, literature and science, media organisations, and other appropriate bodies.

Appendix 4

South Asian Association for Regional Cooperation (SAARC) MAJOR ECONOMIC INDICATORS, 1996-2000 (PER CENT)

Item	Bangladesh	India	Nepal	Pakistan	Sri Lanka
GDP Growth					
'96	5.4	7.8	5.3	5.2	3.8
'97	5.9	5.0	4.0	1.3	6.4
98	5.8	1.9	5.4	5.3	
99	3.6	5.9	2.0	3.4	5.0
'00	5.5	6.0	2.7	4.6	6.2
Gross Domestic Investment (GDP)					
'96	17.0	25.7	27.3	18.7	24.2
'97	17.3	24.8	25.1.	17.5	24.4
'98	16.3	25.2	25.5	17.4	26.6
'99	17.5	25.2	25.0	14.8	28.6
'00	17.0	25.3	25.5	16.2	30.0
Gross National Savings (GNP)					
'96	14.3	24.6	15.6	11.6	15.5
'97	14.8	23.3	15.7	11.3	21.4
'98	14.8	23.5	16.7	15.1	19.3
'99	14.5	23.7	16.1	12.2	20.8
'00	15.0	24.0	17.0	13.0	22.1
Inflation Rate (Consumer Price Index)					
'96	6.6	9.4	8.1	10.8	15.9
'97	2.6	6.9	7.8	11.8	9.6
'98	7.0	14.4	4.0	7.8	9.4
'99	8.0	7.5	9.0	8.0	9.0
'00	6.0	7.0	8.0	9.0	8.0

Money Supply (M2/M3) Growth					
'96	8.2	16.2	14.4	14.9	10.8
'97	10.8	17.6	11.9	12.2	13.8
'98	10.1	19.8	16.9	14.2	13.0
'99	10.0	18.1	16.0	9.0	13.4
'00	8.0	17.5	15.0	12.0	11.5
Fiscal Balance/ GDP					
'96	-5.9	-4.7	-5.7	-6.3	-9.4
'97	-5.6	-5.5	-5.1	-6.2	-7.9
'98	-5.4	-6.5	-6.4	-5.4	-7.7
'99	-6.5	-5.8	-6.5	-4.3	-6.0
'00	-5.5	-5.4	-7.0	-3.3	-5.0
Merchandise Exports Growth					
'96	11.8	5.6	1.9	7.1	7.6
'97	14.0	2.1	10.2	-2.6	13.3
'98	16.8	-5.1	11.7	4.0	6.7
'99	8.0	1.5	9.0	-10.1	6.0
'00	12.0	4.5	9.0	10.2	7.0
Merchandise Import Growth					
'96	19.1	12.1	5.8	16.7	2.4
'97	3.1	4.4	21.6	-6.4	7.6
'98	5.3	0.9	-12.6	-8.2	7.1
'99	10.0	4.5	2.0	-16.9	6.2
'00	8.0	7.7	5.0	10.0	5.6
Current Account Balance/GDP					
'96	-4.1	-1.2	-11.7	-6.7	-5.3
'97	-1.7	-1.6	-9.4	-5.8	-2.9
'98	-1.1	-1.8	-8.8	-3.0	-3.1
'99	-3.0	-1.6	-8.9	-2.5	-5.2
'00	-2.0	-1.4	-8.5	-1.9	-5.2
Debt Service/ Export					
'96	12.1	33.7	5.4	33.9	13.4
'97	11.4	32.5	7.3	38.0	13.4
'98	11.7	31.8	9.0	40.0	12.1
'99	12.0	31.0	8.7	20.0	12.1
'00	12.1	28.5	28.7	22.0	10.8

[*Source* : Asian Development Outlook, 1999, 'Special Chapter-Economic Openness: Growth and Recovery in Asia' Published for the Asian Development Bank by Oxford University Press.]

Appendix 5

HUMAN DEVELOPMENT INDICATORS OF SAARC MEMBER COUNTRIES

	India	Pakistan	Bangladesh	Nepal	Sri Lanka	Bhutan	Maldives	South Asia (weighted average)	Developing Countries
Total estimated population (millions) 1998	987	153*	128	24	19	1.7	0.28	131T	4977T
Total estimated population (millions) 1997	969	148	125	23	19	1.7	0.27	1287T	4715T
Annual Population growth rate (per cent) k1995-2000*	1.8	2.7	2.2	2.5	1.2	2.4	3.2	2.0	1.8
Life expectancy at birth years (1997)	63	64	58	57	73	53	64	62	63
Adult Literacy rate (per cent) 1995	52	38	38	28	90	42	93	49	71
Female literacy rate (per cent) 1995	38	24	26	14	87	28	93	36	62
Combined first, second and third level gross enrolment ratio (per cent) 1995	55	41	37	56	67	31	71	52	57
Infant morality rate (per 1000 liver births) 1997	71	95	81	75	17	87	53	75	65
GNP per capita (US$) 1997	370	500	360	220	800	430	1,180	393	1,250

GNP average annual growth rate (%) 1996-97	4.3	-2.4	4.6	1.7	5.9	7.0	6.3	3.6	3.2
Real GDP per capita (PPS$) 1995	1,422	2,209	1,382	1,145	3,408	1,382	3,540	1,531	3,068
Human development index 1995b	0.451	0.453	0.371	0.351	0.716	0.347	0.683	0.445	0.588
Gender-related development index 1995c	0.424	0.399	0.342	0.327	0.700	0.330	0.668	0.415	0.564

Note:

(a) Population figures for 1990, 1995 and 2000 taken from UN: Ages and Sex Distribution of Population: The 1994 revision (Medium variant). The population growth rate has been calculated by using the formula {(new value/of old value^n)-1}*100.

(b) The Human Development Index (HDI) has three components: life expectancy at birth; education attainment, comprising adult literacy, with two-third weight; and income HDI is based on the old methodology.

(c) The gender-related development index (GDI) adjusts the HDI for gender equality in life expectancy, educational attainment and income.

[*Source* : Human Development in South Asia, 1999, Human Development Centre, Islamabad.]

Appendix 6

HUMAN DEPRIVATION PROFILE OF SAARC MEMBER COUNTRIES

	India	Pakistan	Bangladesh	Nepal	Sri Lanka	Bhutan	Maldives	South Asia (weighted average)	Developing Countries
Population below line (per cent) k1989-94									
.$ a day	53	12	29	53	4	...	...	45	32
. national poverty line	...	34	48	...	24	...	...	40	...
Population without access to safe water 1995									
. number (millions)	143	63	68	...	13	0.60	0.1b	276T	910T
. as a per cent of total pulation	15	45	55	...	7b	35	25c	22	58
Population without access to safe water 1995									
.number (millions)	178	56	25	11	7.7d	0.15k	0.10i	879T	2,687T
	19	40	21	52	42b	30n	34o	70	58
Illiterate Adults 1995									
.number (millions)	291	49	45	9	1.2	0.6	0.01	395T	351T
. as a per cent of total adult population	48	62	62	72	10	58	7.0	51	29

Illiterate Female 1995									
. number (millions)	182	28	26	5.4	0.8	0.3	0.005	243T	544T
. as a per cent of total female population Malnourished children under 5, 1996	62	76	74	86	13	72	7	64	38
.number (millions)	59	9	8	2	0.6	0.1p	0.02q	79T	162T
k. as a per cent of total population	53	38	56	56	38	38s	39s	51	30
Under-five mortality rate (per 1000 live births) 1997	108	136	109	104	19	121	74	110	96
Daily calorie supply 1995									
. quantity	2,382	2,471	2,001	-2,302	2,302	...	2,211	2,350	2,572
. as a per cent of total requirements	1121	110	92	110	101	...	73	111	113
People with disabilities 1992									
. number (millions)	1.80	6.50	9.92	0.63	0.07	...	...	9,92t	110T
. as a per cent of total population	0.2	4.9	0.8	3.0	0.4	...	...	0.83	2.6

Note:

a. year 1985; b&C year 1991, d, g, j & m: year 1994-95; e, f, h, l, k, l, n & o: year 1990-96; p & r: year 1995; q & s: year 1990-97

[*Source* : Human Development in South Asia 1999, Human Development Centre, Islamabad.]

Appendix 7

Speech of Indian Foreign Secretary R.D. Sathe At The First Meeting of the Foreign Secretaries, Colombo, 21-23 April 1981

Mr. Chairman, distinguished colleagues,

Excellencies and fellow delegates,

Please permit me to joint the preceding speakers in extending to you congratulations on your unanimous election as the Chairman of this first meeting of seven Foreign Secretaries of the South Asian region. Mr. Chairman, we are grateful for the deep interest you and the Government of Sri Lanka has taken for arranging this conference. I have no doubts that under you wise chairmanship we shall be able to have meaningful discussion which will help to attain our common objectives. Mr. Chairman, permit me to also our express to you on my own behalf as well as on behalf of my delegation our warm thanks and appreciation for the excellent arrangements for out stay here and the hospitality extended to us.

Our meeting is a very important landmark and a momentous occasion. It is a landmark for the reason that it is first time that an effort is being made at an official level to study, in the words of the paper circulated by the Bangladesh Government, "the feasibility of regional cooperation and policy recommendations on the general approach to such cooperation and the possible areas of cooperation". It is also a momentous occasion because it is the first time that the Foreign Secretaries of the region are getting together. Thus our meeting is a testimony to our political will and determination to use the instrument of regional cooperation for advancing our individual and collective development. My country is particularly happy to be participating in this meeting.

[Source: Statements made by the Foreign Secretaries of India and Pakistan at Some of the Meetings of the Foreign Secretaries (Official Texts), Ministry of External Affairs, Government of India.]

We have had considerable and long experience of cooperating with individual countries of our region on a bilateral and mutually advantageous basis. With some of the countries represented here, we have special relationships based on shared history, tradition and interest and formalised by Treaties and Agreements; with others we have developed mutually beneficial cooperation through arrangements such as joint commission. This cooperation encompasses practically all fields of endeavour, which now form the Agenda for economic and technical cooperation among developing countries. We have also participated in regional programmes of cooperation undertaken in the framework of ESCAP and Colombo Plan. We do not view the proposal now under consideration as detracting in any way from the significance of existing bilateral and multilateral cooperation arrangements. Indeed, we see it as filling a void in the existing pattern of cooperation.

We have studied the paper on the subject of regional cooperation in South Asia which had been circulated some months ago by the Government of Bangladesh. I would like to congratulate the authors of that paper for the lucid manner in which the problems have been set out. As has been correctly pointed out in the paper, unlike other regions, Regional Cooperation in South Asia has not yet taken roots. The Bangladesh paper has articulated the possibilities and advantages in this regards. We fully subscribe to the view expressed therein that in the foreseeable future, regional cooperation in South Asia has to be confined to economic, technical, scientific, social and cultural fields. It is inevitable that there will be some differences of emphasis if not perception in regards to a preliminary documents on this nature. We feel that till detailed examination has taken place it would be premature to consider the institutionalisation of Regional Cooperation through the establishment of a Secretariat, etc. It is our hope that our present meeting will identify positive factors which would be conducive to promotion of regional cooperation. Such cooperation, I must emphasise, must not be a sum total of existing bilateral arrangements. What would be necessary is to carefully identify areas where it is only through collective action of all of us that we are able to remove the handicaps and disadvantages which otherwise we would be facing in these areas.

At this stage it would also be useful to stress that we reach unequivocal agreement on what I would call the ground rules which should govern regional cooperation exercise and which in fact appear in the Bangladesh paper itself. Here I would submit that the principle of avoiding discussions in regional framework of all bilateral and contentious issues and of unanimity as the principle on the basis of which decisions in regard to regional cooperation are taken should be followed scrupulously.

Naturally, all of us would find the present exercise useful only if it is in the nature of a positive sum game. The ideal is, however, difficult to attain. There are certain obvious areas of cooperation where benefits will accure to all of use; in still others benefits may not be immediately perceptible but will become evident may as time goes on. Finally, there are also those areas, where one can see that a common stand through harmonisation and concentration of our policies would benefit us all.

I will spell these out in some detail. The first category can be identified as the cultural field. In this field cooperation can be envisaged in sport, education, films,, theatre, production of textbooks, organisation of seminars, exhibitions, etc. The list can be quite a long one. The second group is what could be considered as infrastructural groups. Here, the Bangladesh paper has already identified quite a number of areas in that group. To recapitulate these are telecommunications, meteorology, transport, shipping, agriculture and tourism. One could add development of appropriate technologies and alternative sources of energy. There is the third area for cooperation among our countries, which relates to negotiations with developed countries and other developing countries in the various international forums. This is particularly true in respect of developmental aid-its quantum and terms, problems of brain drain encountered by most of us; changes in the international monetary system, etc. It should also be possible for us to have a useful exchange of view as to how best we can cooperate with the neighbouring regions. We can also work out cooperation measures in regard to stabilisation of prices of commodities of common interest, for their joint marketing, and measures for facing competition against these from synthetics and other substitutes. There is yet another fourth area where one can envisage cooperation on a regional basis. This is in the field of science and technology and its practical application in joint ventures, exchange of information and data; joint R & D etc. The broader ramifications of programmes in the above-mentioned fields need be discussed and spelt out in considerable detail at technical and expert levels.

I should now turn to some of the measures that need to be taken individually and collectively for facilitating the development of regional cooperation. First and foremost it is important for us to remember that our present exercise has to relate to functional cooperation in areas which are most elevant for the socio-economic development of our peoples. It is basically therefore the involvement of our peoples in this exercise which is of cardinal importance. We have to prepare the public opinion in our importance. We have to prepare the public opinion in our respective countries. Our intelligentsia and academic community should help in this task. Second important step, in my view, is for the economic planners of countries of the region to meet at regular intervals to discuss and exchange our experiences in the field of planning as also to consider long-term planning perspectives. This, in my view would facilitate a better understanding in all our countries of each other's problems and requirements.

I have attempted to sketch these few thought on regional cooperation. The subject will need much more intensive discussion at technical level in the course of which one may expect a number of fields, to be explored in depth. As a result of this some ideas may have to be rejected, some others to be developed further and some implemented as soon as possible. Clearly in the kind of meeting which we are having today and tomorrow such in-deoth discussions would not be possible. It is for this reason, that I would suggest the following methodology.

I suggest that we agree to appoint four technical groups to look into the four broad areas in which regional cooperation is possible and which I have referred to earlier. It would be advisable to lay down some broad guidelines regarding the terms of reference for the meetings of the technical experts though these may have to be adapted and adopted, mutatis mutandis by the groups themselves when they meet. The conveyers for each group could be decide upon at this meeting and thereafter meetings at technical level can be organise by the conveyers to examine the area in which regional cooperation can be envisaged. The work of these groups need to be time-bound but is should be the endeavour of all concerned to complete that task as soon as possible. The reports of these groups will be submitted for examination by the nest meeting of the Foreign Secretaries of the region. That meeting should also consider the inter-sectoral aspects of cooperation, the levels of implementation and other follow-up measures. The task of coordinating the work of the four groups and the decision as to when the next meeting at the Foreign Secretaries should be convened can be left to that country which will host the next meeting of the Foreign Secretaries. It is only when adequate progress in all these fields has taken place that it would be useful and necessary for us to frame recommendations for consideration by our Ministers. The methodology suggested by me may delay the meeting of the Foreign Ministers but it is my submission that it would be necessary to make thorough preparations for the meeting of Foreign Ministers. I believe that the second meeting of the Foreign Secretaries would precisely serve this purpose.

Mr. Chairman and colleagues, at the very outset I referred to the importance of this meeting. I need hardly underline the fact that millions of our people will be following very carefully, the manner in which we move towards establishing regional cooperation. We have an obligation to lay a solid and secure foundation on which regional cooperation can be built. If there are delays one should not become pessimistic. Rome was not built in a day. Neither were other regional groupings established without several meetings and thorough discussions. In fact, I would submit that while we should no doubt profit from the experience of other regions in the world, we should not replicate or copy those patterns. A pattern of regional cooperation in South Asia should evolve itself. We do not have to jump steps ahead and create an organisational superstructure without first agreeing upon arrangements, modalities and programmes of regional cooperation. I submit that by participating in this meeting we have embarked upon a-thrilling journey. We do not know what type of obstacles we shall run into. But the prospect of running into obstacles we shall run into. But the prospect of running into obstacles need not daunt us. So long as our goal is kept clearly in view it should not be difficult to reach it.

Appendix 8

Inaugural Address of Smt. Indira Gandhi, Prime Minister of India, to the Meeting of South Asian Foreign Ministers, New Delhi, August 1,1983

Excellencies, Distinguished Guests,

I welcome you and have pleasure in inaugurating this meeting of South Asian Foreign Ministers. At a political level, this is an important step in the development of mutual relations in our region.

We seven, who are gathered here, are close geographical neighbours. The same monsoon governs our lives. We share experiences, aspirations, challenges. Our region is the cradle of one of the earliest human civilizations. In more recent centuries we have suffered from the political and economic consequences of colonialism. The very process of liberating our people from external rule has renewed awareness of one another's needs and potentialities. Today our major task is to overcome economic backwardness. As members of the Non-Aligned Movement, we seek peace with development among ourselves and in the world as a whole.

Although there are similarities, we are different. Each country has its individual personality, distinctive perception and a different political system. Subscribing to non-alignment, we respect the right of every country to choose and follow its own form of government without interference from others. At the same time, we recognise the duty to resolve whatever differences there might be through discussion and in a spirit of goodwill.

India is big in size and that means the proportion of car problems and difficulties is also gigantic. We don't want to take on more problems. Our policy is not to interfere in the affairs of others.

[Source: India Quarterly, Vol. XL. Nos. 3 and 4, July-December 1984.]

But ours is a troubled region. Most of our countries are multi-racial and multi-religious. It would be idle to pretend that we meet, there are disturbing and tragic developments in our neighbourhood.

We have always believed in cooperation and, as world events unfold, we find that cooperation in solving problems is becoming more vital and necessary to each of us and, I believe, to our region.

The world can survive and progress only with a strong sense of the unity of humankind, and tolerance of the right to political diversity. Within this framework we seven must conduct our affairs so as to eliminate tension and promote greater peace and stability in our region. The regional grouping that bring us together is not aimed against anyone else. Nor are we moved by any ideological or military considerations. Our cooperation in no way limits each country's freedom og judgement. It is allied solely to development and to the strengthening of the economics of our individual countries. Our hope is to work together and to share our experiences in agriculture, rural development, telecommunications, meteorology, health, technology, culture, art and sport.

The past has shown how brittle is the cooperation which is based on narrowness of any type. Beyond the tangible cooperation to which I have referred above is a desirable framework of a people to people relationship. Even if we proceed step by small step, the only lasting cooperation is that which involves all sections of the peoples and gives them a sense of participation.

In our effort to build a better future for our people, we face very similar problems and obstacles. We are all bedevilled by shortages of production and employment, under-nutrition and a too rapid growth of population. Yet there are natural and human resources waiting to be developed and utilised to their fullest potential. There are complementarities between our economies. With better planning and greater exchange of information, we could make the optimum use of our capacities.

Confrontation is dangerous and unprofitable. All the historical, technological and economic forces and factors at work in the world demand cooperation. The threat of nuclear war must be averted. Its consequences are too horrendous to contemplate. We have always spoken out of violence and destruction. These must be curbed. Simultaneously the world must do something to shake free from the grip of the economic crisis which hurts all countries, rich and poor, big and small. But the worst suffers, as each of us knows, are the developing countries. The recent

Conference of Non-aligned Countries here in this city made some constructive suggestions. We are trying to make the industrialised countries recognise the reasonableness of our proposals and the moderation with which we have expressed ourselves.

The more recently concluded session of UNCTAD in Belgrade was an opportunity for some concrete, if not bold and imaginative, steps to initiate the process of restructuring international economics relations and to start an earnest North-South dialogue. The opportunity was allowed to slip by. Some statements have been made recognising the interrelationship between growth in developing countries and economic revival in the advanced. Alas, there is still no sign of this sentiment being translated into positive action.

We do not look for magic deliverance. The only sure road to prosperity is to mobilize our peoples to work. Enduring solutions call for the strengthening of our own economies towards self-reliance. This does not preclude international cooperation. The two are mutually supportive. Hence, along with a North-South dialogue, we urge greater cooperation among developing countries. South-South cooperation is an integral part of the New International Economic Order we envisage. The Non-Aligned Summit suggested that we draw up a comprehensive blue print for cooperation and collective self-reliance among developing countries, taking into account their needs and resources, their exigencies and capabilities.

Experience in other parts of the world has shown that sub-regional and regional cooperation is an important factor in bringing about economic and social progress. The countries of South Asia have been rather slow in realising this. I am glad we are making a beginning. We have had our political differences in the past or have even now, but economic cooperation will give a strong impetus to closer friendship and greater stability in South Asia. I hope that this meeting of Ministers will push forward this programme. In this forum, we should avoid bilateral differences and aim at concentrating on what unites us and helps us in our common quest of peace and development. We are all equals. We are against exploitation and domination. We want to be friends with all on footing of equality. We should be ever vigilant against the attempts of external powers to influence our functioning.

There are many regional organisations, some fully developed, some still at a tentative stage. Even fully developed groupings like the European Economic Community have not been able to sort out their problems merely by a common regional personality. Let us not be disheartened if we have some difficulties and differences to contend with. We are at the beginning of what promises to be a useful journey.

As regional cooperation progresses, new tasks will unfold themselves, bringing in new problems. Let us not be daunted. Our very cooperation will increase our capacity to withstand pressures. With unity we can hope to move ahead to a future of freedom, peace and prosperity.

I declare the Meeting and give my good wishes for your work.

Appendix 9

South Asian Regional Cooperation (SARC)

Text of Prime Minister's Address

The following is the text of the address by Shri Rajiv Gandhi, Prime Minster of India, to the first South Asian Regional Cooperation Summit, Dhaka, on December 7, 1985:

Mr. Chairman, Majesties, Presidents, Excellencies, Distinguished Guests,

Today is an important day in the history of resurgent Asia. Seven neighbours have come together in an act of faith. The South Asian Association for Regional Cooperation is born. So this city, famed for its gossamer weave, capital of golden Bangladesh, witnesses the birth of a promising institution.

Great Crucibles of Human Creativity

The South Asian region has been one of the great crucibles of human creativity. Here, an indigenous civilization, whose origins stretch back into an unfathomed antiquity, interacted with peoples and races who poured in from distant parts of the world. Out of the intermingling of their ideas, philosophies and ways of life grew the noble heritage to which all our seven countries can lay claim.

Through record history, this fruitful interaction continued, both within the region and with those who came from outside. We have venerated the Vedas, the Dhammapada, the Quran, the Bible and Granth Sahib. On our soil have been born saints and sages, seers and epic poets, men and women of profound wisdom who have given to the world some of its great religions and many of its deepest philosophies. South Asia is the home of Mohenjodaro and Anuradhapura and the Taj Mahal; Patan and Kyi-chu; Mainamati and the Mukuru Mosque.

[*Source* : Foreign Affairs Record, Ministry of External Affairs, Government of India, Vol. XXL, No.12, December 1985.]

Nature gave us mighty mountains, fertile plains, lush forests, teeming rivers and bountiful oceans. We developed into world, always in the forefront, sometimes ahead of everyone else. Our agriculture and our textiles, our arts and crafts, our sculpture and architecture, our painting, music and dance matured into one of the great splendorous of the world. The world sought us out. Perilous voyages and dangerous journeys were undertaken to see something of the glory of this fabled land bounded to the north by the majestic Himalayas and on all sides by vast ocean.

And then came the dark age of imperialism, our economies stagnated, our societies stultified, our cultures turned in upon themselves.

We emerged from two centuries of colonial oppression as free, independent, equal countries. We each have our personalities, our particular characteristics, our nuances of culture and spirituality. We vary in size. Our endowments differ. Our paths to development are our own. Our political systems are not all the same. Our political systems are not all the same. But we are all of us animated by a shared spirit of South Asia. Among our peoples, there is an immediate recognition and familiarity, a sense of shared values, fellow-feeling and brotherhood. It is upon this natural goodwill that we build.

Diversity of Region

India welcomes the diversity of our region. We affirm the sovereign equality of the seven States of South Asia. We have much to learn from one another and much to give. We have a profound faith in peaceful coexistence. We are confident we share these beliefs with all our partners in the region.

We of South Asia constitute one-fifth of the world population. Cooperation amongst us constitutes cooperation within a vast segment of humanity. At the Asian Relations Conference in New Delhi in 1947, Jawaharlal Nehru declared, "We meet together, we hold together, we advance together". South Asian cooperation is an important step towards realising the larger Asian consciousness.

The Non-aligned Movement, to which all of us belong, has made the pursuit of peace, progress, prosperity and the establishment of a new world order the centre-piece of its efforts. SARC gives practical form in our region to the Declaration on Collective Self-reliance adopted at the New Delhi Nonaligned Summit.

It was at the initiative of our host country, Bangladesh, that South Asian regional cooperation began taking shape five years ago. We have made modest but important beginnings in key areas of development. We have provided SARC with a functioning institutional base. We have dispelled the suspicions that were thought to exist and demonstrated the possibilities of mutual cooperation in our region. South Asian regional cooperation is now generating its own momentum and itself providing the impetus for further cooperation.

Spirit of Solidarity

Today, we move only having a programme of cooperation to forming an Association. A spirit of solidarity, sharing and unity of purpose has brought s together. We celebrated the completion of the initial phase and together move into the next.

Certainly we have problems and difficulties, and these do impose constraints on us. Enduring cooperation is cooperation adapted to the realities of our condition. The model we have evolved for ourselves is a model which is in accord with our realities, our compulsions and our genius. We have not sought to melt our bilateral relationships into a common regional identity, but rather to fit South Asian cooperation into our respective foreign policies as an additional dimension. We have evolved modalities which do not allow bilateral stresses and strains to impinge on regional cooperation. Our cooperation tempers enthusiasm with pragmatism, and initiative with consensus. At the same time, in the light of our experience of the recent past, we have every reason to hope that the practice of regional cooperation will have a beneficial impact on bilateral relationships.

Turbulent Times

We are living in turbulent times. The world economy remains immersed in deep crisis. International economic institutions are in disarray. The consensus on development has broken down. Multilateralism has come under severe stain. In most developing countries, growth has sharply decelerated or ground to a standstill. On the whole, our region has weathered the crisis well. But all seven of us continue to be confronted with formidable problems of poverty, illiteracy, malnutrition and disease. We have to overcome these problems in a highly adverse external environment. South

Asian cooperation points the way to collective self-reliance. Our endeavours strengthen the forces of multi-lateralism and world-wide cooperation.

This Summit has given rise to great expectations among our peoples and in the outside world. WE have taken a decisive step forward in establishing the South Asian Association for Regional Cooperation. Its success will depend on the involvement of our peoples in their hundreds of million.

The developing countries seek peace and stability to pursue their development. Prevailing tensions and the continuing nuclear arms race pose a serious threat to our progress and prosperity. We must make a conscious efforts to remain outside the vortex of these tensions and conflicts. In the true spirit of Nonalignment, our cooperation should set an example for other.

This Summit broaden the vision of South Asian cooperation. It gives a new impetus and fresh direction to our endeavour. It consolidates the institutional basis of our cooperation. Above all, it fosters peaceful and good neighbourly relations between our countries. We are happy to belong to this family of South Asian nations. Gurudev Rabinderanath Thakur's prayer for his country could well be the prayer for our family:

"Let the earth and water, the air and
the fruits of my country be full,
my God.
Let Homes and marts, the forests
And fields of my country be full,
my God.
Let the promises and hopes, the deeds
And words of my country be true,
my God.
Let the lives and hearts of the sons and
Daughters of my country be one,
my God.

To our Chairman, President Ershad, and to the Government of Bangladesh we extend our grateful thanks for the excellent arrangements they have made. And to the people of Bangladesh our gratitude for the warmth of their welcome and the generous hospitality for which they are renowned.

Thank you.

Appendix 10

Charter of the South Asian Association For Regional Cooperation

We the Heads of State or Government of Bangladesh, Bhutan, India, Maldives, Nepal, Pakistan and Sri Lanka;

1. Desirous of promoting peace, stability, amity and progress in the region through strict adherence to the principles of the United Nations Charter and Non-Alignment, particularly respect for the principles of sovereign equality, territorial integrity, national independence, non use of force and non interference in the internal affairs of other States and peaceful settlement of all disputes;

2. Conscious that in an increasingly interdependent world, the objectives of peace, freedom, social justice and economic prosperity are best achieved in the South Asian region by fostering mutual understanding, good neighbourly relations and meaningful cooperation among the Member States which are bound by ties of history and culture;

3. Aware of common problems, interests and aspirations of the peoples of South Asia and the need for joint action and enhanced cooperation within their respective political and economic systems and cultural traditions;

4. Convinced that regional cooperation among the countries of South Asia is mutually beneficial, desirable and necessary for promoting the welfare and improving the quality of life of the peoples of the region;

5. Convinced further that economic, social and technical cooperation among the countries of South Asia would contribute significantly to national and collective self reliance;

[*Source* : Information and Media Division, SAARC Secretariat, Kathmandu, 1997.]

6. Recognising that increased cooperation, contacts and exchanges among the countries of the region will contribute to the promotion of friendship, and understanding among their peoples;

7. Recalling the Declaration signed by their Foreign Ministers in New Delhi on August 2, 1983 and noting the progress achieved in regional cooperation;

8. Reaffirming their determination to promote such cooperation within an institutional framework;

Do Hereby

Agree to establish an organisation to be known as South Asian Association For Regional Cooperation hereinafter referred to as the Association, with the following objectives, principles, institutional and financial arrangements;

Article I

Objectives

The objectives of the Association shall be:

(a) To promote the welfare of the peoples of South Asia and to improve their quality of life;

(b) To accelerate economic growth, social progress and cultural development in the region and to provide all individuals the opportunity to live in dignity and to realise their full potential;

(c) To promote and strengthen collective self-reliance among the countries of South Asia;

(d) To contribute to mutual trust, understanding and appreciation of one another's problems;

(e) To promote active collaboration and mutual assistance in the economic, social, cultural, technical and scientific fields;

(f) To strengthen cooperation with other developing countries;

(g) To strengthen cooperation among themselves in international forums on matters of common interest; and

(h) To cooperate with international and regional organisations with similar aims and purposes.

Article II

Principles

1. Cooperation within the framework of Association shall be based on respect for the principle of sovereign equality, territorial integrity, political independence, non-interference in the internal

affairs of other States and mutual benefits.

2. Such cooperation shall not be substitute for bilateral and multilateral cooperation but shall complement them.

3. Such cooperation shall not be inconsistent with bilateral and multilateral obligations.

Article III

Meeings of the Heads of State or Government

The Heads of State or Government shall meet once a year or more often as and when considered necessary by the Member States.

Article IV

Council of Ministers

A Council of Ministers consisting of the Foreign Ministers of the Member States shall be established with the following function:

(a) formulation of the policies of the Association;

(b) review of the progress of cooperation under the Associaiton;

(c) decision on new areas of cooperation;

(d) establishment of additional mechanism under the Association as deemed necessary;

(e) decision on other matters of general interest to the Association.

1. The Council of Ministers shall meet twice a year. Extraordinary session of the Council may be held by agreement among the Member States.

Article V

Standing Committe

The Standing Committee comprising the Foreign Secretaries shall have the following function:

(a) overall monitoring and coordinating of programme of cooperation;

(b) approval of projects and programmes, and the modalities of their financing;

(c) determination of inter-sectoral priorities;

(d) mobilisation of regional and external resources;

(e) identification of new areas of cooperation based on appropriate studies.

1. The Standing Committee shall meet as often as deemed necessary.

2. The Standing Committee shall submit periodic reports to the Council of Ministers and make reference to it as and when necessary for decisions on policy matters.

Article VI

Technical Committees

1.Technical Committees comprising representatives of Member States shall be responsible for the implementation, coordination and monitoring of the programmes in their respective areas of cooperation.

2. They shall have the following terms of reference:

(a) determination of the potential and the scope of regional cooperation in agreed areas;

(b) formulation of programmes and preparation of projects;

(c) determination of financial implications of sectoral programmes;

(d) formulation of recommendations regarding apportionment of costs;

(e) implementation coordination of sectoral programmes;

(f) monitoring of progress in implementation.

3.The Technical Committees shall submit periodic reports to the Standing Committee.

4. The Chairmanship of the Technical Committees shall normally rotate among Member States in alphabetical order every two years.

5. The Technical Committee may, inter-alia, use the following mechanism and modalities, if and when considered necessary:

(a) meetings of heads of national technical agencies;

(b) meetings to experts in specific fields;

(c) contact amongst recognised centres of excellence in the region.

Article VII

Action Committees

The Standing Committee may set up Action Committees comprising Member States concerned with implementation of project involving more than two but not all Member States.

ARTICLE VIII

Secretariat

There shall be a Secretariat of the Association.

Article IX

Financial Arrangements

1. The contribution of each Member State towards financing of the activities of the Association shall be voluntary.

2. Each Technical Committee shall make recommendations for the apportionment of costs of implementing the programmes proposed by it.

3. In case sufficient financial resources cannot be moblised within the region for funding activities of the Association, external financing from appropriate sources my be mobilised with the approval of or by the Standing Committee.

Article X

General Provisions

Decisions at all levels shall be taken on the basis of unanimity. Bilateral and contentious issues shall be excluded from the deliberations.

In Faith Whereof We Have Set Our Hands Seals Hereunto.

Done in Dhaka, Bangladesh, On This The Eighth Day of December of The Year One Thousand Nine Hundred Eighty Five.

Hussain Muhammad Ershad
President of the Peoples
Republic of Bangladesh

Maumoon Abdul Gayoom
President of the Republic of
Maldives

Jigme Singye Wangchuck
Dev
King of Bhutan

Birendra Bir Bikram Shah
King of Nepal

Rajiv Gandhi
Prime Minister of the Republic
of Pakistan
of India

Muhammad Zia-ul-Haq
President of the Islamic Republic

Junius Richard Jayewardene
President of Democratic Socialist
Republic of Sri Lanka

Appendix 11

Address by P.V. Narasima Rao Prime Minister of India: Inauguration of the Seventh SAARC Summit At Dhaka Bangladesh April 10, 1993

Madam Chairperson,

Your Majesty

Presidents and Prime Ministers

Excellencies, Ladies and Gentlemen,

I am delighted to be here in the historic city of Dhaka doe this 7th Summit Meeting of the SAARC, May I take this opportunity, Madam Chairperson, to extend our felicitations to you on your assumption of the Chairmanship of this Organisation?

This Session is of particular significance. Our gathering again in Dhaka today signifies the completion of one cycle of our meetings. It is here that the SAARC was inaugurated on 7 December, 1995. Your assuming the Chairmanship of the Movement, at this juncture, is a tribute to the memory of your late husband, President Ziaur Rahman, who was the originator of the idea of cooperation amongst SAARC countries. We are assembled here not only in the shared faith which made us come together in this Organisation, but also in shared purposiveness for cooperation based on our experience of working together for the last seven years. Our attempts to come together in the cultural, scientific, economic and commercial fields, and the full cycle of summits that we have completed, provide the basis for a new beginning, the fusion of our shared faith and common interest which brought the Movement into being. These must be synergised with the experience of our working together in the last seven years and with the changes that have taken place in our

---

[Source: Official Text, Ministry of External Affairs, Government of India]

outlook in keeping with the profound changes in the world around us.

I would also like to acknowledge the significant contributions which Presidents Premadasa made to the Movement as Chairman of the SAARC. We appreciate the deep interest that he showed in discharging the high responsibilities in relation to the SAARC. I would like to place on record our appreciation and gratitude for the thoughtful and active leadership which he provided to our Association.

Madam Chairperson, qualitative changes have taken place in the world around is in the last few years. These have inevitably affected our region. All of us have to adjust to transformed equations in terms of economic influence, political and military power and strategic perceptions which have emerged with the disappearance of Super Power competition and monolithic ideological confrontations. The ramifications of these changes are affecting our existence and our future across the entire spectrum of issues, which are of common concern to us, from security to scientific and technological exploration, from nurturing democracy to sustaining developmental activities. The challenge is not only that of meeting these concerns, but to fashion an international order firmly rooted in the ideals of democracy, and based on the principles of justice and equality, and aimed at ensuring the genuine well-being of the peoples of our region and the world at large. We are witnesses to an international situation subject to contradictory trends of centripetal and centrifugal forces at work. While established political entities and plural societies have disintegrated, there are emerging patterns of socio-economic integration between Nation States underpinned by a unilinear structuring of the global economy.

Our Association must therefore evolve meaningful policy approaches to deal with the world-wide trends in regional cooperation, economic groupings and trading blocs as witnessed in Western Europe, North and South America, ASEAN and the Asia-Pacific region. For economies like ours, particularly at a time when we have liberalised and adopted outward-oriented policies, these trends have important implications. They may well present new trading and economic opportunities for us. Our collective economic strength and weight as a mega-market of over 1 billion consumers and the pooling together of our abundant and manifold talents, skills and resources will alone enable us to be a serious player in the global economy. Hence, the new beginning we must make in the coming years is to focus our energies - political and social - on economic development. Contemporary history tells us that economic development in all its aspects is among the best cures for socio-political ills. We must make a renewed effort to break down the trade barriers between our countries and jettison the irrational past which created and sustained these barrier. A renewal must also mean building upon old and discovering new complementarities, opportunities and avenues for economic collaboration among our 7 countries. In this, our interdependent world, let us begin by recognising, reinforcing and capitalising our own regional inter-dependence. Let not our modest beginnings as regional cooperation movements belie the great potential there is for cooperation. If we believe this, the difficulties we face should not deter us from moving purposively towards the exponential benefits for our peoples that genuine regional cooperation would bring.

Our economic well-being and development objectives are subject to the limitations of the disparities in economic, technological and fiscal conditions that exist within our own region. This lack of symmetry or cohesiveness is likely to be compounded by the inward-looking and self-centres approach to commercial, financial and technological issues which my be adopted by the more advanced and prosperous countries and regions. Our task, therefore, would be to structure a balanced relationship in these spheres with the industrially-advanced countries in a manner in which we safeguard our collective interest, at the same time making sincere efforts to move away from adversary competition or demanding attitudes which earlier characterised our interaction with the prosperous countries.

The efforts to come to fruitful understanding with the advanced countries has to be necessarily predicted on our putting our own houses in order, and structuring a pattern of cooperation amongst ourselves which will project an image and impression to the outside world that their cooperation with us would not be an exercise in one-sided demands but in mutually beneficial relationships. We have to direct our energies to resolve persistent problems of poverty, literacy, health care etc., which affect the quality of life of our peoples. Bringing our experience and expertise together to help each other for this purpose is a pre-requisite for any successful effort at forging a stable and egalitarian relationship with other countries and other regions. As I have had occasion to emphasise before, we must effectively reach out to each other as, or even before, we reach out to the rest of the world.

This Summit marks the beginning of the second cycle of summit meetings of our region. This is a watershed that merits introspection. Introspection leads me to the conclusion that the content and range of cooperation within the SAARC region has been slower than what we wished for. The reasons are the geo-demographic disparity amongst member-countries and inhibitions born of problems inherited from the past. We cannot wish these away. But, we certainly can abide by the stipulation in the SAARC Charter by setting aside issues on which there are differences of opinion, issues which are essentially bilateral. We must purposefully forge cooperation in areas of common interest and which are of more profound relevance to the well-being of our peoples.

I am glad to note that this has been the orientation of our approach as we consolidate our Association and determine its future course of action.

The past year has been characterised by progress in dealing with substantive issues of interest to us. The 6th Summit had given high priority to dealing with problems of poverty. The South Asian Commission on Poverty Alleviation consisting of eminent persons from our countries, has completed its work. The in-depth study carried out by the Commission has resulted in a comprehensive action-oriented report and recommendations. Our deliberations during this Summit should result in decisions which would translate the recommendations into action programmes and policies. Effective social mobilisation of the establishment of appropriate national support mechanisms for poverty alleviation programmes are essential. We endorse the view expressed by the Commission in its report that governments have a central and catalytic role in undertaking this effort and in promoting human development, vocational training and primary health care. This has to be achieved by democratic means in a liberalised socio-economic environment.

We are embarked on a programme of structuring regional economic cooperation to build a dynamic South Asian community. Collectively, we are endowed with natural resources, skilled manpower and the economic incentive of a mass market of nearly one billion people in the South Asian region. Our needs, our products and the services that we can orchestrate can be mutually complementary if backed up by positive political will, mutual trust and confidence.

It is gratifying, therefore, to note that our consciousness about these positive factors has increased. We have commenced considering programmes of cooperation in the important spheres of regional trade, scientific and technological cooperation, environment, and the development of diverse sources of conventional and non-conventional energy. Experts from our region have met and submitted collective recommendations for consideration. I take particular satisfaction in noting the steps taken towards the establishment of the South Asian Preferential Trading Arrangements, SAPTA. India would join in the collective endeavour to implement the decisions in this regard within the time frame stipulated. To the extent that our talents and resources can benefit all the countries in the SAARC region. India places these at the disposal of the SAARC.

It is said in Indian scriptures that the measure of civilisational excellence of any given society is the manner in which women and children are treated in that society. SAARC, as a regional mechanism, over the last two years has acknowledged this norm. The ministerial Resolution on Children adopted by the SAARC Conference in September last at Colombo and the decisions taken by the 7th Meeting of the SAARC Technical Committee on Women in Development held at Male 25th and 26th August, 1992 affirm our collective commitment to ensure the welfare of women and children and to convert them into a dynamic contributive factor for the stability and prosperity of our region.

We are happy that the structure and content of cooperation in SAARC is not being limited to the executive political sphere is terms of summit meeting and derivative activities based on the decisions of these Summits. Arrangements have been put in place for interaction between the presiding officers of our legislatures, between our jurists and between leading figures in the sphere of academy and culture. Our desire to affirm the continuity and common heritage in terms of shared civilisation and culture found expression in the First Asian Cultural Festival of SAARC countries held in India last October. We considered it an honour to host the Festival and it is our hope that such festivals will not only continue in different countries of our region but that they would cover within their ambit cultural, academic, journalistic and science and technology activities.

We must only strengthen and expand cooperation in already identified spheres of activities, but we must move on to new spheres of cooperation animated by a sprit of initiative and imagination. We must forge links to increase our potentialities to harness unconventional sources of energy, search for and utilise natural resources on our land and coastal for and utilise natural resources on our land and coastal seas and put in place projects of cooperation in new field of vocational training, agricultural productivity and high technology. We must encourage exchanges of our experts and create an integrated network for exchanging information and ideas which will serve the overall objective of ensuring our collective well-being by means of sustained cooperative developmental activities.

In recent months we have considered suggestions for the establishment of a South Asian Development Fund to mobilise global resources for development in our region. While mobilising the surpluses available is a desirable effort, we must remain conscious that in the foreseeable future we are subject to limitations of recessionary trends in the world economy, and demands from, and attention to, other parts of the world away from our region. We are therefore faced with an atmosphere of competition where our political stability, our absorptive capacity and our financial, economic and technological attractiveness would be the deciding factors leading to external inputs for our development. A collective effort by all of us to meet these criteria is essential. This is the only way in which we can ensure positive external responses to our needs and aspirations.

Madam Chairperson and Distinguished Friends, we hold our deliberations in a time of ferment and transition. A holistic or historical assessment may be that nations pass through these cycles of crises time and again and that, therefore detachment rather than involvement should be the proper attitude. The point, however, is that detachment in assessment and determining terms of reference to meet challenges is valid and desirable. Equally, purposive activity is necessary for survival and change which are essential for continuity and progress. The scriptures and teachings of all the religions of our peoples tell us that detachment on the one hand and action for the public weal on the other, are not mutually exclusive, but essentially complementary norms and that our efforts should be imbued with the faith and mutual confidence which brought us together at the inception of SAARC. It has been said that the essence of faith is fewness of words and abundance of deeds, it is deeds exceeding words, which lend meaning to life. This should be the ideal which should guide us. Let us work together to make these lands and these peoples of ours endowed with plenty and prosperity, fragrant with the flowering of our efforts to meet the ideals and objectives which we adopted in this beautiful city of Dhaka sever years ago, at the inception of SAAPC. In the words of Shri Rajiv Gandhi, who was present on that occasion, and whose energy and vision helped chart the course that our Association set for itself. "We have much to learn from each other and much to give. We have profound faith in peaceful coexistence. We are confident that we share these beliefs with all our partners in the region".

I thank you.

Appendix 12

Suo-Moto Statement by Prime Minister of India Shri Atal Bihari Vajpayee in Lok Sabha/Rajya Sabha on August 3, 1998

Sir,

1. Over the last few weeks, Government has kept the House regularly informed about developments in the field of international relations and our foreign policy. I take this opportunity to bring Honourable Members up-to-date on the most recent events, especially SAARC, our relations with Pakistan and the recent ARF and ASEAN dialogue meetings.

2. I visited Colombo on 28th - 31st July 1998 to participate in the 10th SAARC Summit. I was accompanied by Commerce Minister, Deputy chairman, Planning Commission, as well as Minster of State for External Affairs who led our delegation at the Ministerial level meeting preceding the Summit.

3. The Summit reaffirmed the common desire of SAARC Member States to strengthen cooperation in the region. There was general agreement with our perception that to meet the challenges and to avail of the opportunities presented by the substantially transformed global economic situation, it was essential to enhance bilateral as well as SAARC regional, economic, social and technical cooperation. The agenda and the discussions during the Summit were focussed on these areas.

4. It was agreed that SAARC must move purposefully towards setting up a Free Trade Area; a group of experts will be set up to negotiate a comprehensive legal framework for this purpose incorporating schedules for liberalised trade and facilitation measures, taking into account least developed countries' concerns. Parallel steps will be taken to conclude the third round of the trade

[*Source* : Foreign Affairs Record, Ministry of External Affairs, Government of India, Vol. XLIV, No.8, August 1998.]

negotiations under the South Asian Preferential Trading Arrangement, and to commence the next round.

5. We have reiterated our commitment to, and readiness for bold initiatives to speed up trade liberalisation. I announced our Government's decision to lift all Quantitative Restriction preferentially, on imports from SAARC countries, with effect from August 1, 1998. This is a decision with far-reaching positive economic and developmental consequences for the region and has been welcomed. We also made known our readiness to enter into bilateral free trade arrangements with interested SAARC countries. Sri Lanka has taken up this offer.

6. In our discussion, it was recognised that the benefits of trade liberalisation would be more extensive and balanced through promoting trade-related joint ventures, investment and trade-in-services such as tourism. India's decision to substantially increase the ceiling for investment for India under the fast track in SAARC countries, from US$ 8 to US $ 15 million has also been welcomed. This will encourage a greater flow of Indian investment and stimulate trade.

7. Important initiatives have been taken in the social sector to illustrate, a Social Charter for SAARC, agreement to finanlise a convention to combat Illegal Trafficking in Women and Children. This is to be signed at the next SAARC Summit. A regional convention on child welfare also be developed.

8. WE underlined the importance of cooperation in energy through networking. India has, further offered to host a special meeting of Science and Technology Ministers to consider a SAARC S&T initiative for regional projects in rural areas, directly benefiting the people. We also underlined the utility of cooperation in traditional systems of medicines and have invited participation in a Health Ministers' meeting in India for this purpose. India has reaffirmed support for comprehensive environment related proposals.

9. I would also like to draw attention to my bilateral meetings on the sidelines of the Summit, with the Presidents of Maldives and Sri Lanka, the Prime Ministers of Bangladesh and Nepal and the Chairman of the Council of Ministers of Bhutan. These meetings provided the occasion for renewing our friendly contact, for fruitful discussions enabling a review of our bilateral relations and of progress in specific areas of cooperation, as well as for sharing our perceptions.

10. I took the opportunity, in my interaction with other leaders, to reiterate our commitment to peace and stability, setting at rest misconceptions about our recent nuclear tests. Our initiatives for confidence building and disarmament have been appreciated. There was agreement on the need to commence purposeful negotiations towards a comprehensive and non-discriminatory global nuclear disarmament regime and a nuclear weapon-free world.

11. We have conveyed our appreciation to the Sri Lankan Government for the excellent arrangements made for the Summit, and in particular to President Chandrika Kumaratunga for the vision and efficiency with which she steered the Summit deliberations. We wish her well in her new responsibility in chairing SAARC. We assure Sri Lanka of our full support.

12. In my interaction with Pakistan Prime Minister, Mr. Muhammed Nawaz Sharif, which included a long meeting on July 29, I reiterated our commitment to developing peaceful and friendly ties with Pakistan, and our interest in a secure stable and prosperous Pakistan. I urged that we should work together to develop trust and confidence, and avail of the many opportunities for mutually beneficial cooperation in the economic, social and other fields so that we can improve the lives of peoples. I further underlined the need to work together to address our differences in a rational and realistic manner. The atmosphere to our discussions was cordial and constructive. I look forward to continuing a purposeful interaction with Prime Minister Nawaz Sharif.

13. My discussions with Prime Minister Nawaz Sharif also focussed on our official level dialogue. Honurable Members will recall that such a dialogue had been resumed last year, and that the subjects for discussion were jointly identified in June, 1997. The modalities for this purpose have not yet been finalised. We directed our Foreign Secretaries to meet and complete this exercise.

14. Indian has consistently underlined its commitment to a direct, composite dialogue with Pakistan. Such a comprehensive an sustained process will contribute to building trust and confidence, promote mutually beneficial cooperation and help address bilateral issues. The dialogue must address the totality of the relationship and not be pursued in a narrow, segmented fashion which would defeat its very purpose which is to build a wide ranging and enduring relationship. A direct bilateral interaction which seeks to generate

confidence and foster cooperation in functional areas, and enhanced people to people contacts would also help create a positive climate, in which difficult issues under discussion could be purposefully addressed. It is recognised by the international community that all outstanding issues between India and Pakistan, including Jammu and Kashmir should be settled bilaterally in a peaceful manner. The modalities which we have suggested would help ensure that the process moves forward on a broad front in a constructive and sustained manner, while at the same time providing a meaningful opportunity for discussions on confidence building measures, cooperation and dealing with outstanding issues, as part of a composite process.

15. Our Foreign Secretaries met in Colombo and exchanged views on this subject. We will remain engaged in the process and continue contacts through diplomatic channels, to work out an agreement, so that the dialogue could be continued.

16. During my talks with Prime Minister Nawaz Sharif, I also emphasised that instigation and support of terrorism was incompatible with our common desire for friendly and peaceful relations and that these activities must cease immediately.

17. Honourable Members are aware that we also participated in this year's ASEAN Post-Ministerial Conference which is an important part of ASEAN Regional Forum (ARF). Meetings held on July 24-29. Our delegation was led by Deputy Chairman, Planning Commission. My government has reaffirmed the policy of strengthening cooperation with countries in ASEAN and the Asia Pacific Region as a whole. Apart from bilateral contacts, we have also established active communication with them in the framework of the dialogue partnership and ARF. Our participation in these meetings this year, was particularly important, as it provided an opportunity to once again clarify our policy on nuclear disarmament in the context of the recent tests, as well as to demonstrate our continued engagement in the economic and political stability of the region and share perceptions on regional and international developments. While the ARF "Chairman's Statement" contained a paragraph disapproving of the recent tests in South Asia, with which we disassociated ourselves, we also found a better overall understanding on the part of ASEAN countries of the rationale of our policy, as well as of the need for purposeful moves by the nuclear Weapon states towards comprehensive, universal nuclear

disarmament on a non-discriminatory basis. We assure the ASEAN countries that we fully respected the status of the Nuclear Weapon Free Zone in South East Asia.

18. Our interaction with ASEAN reflected an understanding that cooperation and dialogue partnership with India had made good progress, and that we needed to jointly consolidate this through implementation of projects and measures under discussion, in trade and investment, infrastructure and human resource development, tourism, culture and people to people contacts.

19. The leader of our delegation also had constructive and forward looking discussion with the Foreign Ministers of ASEAN countries, Russia, China, Australia and New Zealand, the US Secretary of State and the Ministers of State of Japan and the United Kingdom. Our bilateral and multilateral interaction in the ASEAN and ARF meetings has helped our post-Pokharan -II diplomatic efforts. Our overall approach, and importance of the steps we have taken to address international and regional security concerns is better acknowledged. There is also continued recognition that India is a factor for peace, stability in the region.

Appendix 13

Texts of Lahore Declaration, Joint Statement and MOU between India and Pakistan, February 1999.

Lahore declaration

Text: The Prime Ministers of the Republic of India and the Islamic Republic of Pakistan:

Sharing a vision of peace and stability between their countries and of progress and prosperity for their people.

Convinced that durable peace and development of harmonious relations and friendly cooperation will serve the vital interests of the peoples of the two countries, enabling them to devote their energies for a better future.

Recognising that the nuclear dimension of the security environment of the two countries adds to their responsibility for avoidance of conflict between the two countries;

Committed to the principles and purposes of the Charter of the United Nations, and the universally accepted principle of peaceful co-existence;

Reiterating the determination of both countries to implementing the Simla Agreement in letter and spirit;

Committed to the objectives of universal nuclear disarmament and non-proliferation;

Convinced of the importance of mutually agreed confidence-building measures for improving the security environment.

Recalling their agreement of September 23, 1998 that an environment of peace and security is in the supreme national interest of both sides and that the resolution of all outstanding issues,

---

[*Source* : Public Opinion Trends Analyses and News Services, New Delhi. Pakistan Series, Vol. XXVII, No.66, March 1999.]

including Jammu and Kashmir is essential for this purpose;

Have agreed that their respective governments:

- Shall intensify their efforts to resolve all issues including the issue of Jammu and Kashmir.

- Shall refrain from intervention and interference in each other's internal affairs.

- Shall intensify their composite and integrated dialogue process for an early and positive outcome of the agreed bilateral agenda.

- Shall take immediate steps for reducing the risk of accidental or unauthorised use of nuclear weapons accidental or unauthorised use of nuclear weapons and discuss concepts and doctrines with a view to elaborating measures for confidence building in the nuclear and conventional fields, aimed at prevention of conflict.

- Reaffirm their commitment to the goals and objectives of SAARC and to concert their efforts towards the realisation of the SAARC vision for the year 2000 and beyond with a view to promoting the welfare of the peoples of South Asia and improving their quality of life through accelerated economic growth, social progress and cultural development.

- Reaffirm their condemnation of terrorism in all its forms and manifestations and their determination to combat this menace.

- Shall promote and protect all human rights and fundamental freedoms.

Text of Pakistan-India Joint Statement

The following is the text of the Joint Statement issued by India and Pakistan at the conclusion of the two day visit of Indian Prime Minister Atal Behari Vajpayee to Pakistan on February 20 and 21 and the talks held with Mr. Nawaz Sharif:

1. In response to an invitation by the Prime Minister of Pakistan, Mr. Muhammad Nawaz Sharif, the Prime Minister of India, Shri Atal Behari Vajpayee, visited Pakistan from February 20 to 21, 1999 on the inaugural run of the Delhi-Lahore bus service.

2. The Prime Minister of Pakistan received the Indian Prime Minister at the Wagah border on February 20, 1999. A banquet in honour of the Indian Prime Minister of Pakistan at Lahore Fort on the same evening. Prime Minister Atal Behari Vajpayee visited Minar Pakistan, mausoleum of Allama Iqbal, Gurdwara Dera Sahib and samadhi of Maharaja Ranjit Singh. On February 21, a civic

reception was held in honour of the visiting Prime Minister at Governor's House.

3. The two leaders held discussions on the entire range of bilateral relations, regional cooperation within SAARC, and issues of international concern. They decided that:

(a) The two Foreign Ministers will meet periodically to discuss all issues of mutual concern, including nuclear related issues.

(b) The two sides shall undertake consultations on WTO related issues with a view to coordinating their respective positions.

(c) The two sides shall determine areas of cooperation in information technology particular for tackling the problems of Y2K.

(d) The two sides shall appoint a two-member committee at ministerial level to examine humanitarian issues relating to civilian detainees and missing POWs.

4. They expressed satisfaction on the commencement of a bus service between Lahore and New Delhi, the release of fishermen and civilian detainees and the renewal of contacts in the field of sports.

5. Pursuant to the directive given by the two Prime Ministers, the Foreign Secretaries of Pakistan and India signed a Memorandum of understanding on February 21, 1999, identifying measures aimed at promoting an environment of peace and security between the two countries.

6. The two Prime Ministers signed the Lahore Declaration embodying their shared vision of peace and stability between their countries and of progress and prosperity for their peoples.

7. Prime Minister Atal Behari Vajpayee extended an invitation to Prime Minister Muhammad Nawaz Sharif to visit India on mutually convenient dates.

8. Prime Minister Atal Behari Vajpayee thanked Prime Minister Muhammad Nawaz Sharif for the warm welcome and gracious hospitality extended to him and members of his delegation and for the excellent arrangements made for his visit.

Text of Memorandum of Understanding

The following is the text of Memorandum of understanding signed by the Foreign Secretaries of India and Pakistan in Lahore on February 21 on the occasion of Indian Prime Minister Atal Behari Vajpayee's visit to Pakistan, adds the daily.

Text: The Foreign Secretaries of Indian and Pakistan:

Reaffirming the continued commitment of their respective governments to the principles and purposes of the UN Charter;

Reiterating the determination of both countries to implement the Simla Agreement in letter and spirit;

Guided by the agreement between their Prime Ministers of September 23, 1998 that an environment of peace and security is in the supreme national interest of both sides and that resolution of all outstanding issues, including Jammu and Kashmir, is essential for this purpose;

Pursuant to the directive given by their respective Prime Ministers in Lahore to adopt measures for promoting a stable environment of peace, and security between the two countries;

Have on this day, agreed to the following:

1. The two sides shall engage in bilateral consultation on security concepts, and nuclear doctrines, with a view to developing measures for confidence building in the nuclear and conventional fields, aimed at avoidance of conflict.

2. The two sides undertake to provide each other with advance notification in respect of ballistic missile flight tests, and shall conclude a bilateral agreement in this regard.

3. The two sides are fully committed to undertaking national measures to reducing the risks of accidental or unauthorised use of nuclear weapons under their respective control. The two sides further undertake to notify each other immediately in the event of notify each other immediately in the event of any accidental, unauthorised or unexplained incident that could create the risk of a fallout with adverse consequences for both sides, or an outbreak of a nuclear war between the two countries as well as to adopt measures aimed at diminishing the possibility of such actions, or such incidents being misinterpreted by the other. The two sides shall identify/establish the appropriate communication mechanism for this purpose.

4. The two sides shall continue to abide by their respective unilateral moratorium on conducting further nuclear test explosions unless either side, in exercise of its national sovereignty, decides that extraordinary events have jeopardised is supreme interests.

5. The two sides shall conclude an agreement on prevention of incidents at sea to ensure safely of navigation by naval vessels, and aircraft belonging to the two sides.

6. The two sides shall periodically review the implementation of existing confidence-building measures (CBMs) and where necessary, set up appropriate consultative mechanisms to monitor and ensure effective implementation of these CBMS.

7. The two sides shall undertake a review of the existing communication links (e.g. between the respective Directors - General, Military Operations) with a view to upgrading and improving these links, and to provide for failsafe and secure communications.

8. The two sides shall engage in bilateral consultations on security, disarmament and non-proliferation issues within the context of negotiations on these issues in multilateral fora.

Where required the technical details of the above measures will be worked out by experts of the two sides in meetings to be held on mutually agreed dates, before mid-1999, with a view to reaching bilateral agreements.

Appendix 14

First Meeting of Citizens' Commission for South Asia, December 1-3, 2000

We, as citizens of South Asia, are convinced that our destinies are intertwined by our shared history and common interest in the welfare of our people. The Citizens' Commission of South Asia stresses the major role and responsibility of civil society in creating a favourable opinion for promotion of regional cooperation and commits itself to acting as an advocacy group for promoting the welfare of the people of the region.

Our main objective are to:

* Increase public awareness about the importance of South Asian cooperation and the need to intensify cooperation in the next decade and beyond;

* harness the resources of civil society and expand its role in promoting cooperation in South Asia;

* facilitate the task of the opinion, policy and decision makers on South Asian issues: and

* carry out an objective evaluation of progress of regional cooperation.

We urge the governments, opinion makers and the civil society of the SAARC member countries to reaffirm their political will to work collectively for peace, progress and prosperity with a view to improving the quality of life of one-fifth of humankind who inhabit South Asia.

The commission shares the widespread concern over SAARC's slow progress since its inception. SAARC has not had a summit level meeting since the Tenth Colombo Summit of July 1998.

SAARC's inability to meet regularly at a time when challenges posed by globalisation and a rapidly evolving global economic and

---

[*Source* : Circulated by CASAC]

political architecture have created a situation in which the region has been unable to evolve a cogent and a cohesive response at the regional level to these new challenges. Thereby, South Asia has been unable to fully take advantage of the challenges and opportunities offered by the process of globalization. The Commission stresses the need to reconvene the Summit and other meetings and for creating a conducive atmosphere for this purpose. The Commission is of the view that the schedule of the SAARC Summit and other meetings as envisaged in the Charter should be maintained.

The Commission notes with regret that while the rest of the world is moving rapidly in the direction of peace, stability and development, South Asia continues to remain mired in conflict and pervasive poverty. The Commission shares the confidence that it is possible to build a South Asia that is prosperous and secure. For this to happen, significant changes in current approaches and perspectives are necessary. SAARC offers a ray of hope to the impoverished people of South Asia. The choice for South Asia today is simple: it can either pursue a path of purposeful cooperation or sink deeper into hopelessness. The Commission expresses great anguish over the continuing political tensions in the region, which have hampered purposeful and cohesive cooperative efforts. The introduction of nuclear weapons in the region, which has given rise to varying concerns, has further reinforced the urgency of initiating measures and processes for building durable peace in the region. The Commission if of the view that impediments to purposeful and constructive regional cooperation should be removed through appropriate confidence building measures, dialogue and peaceful means.

Although SAARC has largely remained a inter-governmental process, it has received strong support from civil society. The Commission feels that SAARC needs a peoples' focus and to broad base its activities by involving all segments of our societies. The impact of SAARC programmes should first and foremost be felt at the level of common people of South Asia.

The Commission covered a wide range of issues confronting the region. While it feels that all round efforts are needed to make a dent on poverty, environmental degradation, social and other pressing problems through value added regional programmes, it recommends the following areas of activities for immediate action for governments and civil society:

1. The Commission shares the vision that South Asia in the near future would become an integrated community for purposes of trade, investments and movement of goods, services and labour. To this end, the Commission stresses the need to finalize and operationalize SAFTA Treaty by the agree deadline of December 2001. It also emphasizes that meanwhile bilateral or sub-regional arrangements for freeing trade should be pursued in a manner that they serve as building blocks for liberalizing trade in the while region, taking into account the special needs of the least developed countries (like the India-Sri Lanka Bilateral Free Trade Agreement).

2. One of the most significant challenges, particularly for the developing countries, arises out the multi-dimensional process of globalisation and its many complexities. The Commission recognizes that while globalisation offers unprecedented opportunities, the countries of South Asia will have to be watchful of the many imbalances and inequities. Both governments and civil society have a responsibility in working together to enhance efficiency and competitiveness in our economies to cope with the challenges posed by globalisation and to obtain maximum advantages from this process. The Commission feels that it would be most useful for SAARC member countries to share experience and information and evolve common positions, where possible, on issues in a globalised economic order or a newly emerging economic architecture.

3. The Commission feels that the information technology revolution offers an excellent opportunity to South Asia to leapfrog into the knowledge era. It recognizes that human resource and skills is South Asia's greatest asset, which should be purposefully utilized to create capacity in this area with a view to solving the problems affecting the common people. Other areas in which South Asian countries may have competitive advantage also likewise need to be identified.

4. South Asia has had an uneven experience with democracy and governance. The Commission feels that a lot of the region's problems could best be addressed through a responsive and democratic polity and by pursuing the best practices of governance in all areas, including accountable administration, inclusive development, human rights, empowerment and meeting the minimum basic needs of the people of South Asia. It believes that the people themselves must shape and mould their destinies, largely

through their own initiatives, encouraged and supported by the state. The Commission considers corruption prevailing in our societies to be scourge and an impediment to good governance.

5. The Commission believes that governments can and should act as facilitators in promoting measures based on voluntary and civil society initiative for improving the conditions of the people, particularly in the rural areas. It notes the great success of the Grameen Bank and other movements in Bangladesh and South Asia and feels that these experiences could be usefully replicated. There are other similar initiatives, particularly aided by the information revolution, which need to be encouraged by the governments. The Commission urges that the ongoing work on the SAARC Social Charter should be expedited.

6. The Commission feels that in many instances, the people of the region, as elsewhere, are ahead of their governments and that there is need for reconceptualising the functions and roles of governments. In this context, the role and responsibility of civil society also needs to be reexamined and reassessed. The Commission believes that the people themselves must shape and mould their destinies largely through their own initiatives, aided and supported by the State.

The Commission expresses its deep disappointment that progress in eradicating mass poverty, illiteracy and deprivation has fallen far too short to meet the aspirations, resource endowment and the objectives of SAARC. It, therefore, urges both the governments and civil society to greatly intensify efforts at improving the condition of the poor people, particularly in the rural areas. In this context, the solemn commitments made by successive SAARC Summits need to be implemented fully and expeditiously.

The Commission sees its roles as a continuing one in the foreseeable future. It proposes to meet at regular intervals to deliberate on important issues facing our region and create an environment in which the South Asian region could move forward with hope and confidence. Its processes would be open, visible and participatory. The Commission would aim at receiving the broadest range of views and advise on key issues. Until its next meeting in 2001, the Commission assigns studies on the following important subjects by reputed scholars and regional think tanks to enable it to consider the relevant issues in depth:

offered by information technology revolution and preparing South Asia for the knowledge era;

* Impediments to successful regional cooperation

* Democracy and good governance including effective measures to tackle poverty;

* Potential of biotechnology;

* Regional cooperation in energy.

Sd/-
I.K. Gujral
Chairperson

Bangalesh
Kamal Hossain
Farooq Sobhan
Rehman Sobhan
Muhammad Yunus

Pakistan
Asma Jehangir
SartaJ Aziz
Talat Masood

Bhutan
Dawa Tsering
Dago Tshering

India
Manmohan Singh
Muchkund Dubey
Kant K. Bhargava
A.N. Ram

Sri Lanka
Lal Jayawardena
Manel Abeysekera
Saman Kalegama

Maldives
Ibrahim H. Zaki

Nepal
Sher Bahadur Deuba
Devendra Raj Panday
Y.K. Silwal
Sridhar Khatri
Niaz A. Naik

The other members of the Commission who were unable to attend the meeting are:

Amartya Sen (he has sent a message to the Commission)
Abdul Sattar Moosa Didi
Radhika Coomaraswamy

BIBLIOGRAPHY

Government Documents

Government of India, Ministry of External Affairs.

——, *Annual Reports*, (1980-2000).

——, *Foreign Affairs Record*, (January 1979 - November 1999).

Government of India, Ministry of Information and Broadcasting, Publication Division—

Final Communique at the Asian-African Conference, Bandung, Jawa, 1955, (New Delhi, 1955).

Indira Gandhi's Selected Speeches - Years of Challenge, Vol. I, January, 1966-August, 1969, (New Delhi, 1973).

Indira Gandhi's Selected Speeches - Years of Endeavours, August, 1969-1972, Vol. II, (New Delhi, 1975).

——, 1972-1977, Vol. III, (New Delhi, 1978).

——, 1980-1981, Vol. IV, (New Delhi, 1982).

Indira Gandhi's Selected Speeches and Writings, (1982-1984), Vol. V, (New Delhi, 1985).

Jawaharlal Nehru Speeches, Vol. I (1946-1949), Vol. II (1949-1953), Vol. III (1953-1957), Vol. IV (1957-1963), Vol. V (1963-1964).

Panchsheel: Its Meaning and History, (New Delhi - 1958).

P.V. Narasimha Rao Selected Speeches, Vol. I (June 1991-June 1992), Vol. II (July 1992-June 1993), Vol. III (July 1993-July 1994), Vol. IV (July, 1994-June, 1995).

Rajiv Gandhi Selected Speeches and Writings, Vol. I (October 1984 - December 1985), Vol. II (1986), Vol. III (1987), Vol. IV (1988), Vol. V. (1989).

Selected Speeches of Morarji Desai, (1977-79).

Tashkent Declaration, (New Delhi, 1967).

Other Documents

Appadorai, A., (ed.), *Select Documents on India's Foreign Policy and Relations*, 1946-72, Vol. 1, (New Delhi, Oxford University Press, 1982).

——, (ed.), *Select Documents on India's Foreign Policy and Relations*, 1946-72, Vol. 2, (New Delhi, Oxford Univ. Press, 1985).

Asian Relations Conference: Proceedings and Documentation of the First Asian Relations Conference, (New Delhi, Asian Relations Organization, 1948).

Bright, J.S. (ed.), *Before and After Independence: Speeches of Jawaharlal Nehru*, 1922-1950 (New Delhi, The Indian Printing Works, 1950).

Background of India's Foreign Policy, (Resolutions of the Indian National Congress), N.V. Rajkumar, (ed.), (AICC, New Delhi, 1952).

Foreign Policy of India: Text of Documents, 1947-59, (New Delhi, Lok Sabha Secretariat, 1959).

India 1947-50: Selected Documents on Asian Affairs, Vol. II: *External Affairs*, S.L. Poplai (ed.), (New Delhi, Oxford University Press, 1959).

Indian National Congress: Resolutions on Foreign Policy, 1947-59, N.V. Rajkumar (ed.), (New Delhi, AICC, undated).

Indian National Congress: The Glorious Tradition, Texts of Resolutions passed by the INC, the AICC and CWC, (III Vols.), A.M. Zaidi (ed.), (New Delhi, Indian Institute of Applied Political Research, 1987).

The Encyclopaedia of Indian National Congress (Vol. VII to XIII), A.M. Zaidi and S.G. Zaidi (ed.), (New Delhi, Indian Institute of Applied Political Research,1981).

Reports of the South Asian Association for Regional Cooperation (SAARC)

SAARC Committee of the Whole, *Report*, 31 August - 2 September 1981, Colombo.

——, *Report*, 10-13 January, 1983, Colombo.

SAARC Council of Ministers *Report of the First Session*, 12-13 August, 1986, Dhaka.

——, *Report of the Second Session*, 14-15 November, 1986, Bangalore.

——, *Report of the Third Session*, 18-19 June, 1987, New Delhi.

——, *Report of the Fourth Session*, 31 October, 1987, Kathmandu.

——, *Report of the Fifth Session*, 11-12 August, 1988, Kathmandu.

——, *Report of the Sixth Session*, 27 December, 1988, Islamabad.

——, *Report of the Seventh Session*, 8 November, 1989, Islamabad.

SAARC Standing Committee, *Report of the First Session*, 27-29 February, 1984, New Delhi.

——, *Report of the Second Session*, 7-8 July, 1984, Male.

——, *Report of the Third Session*, 5-7 February,1985, Male.

——, *Report of the Fourth Session*, 10-11 May,1985, Thimpu.

——, *Report of the Fifth Session*, 4 December,1985, Dhaka.

——, *Report of the Sixth Session*, 11 August, 1986, Dhaka.

——, *Report of the Seventh Session*, 13 November,1986, Bangalore.

——, *Report of the Eighth Session*, 16-17 June, 1987, New Delhi.

——, *Report of the Ninth Session*, 29-30 October,1987, Kathmandu.

——, *Report of the Tenth Session*, 9-10 August,1988, Kathmandu.

——, *Report of the Eleventh Session*, 26-27 December, 1989, Islamabad.

SAARC Technical Committee on Agriculture, *Report of the Fourth Meeting*, 27-29 May, 1986, Thimpu.

——, *Report of the Sixth Meeting*, 5-7 October, 1987, New Delhi.

SAARC Technical Committee of Education, *Report of the First Meeting*, 6-8 August, 1989, Dhaka.

SAARC Technical Committee on Meteorology, *Report of the Third Meeting*, 19-20 November, 1985,Male.

——, *Report of the Fourth Meeting*, 4-6 October, 1986, Male.

——, *Report of the Sixth Meeting*, 10-11 September, 1987, Kathmandu.

SAARC Technical Committee on Postal Services, *Report of the Fifth Meeting*, 10-12 March 1987.

SAARC Technical Committee on Rural Development, *Report of the First Meeting*, 16-17 January, 1984, Colombo.

——, *Report of the Second Meeting*, 25-26 January, 1985, Colombo.

——, *Report of the Third Meeting*, 15-16 October, 1985, Dhaka.

——, *Report of the Fourth Meeting*, 18-19 October, 1986, Dhaka.

——, *Report of the Fifth Meeting*, 20-21 May, 1987, Dhaka.

——, *Report of the Sixth Meeting*, 18-19 September, 1987, Thimpu.

SAARC Technical Committee on Science and Technology, *Report of the First Meeting*, 16-19 June, 1982, Islamabad.

——, *Report of the Fourth Meeting*, 8-10 October, 1986, Colombo.

——, *Report of the Fifth Meeting*, 14-15 October, 1987, Dhaka.

SAARC Technical Committee on Sports-Arts-Culture, *Report of the Fourth Meeting*, 30 September- 1 October, 1986, Male.

SAARC Technical Committee on Sports-Arts-Culture, *Report of the Seventh Meeting*, 28-29 October, 1988, Katmandu.

SAARC Technical Committee on Transport, *Report of the Eighth Meeting*, 31 October-2 November, 1989, Islamabad.

SAARC Technical Committee on Women-in-Development, *Report of the First Meeting*, 21-23 October, 1986, New Delhi.

——, *Report of the Fourth Meeting*, 13-14 October, 1988, New Delhi.

The SAARC Record - Retrospect and Prospect *Report of the Secretary General on Activities of the Association and Secretariat*, November, 1990, Kathmandu.

Publications from SAARC Secretariat, Kathmandu

Agreement on Establishing SAARC Food Security Reserve, 1987.

Agreement on SAARC Preferential Trading Arrangement (SAPTA), 1993.

Charter of the South Asian Association for Regional Cooperation (SAARC), 1985.

From SARC to SAARC: Milestones in the Evolution of Regional Cooperation in South Asia (1980-1988) Volume I.

From SARC to SAARC: Milestones in the Evolution of Regional Cooperation in South Asia (1983-1989) Volume II.

Agreement between His Majesty's Government of Nepal and the Secretary of the South Asian Association for Regional Cooperation, 1986.

Regional Study on the Causes and Consequences of Natural Disasters and Protection and Preservation of the Environment, 1991.

Report of the Independent South Asian Commission on Poverty Alleviation.

SAARC Documents: *Milestones in the Evolution of Regional Cooperation in South Asia, Volume IV, (November 1991 - April 1993).*

SAARC Documents: *Milestones in the Evolution of Regional Cooperation in South Asia, Volume V, (November 1993 - May 1995).*

SAARC Regional Convention on Suppression of Terrorism, 1987.

SAARC Study on Trade, Manufactures and Services, 1991.

SAARC Summit (1), *Dhaka Declaration and Joint Press Release, 1985.*

SAARC Summit (2), *Bangalore Declaration and Joint Press Release, 1986.*

SAARC Summit (3), *Kathmandu Declaration and Joint Press Release, 1987.*

SAARC Summit (4), *Islamabad Declaration and Joint Press Release, 1988.*

SAARC Summit (5), *Male Declaration and Joint Press Release, 1989.*

SAARC Summit (6), *Colombo Declaration and Joint Press Release, 1991.*

SAARC Summit (7), *Dhaka Declaration, 1993.*

SAARC Summit (8), *Delhi Declaration, 1995.*

SAARC Summit (9), *Male Declaration, 1997.*

SAARC Summit (10), *Colombo Declaration, 1998.*

SAARC Summits (1985—1988), 1988.

SAARC Women in Development (1986—1990), 1990.

SAARC Youth Resolution.

SAARC At a Glance.

SAARC Perspective.

SAARC News Letter.

SAARC Vision Beyond the Year 2000 - *Report of the SAARC Group of Eminent Persons.*

Spectrum, (Nos. 1-4).

Miscellaneous Reports

Human Development in South Asia, (1997, 1998 and 1999), Human Development Centre, (Islamabad, Oxford University Press).

Human Development Report, 1999, United Nations Development Programme, UNDP, (New York, Oxford University Press, 1999).

Asian Development Outlook, (Hong Kong, Asia Development Bank, 1999).

SAARC Survey of Development and Cooperation, 1998-99, (New Delhi, Research and Information System for the Non Aligned and Other Developing Countries [RIS], 1999).

List of Newspapers

The Asian Age (New Delhi).

The Bangladesh Observer (Dhaka).

The Daily News (Colombo).

The Deccan Herald (Bangalore).

The Economic Times (New Delhi).

The Financial Express (Bombay).

The Financial Times (London).

The Frontier Post (Peshawar).

The Hindu (New Delhi).

The Hindustan Times (New Delhi).

The Indian Express (New Delhi).

The Island (Colombo).

The Kathmandu Post (Kathmandu).

The News (Islamabad).

The Pakistan Times (Islamabad).

The Pioneer (New Delhi).

The Rising Nepal (Kathmandu).

The Statesman (New Delhi).

The Telegraph (Calcutta).

The Times of India (New Delhi).

The Tribune (Chandigarh).

Books and Articles

Agwani, M.S. et al. (eds.), *South Asia: Stability and Regional Cooperation*, (Chandigarh, Centre for Research in Rural and Industrial Development, 1983).

Ahmed, Emajuddin, *SARC: Seeds of Harmony,* (Dhaka, University Press, 1985).

Appadorai, A., and M.S. Rajan, *India's Foreign Policy and Relations*, (New Delhi, South Asia Publication, 1988).

Appadorai, A., *Contemporary India: Essays in Domestic and Foreign Policy*, (New Delhi, South Asia Publication., 1988).

Asthana, Vandana, *India's Foreign Policy and Subcontinental Policies*, (New Delhi, Kanishka Publishers, 1999).

Ayoob, Mohammed (ed.), *Conflict and Intervention in Third World,* (New Delhi, Vikas Publishing House Pvt. Ltd., 1980).

——, *India, Pakistan and Bangladesh: Search for a New Relationship*, (New Delhi, ICWA, 1975).

Babu, Ramesh (ed.), *Globalization and the South Asian State*, (New Delhi, South Asia Publishers, 1998).

Bajpai, U.S. (ed.), *India and Its Neighbourhood*, (New Delhi, Lancers Pub., 1970).

Bandhopadhyaya J., *The Making of India's Foreign Policy*, (Bombay, Allied Publisher, 1970).

Banerjee, Dipankar (ed.), *Comprehensive and Cooperative Security in South Asia*, (New Delhi, Institute of Peace and Conflict Studies, 1998).

Bhambri, C.P., *Foreign Policy of India*, (New Delhi, Sterling, 1987).

Bhargava, G.S., *Their Finest Hour - Saga of India's December Victory*, (New Delhi, Vikas, 1972).

Bhargava, K.K. and Hussain Ross Masood, *SAARC and European Union*, (New Delhi, FES, 1994).

Bhargava, K.K. et al (eds.), *South Asia: Towards Dynamism and Co-operation*, (New Delhi, ICRIER, 1994).

——, *Shaping South Asia's Future : Role of Regional Cooperation*, (New Delhi, Madhyam Books, 1999).

Bhutto, Benazir, Pakistan: *The Gathering Storm,* (New Delhi, Vikas Publishing House, 1983).

Bidwai, Praful and Vanaik, *Achin, South Asia on a Short Fuse*, (New Delhi, Oxford University Press, 1999).

Bindra, S.S. *Determinants of Pakistan's Foreign Policy*, (New Delhi, Deep and Deep Publications, 1988).

——, *India and her Neighbours*, (New Delhi, Deep and Deep Publications, 1984).

Bose, Sugata, *South Asia and World Capitalism*, (Delhi, Oxford University Press, 1991).

Bradnock, R.W., *India's Foreign Policy since 1971*, (London, Royal Institute of International Affairs, 1990).

Brecher, Michel, *India's Foreign Policy : An Interpretation*, (New York : Institute of Pacific Relations, 1957).

——, *Nehru: A Political Biography*, (London, Oxford University Press, 1959).

——,*The New States of Asia*, (London, Oxford University Press, 1963).

——, *Succession in India: A Study in Decision Making*, (London, Oxford University Press, 1966).

——, *India and the World Politics: Krishna Menon's World View*, (London, Oxford University Press, 1968).

Chomsky, Noam, *Profit Over People*, (New Delhi, Madhyam Books, 1999).

Das, Debendra K. (ed.), *SAARC, Regional Cooperation and Development: Perspectives, Problems, Policies,* (New Delhi, Deep and Deep Publications, 1992).

Dharmadasani, M.D. (ed.). *South Asian Regional Cooperation,* (Varanasi, Shalimar Publishing House, 1985).

Dixit, J.N., Across Borders: *Fifty Years of India's Foreign Policy,* (New Delhi, Picus Books, 1998).

——, Liberation and Beyond : *Indo-Bangladesh Relations,* (New Delhi, Konark Publishers, 1999).

——, *Anatomy of Flawed Inheritance: Indo-Pak Relations,* 1970-94, (New Delhi, Konark, 1995).

——, *Assignment Colombo*, (New Delhi, Konark 1998).

Dubey, Muchkund and Jetly Nancy (ed.), *South Asia and its Eastern Neighbours*, (New Delhi, F.E.S, 1999).

Dubey, Muchkund, et. al. (eds.), *South Asian Growth Quadrangle : Framework for Multifaceted Cooperation*, (Delhi, Macmillan, 1999).

Dutt, V.P., *India's Foreign Policy*, (New Delhi, Vikas, 1987).

——, *India's Foreign Policy in a Changing World,* (New Delhi, Vikas Publishing House, 1999).

Gangal, S.C., *Indian Foreign Policy: A Documentary Study of India's Foreign Policy since the Installation of the Janta Government on 24 March, 1977,* (New Delhi, Young Asia, 1980).

Ghosh, Partha S., *Cooperation and Conflict in South Asia*, (New Delhi, Manohar, 1988).

Ghoshal, Baladas, *Diplomacy and Domestic Politics in South Asia,* (New Delhi, Konark Publishers, 1996).

Gonsalves, Eric and Jetley, Nancy, *The Dynamics of South Asia: Regional Cooperation and SAARC,* (New Delhi, Sage Publication, 1999).

Gunewardena, Victor (ed), *Regional Co-operation and Integration: Perspectives from Europe and South Asia,* (Colombo, Sri Lanka Foundation Institute, 1998).

Gunetillaka, Godfrey, *Cooperation Among Small Nations in the Context of the Changing Asian Political Economy*, (Colombo, 1979).

Gupta, Karunkaran, *India in World Politics, A Period of Transition*, 1956-1960, (Calcutta, Scientific Book Agency, 1969).

Gupta, S.B. et. al. (ed.), *South Asia as a Dynamic Partner,* (New Delhi, Macmillan, 1994).

Gupta, Sisir, *India and Regional Integration in Asia*, (Bombay, Asia Publishing House, 1964).

——, *India and International System* (New Delhi: Vikas, 1980).

Hussain, Ross Masood, *"SAARC : Evolution and Prospects : A View from Pakistan",* (Islamabad, FES, 1991).

Iftekharuzzaman and Abdul Hafizo (eds.), *South Asian Regional Cooperation*, (Dhaka, Oxford University Press, 1955).

Jain, S.B., *India's Foreign Policy and Non-Alignment*, (New Delhi, Anamika Publishers, 2000).

Jalal, Ayesha, *Democracy and Authorianism in South Asia*, (New Delhi, Cambridge University Press, 1995).

Jansen, G.H., *Afro Asia and Non Alignment* (London, Faber and Faber, 1966).

Jetley, Nancy (ed.), *India's Foreign Policy: Challenges and Prospects,* (New Delhi, Vikas Publishing House, 1999).

Karunakaran, K.P., *India in World Affairs, 1947-50,* (Delhi, Oxford University Press, 1952).

——, *India in World Affairs, 1950-53,* (Delhi, Oxford University Press, 1954).

Kaul, T.N., *Ambassadors Need Not Lie;* (New Delhi, Lancers International, 1989).

Kumar, Satish (ed.), *Year Book on India's Foreign Policy 1985-86*, (New Delhi, Sage, 1988).

Kundra, J.C., *India's Foreign Policy (1947-54)-A Study of Relations with the Western Block*, (Groningn, Wolters, J.B., 1955).

Lama, M.P., *Energy Co-operation in South Asia: Issues, Challenges and Potential*, (New Delhi, South South Solidarity, 1999).

Levi, Werner, *Free India in Asia,* (Minneapolis: University of Minneapolis Press, 1952).

——, *The Challenge of World Politics in South and South-East Asia,* (New Jersey, Prentice Hall, 1968).

Limaye, Madhu, *Problems of India's Foreign Policy*, (New Delhi, Atma Ram & Sons, 1984).

Longer, V., *The Defence and Foreign Policies of India*, (New Delhi, Sterling, 1988).

Mansingh, Lalit et al (eds.), *Indian Foreign Policy: Agenda for the 21st Century,* II Vols., (New Delhi, Konark Publisher, 1998).

Mansingh, Surjit, *India's Search for Power* (New Delhi, Sage, 1984).

Mattoo Amitabh (ed.), *India's Nuclear Deterrent Pokharan II and Beyond,* (New Delhi, Har-Anand Publications Pvt. Ltd., 1999).

Mehrotra, L.L., et al (eds.), *SAARC 2000 and Beyond*, (New Delhi, Omega Publishers, 1995).

Mishra, K.P. (ed.), *Janata's Foreign Policy,* (New Delhi, Vikas, 1979).

—— (ed.), *Foreign Policy of India : A Book of Readings*, (New Delhi, Thompson Press, 1977).

Mishra, Pramod K., *South Asia in International Politics,* (UDH Publishers, Delhi, 1984).

——, *India, Pakistan, Nepal and Bangladesh*, (Delhi, Sundeep Prakashan, 1979).

——, *Dhaka Summit and SAARC: A Broad Overview*, (Calcutta, Netaji Institute for Asian Studies, 1986).

Muni, S.D., *Post-Cold War Regionalism in Asia: With Special Reference to the SAARC Sub-Region,* (Tokyo, Institute of Developing Economics, 1996).

——, *India and Nepal: A Changing Relationship*, (New Delhi, Konark, 1992).

——, *Pangs of Proximity: India and Sri Lanka Ethnic Crisis*, (New Delhi, Sage, 1993).

Muni, S.D., and Muni, Anuradha, *Regional Cooperation in South-Asia*, (New Delhi, National Publishing House, 1984).

Murthy, B.S.N., *Nehru's Foreign Policy*, (New Delhi, The Beacon Information and Publications, 1954).

Murthy, Sachidanand, *India's Foreign Policy*, (Calcutta, Scientific Book Agency, 1964).

Nanda, B.R. (ed.), *India's Foreign Policy : The Nehru Era* (New Delhi, Vikas, 1976).

Naqash A. Nasir, *SAARC : Challenges and Opportunities*, (New Delhi, Ashish Publishing House, 1994).

Narain, Virendra and Upreti, B.C. (eds.), *SAARC: A Study of Perceptions and Policies*, (New Delhi, South Asian Publishers Pvt. Ltd., 1991).

Nehru, Jawaharlal, *An Autobiography*, (London, Bodley Head, 1943).

——, *Discovery of India*, (Calcutta, Signet Press, 1946).

——, *Glimpses of World History*, (London, Drummond, 1939).

Nasenko, Yuri - *Jawaharlal and India's Foreign Policy*, (New Delhi, Sterling, 1977).

Noorani, A.G., *Aspects of India's Foreign Policy,* (Bombay, Allied Publication 1970).

Pai, Pananadikar, V.A. (ed.), *Problems of Governance in South Asia,* (New Delhi, Konark Publishers, 2000).

Pai, Pananadikar, V.A. and Chadha, Navnita,(eds.), *Perspectives on South Asia*, (New Delhi, Konark Publishers, 2000)

Panchmukhi, V.R. and other (eds.), *Economic Cooperation in the SAARC Region: Potential, Constraint and Policies,* (New Delhi, Interest Publications, 1990).

Panda, K.K. and Mishra, P.K., *New Perspectives and India's Foreign Policy: Janata Phase*, (Delhi, Sandeep Prakashan, 1980).

Panikkar, K.M., *The Strategic Problems of the Indian Ocean,* (Allahabad, Kitabistan, 1944).

Panikkar, K.M., *India and the Indian Ocean*, (George Allen & Unwin, London, 1951).

Parmanand, *Political Development in South Asia,* (New Delhi, Sterling Publishers Private Ltd., 1988).

Paulose, Thomas and Kaur, Gurmeet, *India and World Affairs*, (New Delhi, Anmol Publications, 1996).

Poplai, S.L., (ed.), *Asia and Africa in the Modern World*, (Bombay, Allied Publication, 1955).

——, (ed.), *Select Documents on Asian Affairs India 1947-1950, (Bombay*, Oxford University Press, 1959).

Prajapati, Vishnu (ed), *South Asia Power Politics: Studies in Political Identity and Regional Resurgence,* (New Delhi, Commonwealth Publishers, 1998).

Prasad , Bimal, *India's Foreign Policy: Studies in Continuity and Change,* (New Delhi, Vikas, 1979).

——, *The Origin of Indian Foreign Policy*, (Calcutta, Bookland 1960).

——,(ed.), *Regional Cooperation in South Asia: Problems and Prospects*, New Delhi, (Vikas Publishing House, 1989).

Rahman, Attiur, *Political Economy of SAARC*, (Dhaka, University Press Ltd., 1985).

Rajan, M.S. and Ganguly, Shivaji, (eds.), *Great Power Relations: World Order and the Third World,* (New Delhi, Vikas Publishing House, 1981).

Rajan, M.S., *Recent Essays on India's Foreign Policy*, (Delhi, Kalinga Publications, 1997).

Ramakant and Bhola P.L., (eds), *Post-Cold War Developments in South Asia,* (Jaipur, R.B.S.A. Publishers, 1995).

Rizvi, Gowher, *South Asia in a Changing International Environment*, (New Delhi, Sage Publication, 1993).

Sach, Jeffry D. et. al. *India in the Era of Economic Reforms* (Harvard University; Havard Institute for International Development, 2000).

Sankar Ghosh and Somen Mukerjee, *Emerging South Asian Order*, (Calcutta, Media South Asia, 1995).

Satyamurti, K. (ed.), *South Asian Regional Cooperation*, (Hyderabad, Institute of Asian Studies, 1982).

Sen Gupta, Bhabani, *Regional Cooperation and Development in South Asia*, (2 Vols.), (New Delhi, South Asian Publishers, 1986).

——, *SAARC-ASEAN: Prospects and Problems and Inter Regional Cooperation,* (New Delhi, South Asian Publishers, 1988).

Sen Gupta, Bhabani, *South Asian Perspectives: Seven Nations in Conflict and Cooperation*, (New Delhi, South Asian Publishers 1988).

Singh, Jasjit, (ed.), *Nuclear India*, (New Delhi, Institute for Defence Studies and Analyses, 1998).

Singh, Patwant, *India and the Future of Asia,* (London, Faber and Faber, 1966).

Srinivasan, T.N., *Eight Lectures on India's Economic Reforms*, (New Delhi, Oxford University Press, 2000).

——, *The Persian Gulf and South Asia: Prospects and Problems of Inter Regional Cooperation,* (New Delhi, South Asian Publishers, 1987).

Tinker, Hugh, *South Asia: A Short History,* (London, Pall Mall Press 1966).

Umar, Ghulam, *SAARC: Analytical Survey*, Karanchi, (Pakistan Institute of International Affairs, 1988).

Upadhyay, Shashi, *Pakistan and SAARC*, (Delhi, Kalinga Publications, 2000).

Upreti, B.C. (ed.), *SAARC: Dynamics of Regional Cooperation in South Asia*, 2 Vols., (New Delhi, Kalinga Publication, 2000).

Vanaik, Achin, *India in a Changing World*, (New Delhi, Orient Longman, 1995).

Varma, S.P. and Mishra K.P. (eds.). *Foreign Policies in South Asia*, (New Delhi, Orient Longman, 1969).

Wadhva, Charan D. and others (eds.), *Regional Economic Cooperation in Asia: Bangladesh, India, Pakistan and Sri Lanka,* (New Delhi, Allied Publishers Private Ltd., 1987).

Waqif. A. (ed.), *South Asian Cooperation in Industry, Energy and Technology,* (New Delhi, Sage Publication, 1987).

Wingnaraja, Ponna and Hussain Akmal (eds)., *The Challenge in South Asia: Development, Democracy and Regional Cooperation,* (New Delhi, Sage Publication, 1989).

Wolpert, Stanely, *Roots of Confrontations in South Asia: Afghanistan, Pakistan, India and the Super Powers,* (New York, Oxford University Press, 1982).

Articles

Acharya, G.N., "India's Role in South-East Asia : A Review of India's Foreign Policy 1948-61", *Far Eastern Economic Review*, 21 September, 1961, p.p. 555-583.

Adiseshiah, Malcom S., "The Economic Rationale of SAARC", *South Asia Journal*, 1987, p.p. 29-42.

Agarwal, Govind Ram, " Some Avenues for South Asian Economic Cooperation", *South Asia Journal No. 1*, 1987, pp. 43-45.

Ahmad, Aziz, " The Counterpoint of Pakistan", *Mainstream*, Vol. 26, No. 18, 1988, pp. 11-75.

Ahmad, Bashir, "SAARC: Some Reflections", *Regional Studies*, Vol. 5, No.4, 1987, pp. 3-6.

Ahmar, Moonis, "Security Perceptions in the Indo - Pakistan Relationships", *Pakistan Horizon*, Vol. 37, No.1, 1984, pp. 100-99.

——, "The Politics of Conflict and Cooperation in South Asia", *Pakistan Horizon,* Vol. 35, No. 3, Third Quarter, 1982, pp. 44-59.

Ahmed, Emajuddin, "Regional Co-operation in South Asia and India's Role". *IDSA Journal*, 15(3), Jan.- Mar. '83, pp. 405-22.

——, "Regional Understanding through Economic and Socio-Cultural Interaction: *The Case of SAARC", South Asia Journal* Vol. 2, No. 3 January-March, 1989, pp. 233-50.

——, "South Asian Association for Regional Cooperation; A Comparative Perspective", *SAARC Perspective*, Vol. 2, No. 4, December, 1988, pp. 31-35.

Ahsan, Abdul, "South Asian Association for Regional Cooperation in Historical Perspective", *SAARC Perspective*, Vol. 2, No. 4, December 1988, pp. 27-30.

——, "Economic Perspectives of SAARC", *SAARC Perspectives* Vol. 3, No. 5, June 1989, pp. 9-12.

Ahuja, Kanta, "Trends in Regional Economic Cooperation in South and South East Asia", *South Asian Studies*, Vol.12, No. 122, January-June 1977, pp. 145-54.

Anderson, W.K., "India in Asia: Walking on a Tightrope", *Asian Survey*, Vol. 19, No. 12, December 1979, pp. 1241-53.

——, "Domestic Roots of Indian Foreign Policy", *Asian Affairs*, 10(3), 1983, pp. 45-33.

——, "India in 1982: Domestic Challenges and Foreign Success", *Asian Survey* 23(2), Feb. 1983, pp. 11-12.

Ayoob, Mohammad, "India in South Asia: The Quest for Regional Predominance", *World Policy Journal*, 1990, pp. 107-35.

——, "India Matters", *Washington Quarterly, Winter 2000*, pp. 27-39.

Bajpai, U.S., "The South Asian Situation", *World Focus*, Vol. 7, No. 11 & 12, November-December 1986, pp. 38-41.

Baral, Lok Raj, "SAARC, But No SHARK: South Asian Regional Cooperation in Perspective", *Pacific Affairs*, Vol. 58, No. 3, 1985, pp. 411-26.

——, "SAARC as a Dynamic Organisation", *SAARC Perspective*, Vol. 2 No. 4, December 1988, pp. 56-61.

——, "The Emerging Political Demography in South Asia and its Implication for SAARC", *Strategic Studies*, Vol. 1, No. 1, Autumn 1984, pp. 103-16.

Baru, Sanjaya, "The Economic Dimentions of India's Foreign Policy", *World Affairs*, Vol.2, No. 2, April-June, 1998, pp. 88-103.

——"India's Neighbourhood : Economic and Cultural not Physical", *The Times of India*, 2 February, 2000.

——, "Trade and Security : Multilateral and Regional Opportunities", *The Times of India*, 16 November, 1999.

Beg, Masoor Ahmad, "Intra-SAARC Trade: A Dwindling Feature", *India Quarterly*, Vol. XLVI, No.1, January-March, 1990, pp. 47-48.

Bhargava, K.K., "Political Will Key to SAARC's Success", *The Economic Times,* 30 April, 1995.

——, "Delhi SAARC Summit : Malaise and Progress", *Mainstream*, 24 June, 1995 pp. 5-7.

——, "India and SAARC", *World Focus*, Vol. 17, No. 7, July 1996, pp. 11-12.

——, "The Maturing of SAARC", *The Economic Times*, 17 May, 1997.

Bhatt, P. R., "Trade Flow in South Asia", *India Quarterly,* Vol. XL, Nos. 3&4, July-December, 1984, pp. 287-300.

Bhatty, Maqbool Ahmad, "The Future of SAARC", *Regional Studies* Vol.10, No.1, Winter 1991-92, pp. 91-115.

Bhuyan, A.R., "Intra-Regional Trade Expansion in South Asia: Trends, Obstacles and Prospects", *South Asia Journal,* Vol. 4, No.1, 1990, pp. 35-53.

Bokhari, Imtiaz H., "South Asian Regional Cooperation: Progress, Problems, Potential and Prospects", *Asian Survey*, Vol. 25, No.4, April 1985, pp. 371-90.

Brawn, Dieter, *"Conflicting and Converging Trends in Present Day South Asia", Pakistan Horizon,* Vol. 6, No. 4, Fourth Quarter 1983, pp. 11-18.

Chakravarty, Sumit, "SAARC Advances Along Chartered Course", *Indian and Foreign Review,* Vol. 24, No.21, August 1987, pp. 10-19.

——, "SAARC Survives Subversion", *Mainstream*, Vol. 25, No.41, June 1987, pp. 4-5 & 34.

Chari, P.R., "*C.B.M's:* Post-Cold War South Asia", *Regional Centre for Strategic Studies Newsletter*, July 1999, pp. 2-5.

Chopra, Pran, "SAARC-ASEAN: A Comparative Analysis of Aims Structures and Progress," *SAARC Perspective.* Vol. 1, No. 2, October 1987, pp. 12-16.

Corea, Gamani, "Regional Cooperation in South Asia: Perspective and Prospects", *South Asia Journal*, Vol.1, No.1, 1987, 1 & 6.

Damodaran, A.K., "Roots of Foreign Policy", *India International Centre Quarterly,* 14(3), Monsoon, 1987, pp. 53-65.

Danjal, Gursharan Singh, "SAARC on the Move", *Mainstream,* Vol. 30, No.12, January 1992, pp. 11-12.

Datta-Ray, Sunanda K., "New Faces at SAARC: But Old Attitudes Persist", *The Statesman*, 26 November, 1990.

Deshpande, Vinayak S. and Kasikar, Mohan S., "SAARC and Economic Cooperation", *SAARC Perspective*, Vol.4, No. 6, November, 1990, pp. 51-62.

Dhar M.K., "SAARC Summit: India Expects Positive Pak Attitude", *Hindustan Times*, 22 April, 1995.

Dixit J.N., "SAARC Countries and European Community: Towards Stronger Partnership in the 1990's", *South Asia Journal*, Vol. 5, No.1, July-September, 1991, pp. 17-44.

——, "Regional Cooperation in South Asia", *The Hindu*, 2 September, 1993.

——, "Regional Cooperation: Take the Initiative", *Indian Express*, 14 March, 1995

Dubey, Muchkund, "SAARC: The New Imperative", *Strategic Digest*, Vol. 21, No.7, July 1991, pp. 1206-09.

——, "India's Foreign Policy in the Evolving Global Order", *International Studies,* Vol. 30, No. 2, April - June 1993, pp. 117-130.

——, "Kargil Crisis: Limits of Diplomacy", *Mainstream,* 17 July 1997, pp. 7-9

——, "Resuming the Dialogue with Pakistan", *The Times of India*, 15 November, 1999.

Gonsalves, Eric, "An Agenda for the Next Decade", *South Asia Journal,* Vol.1, No.1, 1987, pp. 19-28.

Gujral, I.K., "Indian Foreign Policy: Dilemnas and Challenge", *Lectures delivered on August 18*, 1992 at Colombo, *Mainstream*, Vol. 30, No. 47, September 12, 1992, pp. 9-12.

——, "Foreign Policy Agenda", *World Focus,* Vol. 17, No. 10-12, October - December 1996, pp. 3-6.

——, "Post Cold War Era", *World Affairs,* Vol.1, No. 1, January - March 1997, pp. 44-45.

——, "Interview to Shubhrangshu Roy on SAARC", *The Economic Times*, 12 May, 1997.

——, "Vision of India in the New Millennium", *World Focus*, Vol. 19, No. 10-12, October - December, 1998, pp. 6-10.

——, "Interview to Venkitesh Ramakrishnan", *Frontline*, 14 April, 2000, pp. 21.

Harshe, Rajan, "South Asian Regional Cooperation: Problems and Prospects", *Economic and Political Weekly,* Vol. 34, No. 19, May 8, 1999, pp. 1100-1105.

Hasan, Muzaffar, "The SAARC Summit: An Appraisal Focus on Peripheral Issues", *Pakistan and Gulf-Economist*, Vol. 9, No. 48, December, 1990, pp. 6-9.

Huntington, Samuel O.,:"The Clash of Civilizations", *Foreign Affairs*, Summer, 1993, pp. 22-49.

——, "If Not Civilizations, What? Paradigms of the Post - Cold War World", *Foreign Affairs,* November-December 1993, pp. 186-194.

Huq. Muhammad Shamsul, "Beyond Bangalore", *South Asia Journal,* Vol.1, No.1, 1997, pp. 7-18.

——, "The SAARC: An Evaluative Study", *SAARC Perspective,* Vol.2, No.4, December 1988, pp. 1-6.

Hussain, Ross Masood, "Promotion of Inter-Government, Inter-People and Inter-Institutional understanding in South Asia", *South Asian Survey,* Vol. 2, No. 2, 1995, pp. 18-200.

Ibrahim, Anjum, "Economic Cooperation in South Asia: Pros and Cons", *Regional Studies*, Vol. 7, No. 4, Autumn 1980, pp. 54-63.

Iftekharuzaman, "Bilateral Impediments to SAARC: The Indo-Sri Lanka Crises over IPKF Withdrawal", *BISS Journal,* Vol. 10, No.3, July 1989, pp. 249-73.

——, "South Asian Trade Cooperation with SAARC and the ASEAN: Rationale, Prospects, Realities", *BISS Journal,* Vol. 10, No.1, January 1989, pp. 1-38.

——, "The SAARC in Progress: Achievements, Old Problems, New Dimensions", *Regional Studies*, Vol. 6, No.1 Winter, 1987-88, pp. 12-26.

Jha, Prem Shankar, "India after the Cold War", *The Hindustan Times*, 7 October, 1999.

Kanesalingam, V., "General Overview of SAARC's Achievements", *Marga*, Vol.12, No. 1, 1991, pp. 1-16.

Katyal, K.K., "Indo-Pakistan Ties: A Queer Mix", *Frontline*, Vol. 2, No.8, April-May, 1985, pp. 18-19.

——, "Pakistan Wants SAARC to Address Bilateral Rows", *The Hindu*, 19 December, 1995.

——, "SAARC: A Long Trek", Vol. 3, No.22, *Frontline*, November 1986, pp. 4-9.

——, *"So Near, Yet So Far"*, Vol. 2, No. 25, *Frontline*, 1985, pp. 4-12.

——, "Building Bridges in South Asia", *The Hindu*, 24 July, 2000

——, "Foreign Policy Challenges", *The Hindu*, 15 November, 1999.

Khatri, Sridhar K., "A Decade of South Asian Regionalism: Retrospect and Prospect", *Contemporary South Asia*, Vol. 1, No.1,

1992, pp. 5-23.

——, "Democratization and Regional Cooperation in South Asia", *Everest Herald*, 26 April, 1996.

Khosla, I.P., "SAARC and India, an Overview", *South Asian Survey*, Vol. 6, No.1, January - June 1999, pp. 9-22.

Kizibash, Hamid H., "The Super Powers and SAARC", *Pakistan Horizon*, Vol. 17, No.1, *January, 1989, pp. 76-92.*

Kodikara, Shelton., "Political Dimensions of SAARC", *South Asian Journal,* Vol. 2, No. 4, 1989, pp. 249-71.

Kumar, Rajiv, "Cooperation of Economic Policies in South Asia: Prospects, Problems and Modalities", *South Asia Journal*, Vol. 1, No. 3, 1988, pp. 299-315.

Lama, Mahendra P, "Economics of SAARC", *World Focus* Vol. 17, No. 7, July 1996, pp. 11-12.

——, *"Foreign Investment Regimes in South Asia: Some Critical Issues" South Asia Economic Journal*, Vol. I, No.1, March 2000, pp. 53-78.

Lashkar, M.I., "SAARC: An Economic Perspective", *Pakistan & Gulf Economist*, Vol. 8, No. 2, 14-20 January 1989, pp. 28-29.

Malik, Iftikhar H., "Indo-Pakistan Relations: A Historical Reappraisal", *Contemporary South Asia*, Vol.1, No.1, 1992, pp. 127-42.

Memon, Noor Ahmed, "Pak SAARC Economic Relations: Trade Potential", *Pakistan & Gulf Economist*, Vol. 8, No. 2, January 1989, pp. 25-27.

Mishra, P.K., "Determinants of Inter-Regional Relations in South Asia", *India Quarterly*, Vol. 36, No.1, January-March, 1980, pp. 68-83.

——, "Indian Support for the SAARC", *Strategic Studies Journal*, Vol. 3, No. 122, 1990, pp. 92-105.

——, "Kathmandu Summit and After", *Patriot*, 21 November, 1987.

——, "Towards a Framework of South Asian Regional Cooperation: Colombo to Kathmandu", *Foreign Affairs Record,* Vol. 31, No. 12, December, 1982, pp. 213-32.

Mukherjee, Indra Nath, "Regional Trade, Investment and Economic Cooperation among South Asian Countries", *South Asian Studies*, Vol.25, No.122, December 1990, pp. 34-63.

——, "Indo-Sri Lanka Trade and Investment - Linkages: with Special Reference to SAPTA and Free Trade Agreement", *South Asia Economic Journal,* Vol. 1, No. 1, March 2000, pp. 53-78.

Muni, S.D., "Confidence-Building Exercise", *World Focus*, Vol. 10, No. 1, January 1989, pp. 3-6.

——, "Lanka Deals SAARC A Severe Blow", *The Times of India*, 21 July, 1989.

——,"SAARC: The Villingile Ministerial Meeting", *Strategic Analysis*, Vol. 8, No. 5, August, 1984, pp. 421-30.

——, "SAARC: Building Regionalism from below", *Asian Survey*, Vol. 25, No. 4, April 1985, pp. 394.

——, "SAARC and Security", *Mainstream*, Vol. 25, No.9, 15 November, 1986, pp. 5-6.

——, "SAARC Summit Perspective", *Mainstream*, Vol. 26, No. 4, November, 1987, pp. 5-6.

——, "SAARC as an Approach to Mutual Confidence Building", *SAARC Perspective*, Vol. 2, No. 4, December, 1988, pp. 13-26.

——, "Strategic Aspect of SAARC", *Strategic Analysis*, Vol. 8 No. 1, April 1984, pp. 23-34.

——, "India and Its Neighbours: Persisting Dilemmas and New Opportunities", *International Studies*, 30(2), 1993, pp. 185-206.

——, "India Enters ASEAN Strategic Equation" *The Times of India*, 17 May, 1996.

Murthy, Padamja, "BIMST-EC Making Positive Moves", *Strategic Analysis*, Vol. XXIV, No. 4, July 2000, pp. 833-36.

Naidu, G.V.C., "Future of Institutionalisation in Asia Pacific: The ARF its Implications for India", *Strategic Analysis*, September 1999, pp. 965-991.

Naik, Naiz, A., "Restructuring SAARC", *SAARC Perspective*, Vol. 4, No. 6, November, 1990, pp. 38-40.

Nuruzzamman, M.D., "SAARC and Sub-regional Co-operation: Domestic Policies and Foreign Policies in South Asia", *Contemporary South Asia*, Vol. 8, No. 3, November, 1999, pp. 311-23.

Panchmukhi, V.R., "Co-operation in Industrial Development in the SAARC Region: Some Reflections" *South Asia Journal*, Vol. 4, No.1, 1990, pp. 55-65.

——, "Regional Cooperation and Development", *The Economic Times*, 4 April, 1991.

—, "Significant Role of India in SAARC", *The Economic Times*, 13 May, 1993.

Raja Mohan, C., "No Tears for the SAARC", *The Hindu*, 27 November, 1999.

——, "America's Expanding Asian Alliance", *The Hindu*, 3 May, 1999.

——, "India Gains from ARF Meet", *The Hindu*, 29 July, 1998.

Raje, Vasundhra, "Building Regional Cooperation: India's Role," *South Asian Survey*, Vol. 6, No-1, January- June, 1999, pp. 3 -6.

Sen, Chiranjib, " Globalization, India and East Asia,", *Seminar* No. 487, March, 2000, pp. 51-57.

Senadhira, Sugeswara, "India Needed in Taming the Tigers, feel, Lankan Experts", *The Economic Times*, 7 June, 2000.

Sengupta, Bhabani, "India in the Twenty First Century", *International Affairs,* Vol. 73, No.1, January 1997, pp. 297-314.

Singh, Jasjit, " India's Nuclear Doctrine" *Asian Strategic Review* 1998-99, November 1999, pp. 9-23.

——, "Our Eastern Neighbour", *Seminar,* No. 487, March, 2000, pp.48-50.

——, "Pakistan's Fourth War", *Strategic Analysis, IDSA,* Vol. XIII, No. 5, Aug. 1999, pp. 685-702.

Singh Jaswant, "A Chance to Shed Preoccupations of the Past", (Interview to C. Raja Mohan), *The Hindu*, 25 July, 1999.

——, "Interview to Shastri Ramachandran and Rahul Shivshankar", *The Times of India*, 24 July, 2000.

Singh, Natwar K., "India and her Neighbours", *Link*, Vol. 28, No.11, 6 January 1990, pp. 7-8 & 32-33.

Singh, Udai Bhanu, "India and ARF: The Post Pokharan II Phase", *Strategic Analysis*, January 1999, pp. 1591-1607.

Sobhan, Rehman, "Future of SAARC: Towards Building a South Asian Community", *Journal of International Affairs*, July-December 1997, pp. 1-22.

——, "Regional Cooperation in South Asia : Quest for Identity", *South Asia Survey*, Vol. 5, No.1, January - June, 1998, pp. 3-26

V. Suryanarayana, "Prospects for a Bay of Bengal Community", *Seminar No. 487,* March 2000 - pp. 58-61.

Wadhwa, Charan D., "Regional Blocs: Trade Opportunities for SAARC-I and II", *The Economic Times*, 8 May, 1991.

——, "SAARC Countries and European Community: Towards Stronger Partnership in the 1990's", *South Asia Journal*, Vol. 5, No. 1, July-September, 1991, pp. 17-44.

Waqif, Arif, A., "Exploring Potential Areas of Industrial Cooperation in South Asia", *South Asia Journal*, Vol. 1, No.1, 1987, pp. 51-63.

Waslekar, Sundeep, "Forging Strong Ties", *The Times of India*, 21 January, 1991.

Zaidi, Syed A.R., "A New South Asia", *South Asia Journal,* Vol. 5, No. 1, July-September, 1991, pp. 65-73.

Zaki, Ibrahim Hussain, "No India-Bashing at SAARC," *The Economic Times*, 3 March, 1992.

Seminars / Conference Papers

Bhargava, K.K., "India and its South Asian Neighbours: Obligations and Privileges", Paper presented at the National Seminar on *India's Pivotal Role in South Asia: Optimizing Benefits and Minimizing Apprehensions, Organized by CASAC,* India Chapter, New Delhi, 21 April, 2000.

——, "Regional Political Consultations on Foreign Policy and Security Issues ", Papers presented at the International Conference on *South Asia 2010: Challenges and Opportunities,* Organized by CASAC, Kathmandu, December 1-3, 1999.

Dubey, Muchkund, "Keynote Address on India's Pivotal Role in South Asia", at the National Seminar on *India's Pivotal Role in South Asia: Optimizing Benefits and Minimizing Apprehensions, Organized by* CASAC, India Chapter, New Delhi, 21 April, 2000.

Haq, Khadija, "Mahbub-ul-Haq and the Concept of Human Development in South Asia", *Paper presented at the South Asia Conference* Organized by Institute of Social Science on Legacy of Mahbub-ul-Haq and the Concept of Human Development in South Asia, New Delhi, 19-22 May, 2000.

Kalegama, Saman, "South Asia and Other Regional Economic Groupings", paper presented at the International Conference on *South Asia 2010; Challenges and Opportunities*, organised by CASAC, Kathmandu, December 1-3, 1999.

Lama, M.P., "Economic Cooperation as Confidence Building Measures: Role of India in South Asia", Paper presented at National Seminar on *India's Pivotal South Asia: Optimizing Benefits and Minimizing Apprehensions,* organised by CASAC, India Chapter, New Delhi, 21 April, 2000.

Mukherji, I.N., "South Asian Preferential Trading Arrangement: Role of India", Paper presented at the National Seminar *Organized by* ICSAC Building Regional Cooperation: India's Role, New Delhi, 11-12 December, 1998.

Muni, S.D., "India in SAARC: A Reluctant Policy Maker", *A Paper prepared for the United Nations University Project on*

Globalism and New Regionalism, Directed by Professor Bjorn Hettne of the Peace and Development Research Institute, Gothenburg University, Sweden, July 1996.

Saeed, Amera, "Track II Interaction - Impact on Intergovernmental Processes and Regionalism in South Asia" Paper presented at International Conference on *Regional Co-operation in South Asia : Interfacing New Dimensions and Perspectives* jointly organised by the Bangladesh Institute of International and Strategic Studies (BIISS) and German Embassy in Dhaka, Dhaka 22-24 October, 2000.

Upreti, B.C., "Sub-Regional Cooperation in South Asia : Perceptions, Potentials and Problems of Cooperation among the Countries of the Eastern Himalayan Region", Paper Presented at the National Seminar on *Building Regional Cooperation-India's Role,* Organised by ICSAC, New Delhi, 11-12 December, 1998.

Waqif, Arif A., "India's Contributory Role in Economic Development of SAARC Countries with Special Reference to Trade and Investment", Paper presented at the National Seminar *Organized by CASAC,* on *India's Pivotal Role in South Asia: Optimizing Benefits and Minimizing Apprehensions*, *India Chapter*, New Delhi, 21 April, 2000.

INDEX